The State Of Academic Science

Background Papers

Walter S. Baer

David W. Breneman

Sanford A. Lakoff

Dael Wolfle

Carl M. York

Edited by
Bruce L. R. Smith
Joseph J. Karlesky

Change Magazine Press
New York

The State of Academic Science

Volume I: Summary of Major Findings
LC 77-72979
ISBN 0-915390-09-4
(Published June 1977) $5.95

Volume II: Background Papers
LC 77-72979
(Published January 1978) $5.95

The State of Academic Science is based on a
study supported by the National Science
Foundation and is being published with funding from the Alfred P. Sloan Foundation.

Change Magazine Press
NBW Tower
New Rochelle, N.Y. 10801

Contents

Preface

T his volume presents the background papers for the first volume of The State of Academic Science *published in the late spring of 1977. We were pleasantly surprised at that time by the strong public reaction that the study stimulated. Indeed, some of the concerns over the future course of basic science brought to light by the study found a response in the President's 1978/79 budget. Mr. Carter requested an 8 percent boost in federal R&D obligations at academic institutions and a 5 percent growth in real dollars for basic research. Publication of the background papers provides a welcome opportunity for further comment on the issues raised as well as detailed discussion of technical and methodological points.*

The present volume is necessarily somewhat more technical than the first and will appeal particularly to specialists in the field. The initial volume relied extensively on supporting data provided by these papers. The paper by Walter Baer appeared in abridged form as Chapter 3 in the first volume. The treatment of such issues as graduate education, government regulations, and trends in research activity is more detailed and comprehensive in the papers than in the original volume. We believe that the background papers will also make a substantial contribution to the debate of public policy issues. The papers are published with our gratitude to the authors for their contributions to the overall project and presented in the hope of stimulating additional debate and discussion on academic science issues by scholars and the attentive public.

Once again we are grateful to George Bonham, editor-in-chief of Change *Magazine, for his support and encouragement in the publication of this second volume. Our editor, Joan Stableski, and the staff of* Change *provided invaluable assistance; they all have our warmest appreciation.*

Bruce L.R. Smith
Joseph J. Karlesky

The Future Research Role of American Universities

Bruce L. R. Smith
Joseph J. Karlesky

I n the first volume of *The State of Academic Science*, published in May 1977, we assessed the condition of university science in mixed terms: There was no sign of a general breakdown in the quality of American science, but at the same time there were indications of serious trouble in the future. The troublesome signs included a decline in research opportunities for young scientists, the deterioration in many universities of instrumentation and other supporting resources for research, and the increase both in burdensome procedures for obtaining funding and in controls limiting the flexibility of individual researchers in the use of research funds. Changes in the funding patterns of federal granting agencies—in particular, the trend toward less diversity in funding sources for a number of fields—also presented worrisome problems for the future. State governments seemed destined to play an important role in shaping the future of American science—a role that we believed was not fully appreciated by many observers. Potential conflicts between state and federal policies constituted an area in need of careful thought and attention. Perhaps most important, we found that many of these trends seemed to converge and to point in a disturbing direction: toward a less speculative and venturesome science as researchers sought relatively safe and predictable avenues of inquiry.

Another finding in the initial volume concerned the differential impact of these adverse trends on various science departments, investigators, and universities. The evidence appeared to suggest that the preeminent science departments thus far have been more successful than most others in maintaining their research efforts. Graduate education seemed to face particular strains as enrollments in some fields declined. Some state governments responded to declining enrollments and increased costs by reviewing the status and quality of graduate programs.

These broad conclusions contain many shadings of argument and meaning, and the links between the data and the interpretations drawn are complex. The papers in this volume, as described in the preface to Volume I, were written in the summer of 1976 to provide background for the general conclusions, to spell out the areas of agreement, and to define more clearly the issues on which there is ambiguity or differences of emphasis or opinion concerning the future of academic science in the U.S. Each author addresses an aspect of the general health of American science. Taken together, the papers present a composite picture that reflects the shifting fortunes of American universities at the end of a decade of substantial change.

The papers are arranged to permit the reader to move from a discussion of the overall context of academic science and the broad trends affecting the research efforts of universities to a detailed review of each of the major trends. First, Dael Wolfle presents a general picture of university research since World War II, with particular reference to the trends of the past decade. He thus establishes the framework within which the other authors take up particular themes. Walter Baer explores the shifting interaction between universities and other R&D performers, and in particular he devotes attention to industry/university ties, which have undergone significant changes in the past decade. Carl York follows with an analysis of the trend toward targeting in research practices, tracing the links between the current emphasis by research sponsors on applications and the historic patterns in America's use of research to serve national needs. David Breneman then examines in detail the trend toward declining graduate enrollments in certain fields, and he draws some cautious inferences about the meaning of the evolving patterns for the research efforts in various kinds of institutions. Sanford Lakoff, in the final chapter, addresses another major trend affecting academic science: the growth of more detailed regulations on the conditions of research support and the emergence of greater pressures for accountability in the partnership between the universities and the federal and state governments.

In this introductory chapter we attempt to provide some of the connective tissue between the papers as a guide to the reader, and also to highlight topics of particular interest for future research and public policy debate. The papers share the general notion, as a point of departure for their respective analyses, that the university research effort as a whole remains generally strong even after the rapid changes of the recent past. Despite the increased emphasis on targeted research, the shifts in sponsorship among the federal agencies, the growth of regulations, and other trends, many universities have managed to adapt;

their research activities typically have not yet been curtailed in a major way. Further, the papers all appear to suggest that the "boom" period in federal support for science, lasting roughly from the mid-1950s to the late 1960s, was historically unique. In a sense, what has to be explained is not why the support for science now has slackened but why it exploded in the previous era and lasted for over a decade.

By inference at least, it is clear that each author feels some discomfort over the reasons typically given for the support of science in the boom years. The exaggerated belief in links between basic research and quick practical payoffs, the unrealistic promises of results, the certain air of hucksterism, and other elements seemed bound to lead to disenchantment. At the same time, the rapid shift in government research support policies in recent years has disrupted the system. Discontinuities in support pose a major problem for U.S. science. Stability of funding may be as important as the overall level of funding, and even a somewhat lower level of research support might be preferable if it were provided on a more stable, long-term basis.

There also appears to be substantial evidence that the universities and the research efforts they undertake are growing less alike as a result of the trends of recent years. In the initial volume, we referred to this as "stratification" of the university research system. [1] It is apparent from the papers presented here that this term has several meanings. Universities have become more stratified in the sense that fewer departments are fully equipped to carry on research at the frontiers of knowledge in various fields. Universities also have begun to define their missions differently. The research programs they carry on are increasingly tailored to their own particular strengths or to other local circumstances (the presence of local industry, peculiarities of the job market, and the like). Degree programs also may emphasize certain kinds of skills.

The attitudes toward targeted research, as analyzed by Carl York, show striking differences. Some universities seek to build on traditional strengths to capitalize on the trend toward applications, while other universities are hesitant or ambivalent. The universities, moreover, are exhibiting sharper differences of opinion internally on this point as on numerous other matters. The concept of the university as a coherent entity, while always something of a myth, is likely to undergo particular strain in the future as the separate areas of an institution pursue their own interests. It is unclear, as a result, whether universities will come to be managed to a greater extent by central administrators or whether there may develop a loosening of institutional loyalties. But the authors are agreed that the traditional modes of internal academic governance will undergo some transformation.

Although it seems likely that universities will both cooperate and compete with other research performers to a greater extent in the future, none of the authors envisages a drastic shift in division of labor among the nation's various categories of research performers. As seen particularly in Walter Baer's cogent analysis, the universities have consolidated their role as performers of the largest share of U.S. basic research despite the leveling off in the expansion of research support during the past decade.[2] There are limits to how far the universities can move from their traditional research functions, particularly in light of the difficulties of achieving closer links with industry. The rhetoric to date has been somewhat overblown, and the actual developments limited. Some changes, however, have occurred, and strong sentiments exist within many universities that the neglect of relationships with industry in the 1960s was a mistake.

There is also no sign that the federal government will cease to support basic research at universities or that it will shift such support to other performers, even though the funding levels may not always match university expectations. A major uncertainty here, however, as examined in several of the papers, relates to whether the mission agencies of the federal government use a broad or a narrow definition of research relevant to their missions. Dael Wolfle considers the practices of the mission agencies in this respect to be of major importance for the future of academic science; a restrictive view of mission-related research could put the academic community at a great disadvantage. And such administrative details as the preparation of requests for proposals (RFPs), which put a premium on quick response, may also be factors of considerable importance. Other R&D performers may be better equipped than universities to prepare proposals under pressure of an early deadline, although they are not necessarily better equipped to perform the actual research.

The old issue of the "balance wheel" function for the National Science Foundation is involved in this aspect of the debate.[3] In the early 1960s it was generally believed that the major share of support for university research would come from the mission agencies. NSF would act as a balance wheel: providing extra support for areas inadequately funded by the mission agencies, supporting some fields for which no mission funds were available, and funding projects that otherwise would qualify for mission support only after demonstrating their potential for social benefits. It is, of course, still the case that the mission agency role is critical, but some significant changes in the underlying assumptions have occurred. Few mission agencies now appear to recognize any broad obligation for the health of particular scientific fields.[4] NSF has grown larger than could have been readily imagined a decade ago, but it is still without the budgetary resources to enable it to fulfill the same function that the mission agencies, taken together, did a decade ago. To the extent that NSF has taken on responsibilities for long-term support of large facilities and laboratories that were once supported by mission agencies, there have been fewer resources available for new fields, for individual investigators, and for expanding support for unforeseen developments. What, then, is the modern balance wheel function that should be performed by NSF? No easy answers come to mind, but in several of the papers a concern is expressed that NSF has either grown too large for its traditional role or is not large enough to perform its new role adequately

There are similar uncertainties expressed about the future role of the mission agencies. None of the authors wishes to see the mission agencies withdraw from the support of basic research in the universities; rather they hope that mission agencies will take a broad view of research needs. Yet several authors suggest that some of the adjustments that have taken place over the past decade are natural and desirable. Walter Baer, for example, views the shift of defense laboratories to off-campus sites as a logical development in the best interests of both the universities and the Department of Defense (DOD). But this shift undoubtedly created some adjustment problems for various universities. MIT, for example, lost substantial overhead allowances when the Instrumentation Laboratory formally ceased its affiliation with the University. Yet when a lab reaches a certain size and the character of the research effort becomes closely geared to a government mission, it is reasonable for the activity to acquire its own identity apart from the parent institution. In general, given the strains of the Vietnam period, the question of how close the ties between defense agencies and universities could or should be is a troublesome one, with good arguments on each side. For certain fields within the physical sciences and engineering, the question is particularly pressing because the loss or further diminution of defense research support could affect significantly the level of research activity in these fields.

But even more than those of DOD, the actions of the Department of Health, Education, and Welfare appear to pose a major issue for universities. Dael Wolfle asks whether the sheer magnitude of the HEW presence in supporting academic research has not already upset the fundamental pluralism of the research support system. The dramatic rise of HEW as the major supporter of university research over the past decade has created a relationship of such dependency that any significant change in HEW policies creates shock waves throughout the universities. Some advantages, however, also result from having one agency in such a predominant position. The agency can assume substantial responsibilities for the overall health of various fields and for the strength of the institutional base underlying the science effort. HEW, alone among the research-sponsoring agencies of the federal government, continues a significant program of formula-type support to universities in addition to support for individual projects or departments.[5]

Several other issues of fundamental importance are mentioned in the papers but are not fully resolved. They deserve special attention as matters likely to be in the forefront of policy debate, and they also present particularly difficult analytical puzzles. Although agreeing that research of excellent quality continues to be done at American universities, the contributors differ somewhat in their assessments of the dangers facing American science and the immediacy of the threat. Wolfle, relying heavily on the aggregate measures compiled in the 1974 *Science Indicators*,[6] finds evidence of a potentially serious decline in American science. He sees a relationship between factors such as a decline in the U.S. share of world publications in certain fields and other evidence of decay in the scientific effort, and he is inclined to see the dangers as imminent unless corrective action is taken. For Baer, who approaches the question from a different perspective, U.S. science (and particularly the link between the generation and the application of knowledge) is still widely admired by other countries. By implication, at least, he seems less concerned about a possible deterioration of the American science effort. Breneman appears closer to Baer's position in his analysis of doctoral enrollment trends insofar as he finds little evidence that enrollment reductions in some fields have as yet substantially affected the research efforts. Over time, however, declining graduate enrollments could pose a danger in certain fields and in certain universities. Lakoff's view lies closer to that of Wolfle, seeing the threats to the university research environment in urgent terms. His argument is based less on output measures or other quantitative indices than on his general analysis of the corrosive influence of federal regulations on the climate of inquiry.

An important related issue that is not resolved in the papers concerns the role of the second- and third-tier universities in the overall academic research effort. The most serious problems to date have been found in the scientifically less-distinguished universities or in those with rather recently developed research programs and advanced education and training. The problems have not affected all second-tier institutions; many have avoided difficulties by specializing in certain fields of research and advanced training where the university has a natural advantage due to the presence of local industry, special faculty skills, or other factors. But the damage felt in a number of the second-tier universities and in certain regions of the country is serious enough for us to take notice. Has there been a significant loss to the nation as a result of this contraction? Or does the retrenchment reflect a healthy readjustment in a system that has squeezed out inefficient performers? Is there a minimum coverage of science fields that must be maintained if a university is to have a significant research effort? How much research strength must be present in every region of the country?

The questions that suggest themselves are numerous. The contributors struggle with the problem but find no easy way to resolve it. Most, but not all, important research contributions come from the major research-intensive universities. But the students who will become the next generation of scientists are recruited from a much broader range of academic institutions, including state universities and liberal arts colleges throughout the country. The broad base of the American science effort, furthermore, has seemed to play an important part in making possible the outstanding achievements of the most gifted scientists. With a narrower national base of scientific research, the competitive and dynamic system that has produced spectacular achievements in science could be gradually eroded.

A key concern that troubles the contributors is whether a new equilibrium can be achieved in a somewhat trimmed but still competitive system. The concept of "steady state" conditions is relevant here. Granting that a return to the rapid growth conditions of the 1950s and early 1960s is unlikely, can a vigorous and dynamic research effort be maintained with relatively fixed resources? Part of the answer depends on the state of the economy, including in particular the rate of inflation. If inflation continues at very high levels, there is a danger that the research efforts of more and more universities will be adversely affected until, finally, too few centers of high quality research remain. The process that already has led to the constraints felt by some weaker institutions might continue to operate with similarly damaging consequences for the research activities at other institutions. Yet in principle there is no reason why the research system could not achieve stability with a somewhat smaller number of universities and fewer investigators if adequate support were provided for the institutions and individuals that survive a shake-down period. The question of the number of research-intensive universities and science departments needed should, under this perspective, be kept analytically distinct from the effects of a factor like inflation that has a broad impact across all categories of institutions.

Of particular importance to several of the authors is the preservation of the competitive system of awarding research grants and contracts on the basis of merit as judged by scientific peers. Only if merit continues to operate will the nation have reasonable assurance that the "right" institutions survive the process of contraction.[7] Other of the authors seem less confident that the peer review system can survive the strains that will be placed on it in the troubled period ahead; and, according to this view, some departures from the strict application of merit principles may have to be contemplated. For example, "sheltered" competition according to geographical region for a limited part of total federal R&D funds might become necessary if the nation were to decide as a matter of policy that each region of the country must maintain a certain minimum level of scientific research capability. A simple increase in the federal R&D funds available, it is generally agreed, would not result in an appreciable increase for those investigators in the scientifically less-distinguished universities who have lost out in the more austere funding climate of recent years. Beyond this it is apparent that peer review, at least in its traditional disciplinary form, cannot function in the awarding of large-scale inter-disciplinary grants or in the designation of funds for targeted research projects. In these instances the criteria that guide selection are less determined by the scientific merits of any particular individual or any single research proposal. The commitment of the institution to manage a large-scale project and other factors necessarily will play a larger part in the decision. Considerations of quality should still be maintained, and it will be a considerable task for science policymakers to identify surrogates for peer review within the disciplines in the case of large projects where one has difficulty identifying peers in the traditional sense. But unquestionably as research projects become larger in scale and also more targeted in character (often the two will go together) they will also grow more political. Awards will hinge on a broader range of considerations than merely the scientific merit of a few individuals. The task will not be to eliminate such broad considerations from the decision—plainly an impossibility—but to assure that objective judgments by knowledgeable persons are also part of the decision process.

Only hinted at in several of the papers is one concern that follows from the interaction of the various trends discussed above. Briefly, we might refer to it as the fate of the good but not preeminent scientist, science department, and science university. The preeminent investigators will likely continue to be relatively well supported in the near future if recent experience is a guide. [8] The regional universities, specializing in applied work, increasingly may benefit from the trend toward more targeted research priorities. Hence, the investigators that are just below the top, and the institutions they work in, may face the most severe problems of readjustment. They have neither the rationale for maintaining the highest quality of American science nor that for providing practical service to the nation. The evidence on this point, however, is not sufficiently clear to permit a confident assessment at this time.

All the contributors agree that to understand the trends affecting university research an improved analytical base is needed. Despite the impressive data-gathering efforts by the National Science Foundation, the kind and quality of information available on university research efforts leave the observer troubled by large uncertainties. No one suggests that information alone will provide solutions to the emerging problems or that statistics will relieve the necessity of making hard choices in the future. Moreover, the contributors are uncomfortable at the prospect of a large-scale attempt to gather new data from the universities; the authors fear that just such administrative demands are part of the problem. Data requests from a multiplicity of federal and state agencies comprise a substantial share of the workload of many university officials. Nonetheless, the gaps in present information and the disparities that can be found in current data are of such a character as to make improvements highly desirable. Ways must be found, without imposing burdensome requirements, to gather more accurate and refined data that will provide a better basis for systematic and timely assessments of the state of academic science.

No straightforward answers emerged from Volume I of this study, nor will they be found in the present volume. But the analyses presented here make an important contribution to the debate on the future of academic science in the U.S. All of the papers have a final, common, underlying theme: A stable, long-term relationship between society and the research-intensive universities in the pursuit of science is the critical goal. The panacea for today's problems, the hasty improvisation, the quick fix are all to be eschewed. The trends examined here will leave the reader with the sense that the future is by no means entirely untroubled. But there is also the hope that, out of the crucible of recent experience, a more stable partnership between society and the academic science community may result. Growth in understanding of the conditions that nurture science will at least give society clearer choices on the use of its intellectual talents in the pursuit of broad national goals.

---

1. Bruce L. R. Smith and Joseph J. Karlesky, *The State of Academic Science: The Universities in the Nation's Research Effort* (New Rochelle, New York: Change Magazine Press, 1977), pp. 229-235.

2. See Walter S. Baer, "The Changing Relationships: Universities and Other R&D Performers," especially pp. 71-72 in this volume.

3. On the notion of the balance wheel, see National Academy of Sciences, *Basic Research and National Goals*, Report to the Committee on Science and Astronautics, U.S. House of Representatives, March 1965, pp. 23-24. In general, see also *The National Science Foundation: A General Review of Its First 15 Years*, Report of the Legislative Reference Service to the Subcommittee on Science, Research and Development of the House Committee on Science and Astronautics, Eighty-ninth Congress, First Session, April 1965. See also *The National Science Foundation, Its Present and Future*, Report of the Subcommittee on Science, Research and Development of the House Committee on Science and Astronautics, Eighty-ninth Congress, Second Session, January 1966.

4. On August 15, 1977, then Office of Management and Budget Director Bert Lance sent to all executive department and agency heads a memorandum expressing support of basic research funding consistent with mission needs. It read in part: "The President is particularly concerned with the identification of critical problems currently or potentially faced by the Federal Government where basic or long-term research could assist in carrying out Federal responsibilities more effectively or where such research would provide a better basis for decision making.... We are asking that in the context of developing your 1979 budget you identify whether there are specific problems in your area of responsibility that might be better addressed through basic research and then use the results of your review to determine whether available resources can be better applied to basic or long-term research associated with those problems.... There is a

tendency to defer needed basic or long-term research to meet more pressing near-term problems. We urge that in developing budget proposals for your agency you take a balanced view in dealing with your R&D programs and be sensitive to this tendency."

5. An NSF Basic Research Stability Grant Program has been funded at $4.5 million for FY 1978. This initiative is a new formula grant program designed to provide discretionary funds to more than 300 colleges and universities for the purpose of undergirding the project grant system. Calculated on the basis of NSF basic research support, the formula grant provides resources that can be used either for seed money or for expenditures such as instrumentation or start-up programs. But as of this writing, OMB had "deferred" any expenditures under the program. For a general review of Carter administration policies toward science, see Daniel S. Greenberg, "Science Under Carter, A Year-End Review," *Science and Government Report*, December 15, 1977, pp. 1-4.

6. National Science Board, *Science Indicators—1974: Report of the National Science Board, 1975* (Washington, D.C.: National Science Foundation, 1975).

7. For background studies on the working of peer review systems, see Thane Gustafson, "The Controversy Over Peer Review," *Science*, Vol. 190, No. 4219, December 12, 1975, pp. 1060-1066; and Stephen Cole, Leonard C. Rubin, and Jonathan R. Cole, "Peer Review and the Support of Science," *Scientific American*, Vol. 237, No. 4, October 1977, pp. 34-41.

8. See our discussion in Chapter IV, "Current Developments in Academic Science and Engineering," in *The State of Academic Science*, op. cit., pp. 81-158.

Forces Affecting the Research Role of Universities

Dael Wolfle

S cientific knowledge has advanced spectacularly since World War II and so have the applications of this knowledge to agriculture, medicine, and technology. In the United States these advances were the intended results of important policy decisions made at the end of World War II: the decision to spend substantial amounts of public money on research and development; to conduct most of the R&D in universities and in industrial and other research laboratories, rather than within government agencies; to include considerable basic research in the total program; and to assign to scientists themselves a significant part of the responsibility for deciding how the research budget could best be utilized. These policies were backed by the public confidence in science that followed the dramatic inventions of radar, penicillin, and the proximity fuse; the release of nuclear energy; and other wartime developments that gave hope of comparable contributions to a peacetime economy if research and development could only continue to be supported as they had been during the War.

Military, economic, health, and welfare improvements were the objectives, but it takes time—sometimes a great deal of time—to achieve scientific objectives, and even more time to translate scientific findings into practical applications. Much of the basic research underlying major developments of recent years was conducted 10, 20, or even 30 years before the technological or medical innovation was successfully achieved.[1] Thus, all the results of the research conducted in the two decades before 1970 still cannot be predicted today.

But some positive evidence is available.[2] The United States produces a large portion of the world's scientific literature, and it increased its proportion during the 1950s and 1960s. The U.S. has been responsible for two thirds of the major technological innovations since the early 1950s. As research in universities has increased, so have the specifically identifiable contributions of that research to practical applications. Whether one measures the payoff in advances in the state of scientific knowledge, or in terms of new patents and technological innovations, the expansion of research and development has brought substantial gains. The strategy adopted at the end of the War has been successful.

Universities that are deeply engaged in research and graduate education have been an important part of that strategy and success. For a variety of reasons, the research activities of those universities now are in trouble. Among all the institutions of higher education in the U.S., the leading research universities are the largest, most expensive, and most prestigious. But they are also the institutions whose programs and objectives often seem most at odds with the goals and values of the public. After two decades of rapid expansion, research-oriented universities are having to adjust to much slower growth and even to the curtailment of some of their activities. This change came quickly, beginning about 1968 when federal funds for research stopped growing. By 1970 it was widely recognized that more students were receiving bachelor's and PhD degrees than could be fully utilized by the available jobs. State appropriations for public universities began to falter. And all of these changes were exacerbated by the general economic sluggishness of the early 1970s.

Had history been a bit different, some of the resulting pressures on universities might have been distributed over a longer period of time, or perhaps been avoided altogether. But universities could not have put off for long the more searching public scrutiny and the greater external pressures that have mounted rapidly in recent years. They could not have escaped these pressures because they have become too large, too expensive, and too important to be left undisturbed.

Pressures from outside have been increasing. There have been stepped-up efforts to use universities to achieve objectives that have not been part of the traditional academic program. Some students and faculty members would like to see universities become agents of social action, devoting their efforts to problems of major societal concern—problems whose importance is unquestioned but which are quite different from those to which universities have usually made their greatest contributions. Government agencies have used the threat, and the fact, of withholding research funds to force compliance with important but educationally unrelated changes in social practice. As these pressures have mounted, the amount of research money per faculty member has dwindled, inflation has soared, graduates have had greater difficulty in finding appropriate jobs, forecasters have predicted a period of declining enrollment, and government regulations have proliferated.

The university has become a much buffeted institution. Although still conducting research of high quality, still educating students in a wide variety of specialized fields, and still contributing many types of public service, the university—much more than 10 years ago—is working under financial constraints, grappling with a variety of external controls that reduce its ability to make internal adjustments, and greatly worried about the possibility of the even more severe dilemmas that seem to be on the horizon.

Changes in Financial Support

From 1953 through 1967 national expenditures for R&D increased by 350 percent. The federal portion increased even more rapidly—by 425 percent—and by 1967 it was responsible for 62 percent of the total. Since 1967 growth has been much slower, with the 1976 total 64 percent greater than in 1967 and the federal portion only 40 percent above 1967.

If the figures are converted to constant dollars, growth from 1953 to 1967 still appears very swift, for inflation was modest during those years. After 1967 inflation was more rapid, and converting to constant dollars changes the picture dramatically. In constant 1972 dollars, the national total for R&D declined by 5 percent from 1967 to 1976, and the federal portion dropped by 19 percent (see Table 1).[3]

Within these general trends, universities fared considerably better than the average research institution. Funds for university research grew more dramatically than the average during the period of rapid total growth, and even in constant dollars they have continued to grow, albeit slowly, in the years since 1967. The whole R&D pie has grown smaller, but academic scientists have been given a slightly larger piece. University research funds from the federal government were 3 percent greater in 1976 than in 1967, and the total from all sources was 13 percent greater, with most of the increase provided by university funds.

Thus the academic component has become an increasingly larger fraction of the nation's total research effort. Early in the 1950s, universities were responsible for about 5 percent of the national total. By 1963 their portion had grown to above 6 percent, and by 1971 it exceeded 9 percent. Of the portion funded by federal sources, academic research increased from 7 percent in 1963 to 12 percent in recent years. In keeping with the special competence of universities, most of their work has been in basic research. Universities are responsible for over half of the basic research conducted in the U.S., for about 10 percent of the applied research, and for about half of 1 percent of the development work.

Table 1

Support of Research and Development, 1963-1976
(in millions of constant 1972 dollars)

Year	Total Support		University Support	
	All Sources	Federal Government	All Sources	Federal Government
1963	$23,829	$15,651	$1,510	$1,062
1964	25,930	17,241	1,754	1,260
1965	26,970	17,508	1,983	1,444
1966	28,460	18,198	2,234	1,644
1967	29,291	18,217	2,431	1,783
1968	29,798	18,077	2,603	1,905
1969	29,550	17,170	2,560	1,839
1970	28,355	16,055	2,556	1,804
1971	27,697	15,509	2,604	1,795
1972	28,257	15,795	2,676	1,839
1973	28,642	15,491	2,779	1,926
1974	27,712	14,495	2,592	1,746
1975	27,158	14,387	2,666	1,796
1976	27,927	14,766	2,736	1,831
1976/1967	95%	81%	113%	103%

*Figures for 1976 are National Science Foundation estimates.

Source: National Science Foundation, *National Patterns of R&D Resources*, NSF 77-310, 1977.

Individual Grants

Although the total amount of money for university research has grown slightly since 1967, as measured in constant dollars, there has been less available for each faculty member interested in conducting research. Faculty growth has been slower in recent years than in the 1950s and early 1960s. Yet university enrollments have continued to increase and so has the size of most faculties. As a result, the number of academic scientists and engineers interested in research has increased. Research funds per full-time equivalent scientist and engineer employed in universities granting doctoral degrees decreased from $15,300 a year in 1967 to $11,700 a year in 1974. The comparable figures for research funds from the federal government were $11,200 in 1967 and $8,400 in 1974. Thus, per faculty member, there was a real loss of 25 percent in research funds in the seven-year period from 1967 to 1974. [4]

This loss does not appear to have weakened the research motivation of faculty members. National surveys conducted in 1968, 1974, and 1975 of departments that grant the doctorate all showed from 83 to 85 percent of the faculty members to be spending 20 percent or more of their time in research.[5] However, the percentage of these faculty members who received federal support for their research dropped from 65 percent in 1968 to 57 percent in 1974.

Moreover, in order to secure support, a number of faculty members have had to shift their fields of research. In 1968, 78 percent of the doctoral-granting departments reported that their younger faculty members could generally secure support for the research areas of their own choice, and 88 percent reported that senior members of the faculty could generally get such support. Comparable figures for 1974 had dropped to 56 percent for younger and 53 percent for more senior faculty members.[6]

Another study, based on 1975 data, found 31 percent of the doctoral-granting departments reporting that 10 percent or more of their faculty members were conducting research in areas other than their preferred ones. Most of these research shifts were relatively minor, to a different specialty within the same subfield of science, for example. But some were major shifts to an entirely different field or discipline. Regardless of the size of the shift, the availability of research support was the principal reason for transferring to a nonpreferred area.[7]

The availability—if not abundance—of research support was illustrated by a number of comments from faculty members interviewed during site visits for this study: "Overall support is holding up"; "most people who are good still get money for basic research"; "some of our proposals are turned down, but the department hasn't lost any that I would really want to fight for"; or even, "our people are getting more grant funds now than in the early 1970s and doing the research they want."

There has been room, then, for at least some optimism. Comparing 1974 and 1975 with 1968 it is clear that faculty members in PhD-granting university departments are today, one way or another, spending as much time on research as they did in 1968, whatever the limitations on that research.

But whether one interprets the academic research mood as sanguine or pessimistic, it is also clear that agency funds do not go as far as they used to. The National Science Foundation (NSF) increased its annual number of grants by maintaining an essentially constant average size in current dollars. The National Institutes of Health (NIH) followed a different course. The average project grant more than doubled between 1962 and 1974 and thus kept well ahead of inflation, but the number of grants declined by nearly 50 percent from 1963 to 1970, after which time new funds for the National Cancer Program permitted a substantial increase in the next few years.[8]

In both cases, inflation took its toll: Academic research costs went up about 50 percent between 1967 and 1975.[9] Not only are grants effectively smaller today, but it is also necessary to work harder to get them. The number of potential grantees has increased. Many try to improve their chances by writing more detailed descriptions of their proposed work and by submitting fuller documentation. In some cases, shortening the time periods of grants has allowed agencies to increase the number of grants and thus spread their funds more widely. But for grantees, this practice requires frequent reapplications and the division of their research plans into short, safe, and what they hope will be appealing segments. In a letter that ironically was published on Christmas 1970, a Princeton biologist reported that in response to a grant request he had been informed that "we aren't supporting that big a research project anymore" and was advised to break it up into a few smaller projects, describe them in much more detail, and submit 20 copies of each.[10]

Scientists generally would agree that research grants should continue to be made on a competitive basis; competition with critical peer review is the best method yet devised to ensure that the most important problems are tackled by the most competent investigators.[11] But now it seems to many that an inordinate amount of time goes into preparing, revising, negotiating, and attempting to renew the grants on which their work depends. The time involved must be subtracted somewhere else—often from hours in the laboratory or field—and this constitutes one of the hidden costs of the present situation.

Other Forms of Support

Although funds for project grants have kept slightly ahead of inflation, other forms of support for academic science have been greatly reduced. In 1967, in addition to $1,324 million of research funds from the federal government, colleges and universities also received obligations for another $1,000 million of federal funds—three quarters again as much—for the purchase of scientific equipment; for the construction of new laboratories, oceanographic research ships, and other facilities; for fellowships and traineeships for graduate students; and for other costs of maintaining or improving scientific capabilities.

By 1975 this additional support had declined to about $350 million (in 1967 dollars). Total federal support for academic science was thus about 26 percent less in 1975 than it had been eight years earlier. This decline in funding considerably reduced university flexibility. Funds for individual projects were adequate. But institutional funds, funds that could be used however the university saw fit, were largely gone. There was much less money to fill in research gaps, to start new exploratory studies before they reached the stage of project support, or to meet other special and changing needs.

The reduction or disappearance of these funds also signaled an extremely important change in the federal government's relationship with universities. Ever since the expansion of R&D started shortly after World War II, federal funds have been used both to "buy" research the government deemed desirable and to "support" research planned by the grantee. But in addition to these relationships, there was also high-level acceptance of a federal obligation to help sustain the general health and development of the universities, upon which the nation was heavily dependent.[12] In working-level committees that commitment is still sound,[13] and the National Science, Engineering, and Technology Policy, Organization, and Priorities Act of 1976 (PL 94-282) instructed the President's Committee on Science and Technology to consider "ways to strengthen the nation's academic institutions' capabilities for research and education in science and technology." But not since President Johnson's day have such affirmations of support for academic research been initiated by the White House itself.

Changing Sources of Support

Every research-supporting agency has characteristic expectations for the use of its funds, and those funds bring somewhat different opportunities and problems to the recipient. Early in the 1950s universities received 54 percent of their separately budgeted research funds from the federal government, 28 percent from their own resources (including tax funds for public universities), 10 percent from foundations and other nonprofit organizations, and 8 percent from industry. By 1966-68 the federal portion had climbed to 73 percent while all of the others had declined. By 1973-75 the federal portion had fallen back to 68 percent; universities were filling nearly all of the gap from their own resources— sometimes by dipping into capital—and were providing 22 percent of the total; nonprofit organizations contributed 7 percent; and the industrial share was down to 3 percent.

A few agencies have always provided the major part of the federal support. Following World War II, the Department of Defense (DOD) took the lead in supporting academic research, and even as late as 1954 it was providing over 70 percent of total federal funding. By the early 1960s its share was down to less than a quarter, and since then its percentage has dropped steadily as other agencies have grown and as defense funds allocated to academic research either have declined or shown only minor growth. In 1974 and 1975 defense funds supported less than 9 percent of all academic research.

In the meantime, the NSF share grew fairly steadily to the point of now providing about one fifth of the academic total. But it is the Department of Health, Education, and Welfare (HEW)—and chiefly

NIH—that has become the new giant. It now regularly provides more than half of all federal funds transferred to colleges and universities for research support.

This system of support is often described as pluralistic, and it is. Yet a single agency provides over half of all federal research funds going to universities; two agencies together provide three quarters; and a total of five agencies provide more than 90 percent. These, like the smaller agencies, tend to work within their individual spheres of interest and to support somewhat different types of research. As a result, the sources of potential support for any one investigator or department are normally fewer than a full list of funding agencies would suggest. Besides, HEW has become so much the dominant agency that every change in its policies, priorities, regulations, and procedures must be of critical concern to every university.

Applied and Targeted Research

Common to all the federal funding agencies has been an increased emphasis on applied or targeted research. The newer agencies have primarily applied missions. And the more established agencies have shifted significantly in emphasis, such as the favored budgetary treatment accorded the highly targeted National Cancer Program in HEW or the rapid expansion of the RANN (Research Applied to National Needs) program of NSF, which went from 0.56 percent of the total NSF budget in 1968 to nearly 12 percent in 1974 and 1975.

The distinctions between basic and applied or between targeted and nontargeted categories are often fuzzy, and in many individual cases it makes little difference whether a project is formally classified as basic research or as applied research, or whether it is supported from general purpose or from targeted funds. Often it is impossible to tell from the name of an agency or program just how its funds will be used. DOD long supported some very fundamental scientific work, and substantial funds of the National Cancer Program are also used for that purpose.

Yet the decrease in the amount classified for basic research is of some significance to universities, and especially to the more prestigious ones, which are most solidly dedicated to the advancement of basic knowledge. They have been affected by the fact that from 1967 to 1974 all of the major federal agencies supporting research in universities, except for NASA, decreased the percentage of their funds allocated to basic research. In HEW the decrease was from 32 to 25 percent and in NSF from 91 to 79 percent.

Correspondingly, the percentage of university research funds classified as basic research declined. Yet the change was small compared with that of earlier years. In 1953, 43 percent of the research funds used by universities went to basic research. It climbed to 79 percent in 1964, remained above 75 percent through 1972, and then dropped back to 70 or 71 percent in 1973 through 1976.

Although significant, this change alone was not great enough to account for the decrease referred to earlier in the percentage of faculty members able to secure support for the kind of research they wished to pursue. There are many reports that some agency program officers who are responsible for funds nominally intended for basic research have become increasingly insistent that the projects they support be clearly relevant to topics of current societal concern, or that potentially applicable results be foreseen. Although it is not possible to document the extent of this hidden shift, the change seems to be a real one. It would be surprising if it were otherwise; for a decade there has been public and governmental pressure to effect just such a change.

Field Differences

In 1974, 84 percent of faculty members in doctoral-granting departments were spending 20 percent or more of their time in research, but the percentage varied substantially from field to field—from 97 percent in biochemistry down to 71 percent in electrical engineering. And the percentage of faculty engaged in research on topics of their own first choice also varied widely; only a little over one third of the mathematics departments reported that their members could generally secure support for the kind of research they wanted to do, while two thirds or more of the departments of biochemistry and biology gave such reports. These reports are consistent with changes in the allocation of federal research funds: The physical sciences experienced a loss of 17 percent (in constant dollars) between 1966-68 and 1973-74, while the environmental sciences gained 44 percent and the social sciences increased 24 percent. Within the life sciences, funds for research in the area of clinical medicine went up 13 percent while the support in other areas declined.[14]

Behind these general trends, more detailed analysis shows a number of finer distinctions—by subfield, by strength of university department, and in some cases by the age of the investigator. Therefore both a high degree of satisfaction and considerable dissatisfaction with the availability of research funds may coexist on the same campus or within the same discipline as it is represented on different campuses. Overall, though, the picture is clear: University research continues at a high level, but the power of the federal purse is pushing more of that research in directions that are determined by federal agencies, and there are fewer opportunities to secure support for work on the basis of scientific interest alone.

Younger Investigators

There has been considerable concern that the changes summarized above have had an unduly adverse effect on younger investigators. In the social sciences it appears likely that they have. Reviewing several lines of evidence, a National Research Council report concluded that political scientists, social psychologists, and sociologists who had held their doctorates for less than seven or eight years had suffered a disproportionate decline in the percentages of their numbers receiving federal support for research.[15]

In most other fields there does not seem to be such a decline. Analyses of grants from the NSF, NIH, and the National Cancer Institute all show a higher percentage of grants being made in response to proposals from younger investigators than to proposals from older ones.[16] In a national sample of 5,000 faculty members, a multivariate analysis of the characteristics associated with successful grant proposals showed two factors standing out above all the rest. Most important was the record of recent research publications. Applicants with several recent publications were more likely to get grants than were others. The second factor was the field of work; as pointed out above, more support is available in some fields than in others. Beyond these two major variables, no other characteristic of the individual or the individual's institution explained more than a tiny fraction of the variance. However, after full account was taken of differences in research records and fields of science, being young gave an applicant a slight edge in getting grants.[17]

When asked a judgmental question concerning the appropriateness of the division of research funds between their younger and older colleagues, most department chairmen were reasonably well satisfied. There was dissent from this majority opinion, but less in 1974 than there had been in a similar study in 1968: 27 percent thought the split inappropriate in 1974 as compared with 32 percent in 1968. Of the dissenters, about four out of five considered their younger faculty members to be the disadvantaged group.[18] Except in the social sciences, distribution of research funds by age does not seem to be a major problem. There is less support than younger investigators would like, and a considerable number of them have to work in areas other than those they prefer. But their senior colleagues, in about equal proportions, are experiencing the same difficulties.

External Controls

Universities have never been free of external controls. Politics, patronage, and religion have sometimes intervened in internal policy decisions to determine who was hired or fired, or what was taught or done. In the past, whenever universities diverged too greatly from orthodoxy or populist views of the public interest, someone tried to bring them back into line. But for much of this century universities have been relatively free to make most of the decisions concerning the use of their resources. Public universities have been able to allocate their state appropriations as they thought best, and private universities have had even greater freedom in using most of their funds. Additional funds from foundations, industry, or government have been small enough in amount and diverse enough in purpose that they have carried little threat to university autonomy.

In recent years, external controls have been growing stronger. In the 1940s, when the large-scale postwar support of research was being debated, scientists were warned that this result was inevitable—that whoever paid the piper called the tune. But many sources of money were becoming available, and many options were open to researchers. If one agency could not support a particular project, another might; if one university did not wish to conduct a particular program, another would. There were enough pipers and enough tunes to be played that there was little need or opportunity for coercion, and for an extended period both the pipers and their patrons were well satisfied. What is surprising is that the problem of external controls did not become acute for so long.

As enrollment has mounted and as costs have multiplied, all of higher education has come under increasing examination. But it is the universities that usually seem to be in the spotlight. Universities are typically bigger than colleges; they charge a higher tuition; and they are more likely than colleges to be the scenes of conflict over ideas that run counter to public standards of morality, conduct, or propriety. The degree of their academic freedom—their right to inquire into any field and to subject any orthodox belief to critical skepticism—has long been a right (or privilege) treasured by universities and it places them further away from populist ideals than colleges and much further than community or junior colleges.

For this reason, state governments recently have been strengthening their controls over public universities. One method has been to assign greater responsibility to the state coordinating boards that now make a number of decisions for all the institutions of higher education in a state system. At the same time, state legislatures and fiscal planning agencies have come to specify in much greater detail than formerly just how state appropriations (and sometimes other university funds as well) are to be spent. In order to provide a rationalized basis for allocating state funds, legislative bodies and state coordinating boards have come to require more detailed information from all state institutions of higher education so that comparative data on enrollments, faculties, class sizes, expenses, and other operating details can be used as bases for more or less uniform statewide funding formulas. Universities are the institutions that have the most to lose from these state controls.[19]

Government Use of Universities

Initially colleges were expected to serve society by educating ministers, doctors, lawyers, teachers, members of government, and other national leaders who would contribute to a progressively better future. This was the climate of opinion when research came into American colleges and universities. Just as the federal government did not try to direct the educational activities of colleges, so also a hands-off policy was the standard with respect to research. But gradually the universities that originally served a broad national purpose by educating young men and women and by following their own particular goals more and more became instruments of national purpose, used to achieve specific objectives that were determined by government agencies. Universities have not been the only institutions involved in this mutation; they are part of a larger blurring of distinctions between the public and private sectors. In a variety of ways, and especially since World War II, the federal government has provided funds to industry, to universities, to states, to private research institutes, and sometimes to new and specially formed corporations—all to provide goods or services selected by Congress or by the executive branch.[20]

The primary reason for federal support of university research has been practical—to strengthen national defense, to improve health, to win the space race, to enhance national prestige, to stimulate economic growth. Some university research has contributed to the achievement of these goals, but since the mid-1960s there has been increasing insistence that academic research be more directly and immediately aimed toward such goals. On June 15, 1966, a day perhaps symbolic of the impending change, President Johnson announced to a group of medical and hospital leaders:

> I think the time has now come to zero in on targets by trying to get our knowledge fully applied.... Presidents, in my judgment, need to show more interest in what the specific results of medical research are during their lifetime and during their administration. I am going to show an interest in the results.[21]

Since then federal agencies have increased their emphasis on applied research and targeted programs.

It is unlikely that a formal declaration of the universities' role as instruments of national purpose for the achievement of federal objectives will ever be made. Such a declaration would unnecessarily create dissension over traditional American principles and would imply federal responsibility for continuing institutional support, an obligation that recent administrations have tried to avoid. Nevertheless, federal spokesmen are making increasingly frank statements of their intent to exert control on specific issues. In 1976 an HEW official told the Association of American Medical Colleges: "It is important to see clearly that the direction in which we are moving is toward increasing federal domination of the American health enterprise."[22] This statement is surprising not for its content but for its frankness—a kind of frankness that suggests HEW has the requisite power to assert itself and has overcome any past reluctance to use that power.

Details may change, and new accommodations may be worked out, but the basic shift toward greater public and government control over higher education is irrevocable. There can be no going back to the more peaceful days of small size, low budgets, and almost complete internal control over university decisions. Universities simply are of too great importance in the scheme of national affairs to be left to themselves. As Don Price has pointed out, the American people have always wanted to hold their governors responsible.[23] For this reason frequent elections and a variety of checks and balances were made integral parts of American government. As education has become more widespread and as its practical applications have grown more capable of influencing the health, wealth, and general welfare of the entire country, universities have joined the ranks of the governors. In that status they must expect to continue to have to cope with demands for accountability, with skepticism over their motives and their management, and with further attempts to control their activities and define their objectives.

Federal Regulations

Goals are primary to procedural details, but they are usually flexible enough to accommodate a wide range of means to their achievement. Procedural details are often less flexible, and that inflexibility makes them particularly irksome to men and women who insist that they know how to apply general principles to their own special circumstances. Yet researchers have been faced with increasingly detailed regulations governing their use of federal funds—both in terms of the records they must compile and the reports they must submit.

Clashes have been inevitable as scholars and university administrators, operating on the basis of the goals, traditions, and the essential nature of research and graduate education, have dealt with government auditors, lawyers, and management specialists operating on the very different goals and customs of their professions and agencies. The government representatives come from hierarchical organizations that differ fundamentally from the decentralized, collegial nature of a university. As the literature on organizational behavior demonstrates, hierarchical organizations tend to emphasize maintenance of the status quo, conformity with prescribed forms and modes of behavior, and the allocation of decision-making responsibility in a highly structured fashion. In sharp contrast, universities emphasize independence and are oriented toward the achievement of major institutional goals rather than the preservation of the status quo.

It is not easy to bridge this gulf. On the one side are scientists and university administrators whose interest is in advancing the state of knowledge. They have been apprenticed and acculturated in a system that encourages great freedom in planning their own research activities. The state of knowledge, the outcome of an experiment, the sudden appearance of a new finding or a promising lead, their own judgment and the judgment of scientists they respect—these are their guides in determining how time and the resources at their disposal can best be used.

On the other side are persons trained in management systems, in accounting, or in the interpretation of contracts. They may have little appreciation of the relative merits of one or another scientific experiment or line of research, but they know the terms of the grants and contracts they review, and they have found a considerable number of lapses from those terms, occasionally flagrant, sometimes minor. Some scientists have considered grants as essentially unrestricted, to be used as they saw fit without regard to the specifics of the original proposal. And in the more common cases in which the investigator did follow the original plan, financial and other records have often been missing, incomplete, or inaccurate. Government auditors believe they have had much to complain about.

In the absence of a common background and a common understanding to unite the two sides, written regulations become more lengthy and more numerous. There is more insistence on the details of how records are kept and reports prepared. There is more insistence on controls to make sure that the university performs exactly as it said it would in a grant application, and as the agency thought it would in approving the grant—all of this to assure the auditors that public funds have been properly used and that the university is held fully accountable. But from the viewpoint of university representatives, exactly the same proliferation of regulations frequently seems to interfere with the substance involved, the purpose for which the grant or contract was made in the first place.

The adversarial relationship that has developed is marked by frustration, irritation, and suspicion on both sides. An illuminating, and one would hope rare, example was recently reported during a site visit for this study by a university officer responsible for coordinating sponsored research activities. The regional representative of HEW, which had become the auditing agency for the university, told him, "If you think you had trouble before, we're really going to get you now." It is almost inconceivable that such a threat would have been made—or even secretly thought—a quarter of a century ago when federal agencies were building the foundations of the government/university partnership in research. The attitude then was largely one of mutual trust—one of the good legacies of the World War II cooperative relationship.

Since then, arguments over indirect costs, insistence upon cost sharing, a few flagrant abuses by grant recipients, congressional probing of occasional agency laxness, and the changing attitudes and values described earlier have created so much antagonism and suspicion that months of negotiations now lead to a lengthy grant or contract that incorporates many pages of detailed regulations and implies many more. The difference symbolizes the change from trust to suspicion that constitutes one of the great costs of the present government/university relationship.

Another result has been a substantial increase in dollar costs. The additional data that must be compiled and analyzed, the new records that must be kept, the extra reports that must be filed, and the additional negotiations that must be entered into all require more filing cases, more clerks and statistical analysts, more office space, more vice presidents, more computer time, more telephone calls, and more of all the supporting services, supplies, and equipment that grow with staff size. Above all, they require more administrative work by scientists who frequently are not very good administrators—all resulting in a corresponding reduction in the research produced per dollar spent.

The Costs of Compliance

No one knows the total costs of compliance with all the government regulations, but several estimates and sample studies indicate that the amount is substantial. In one of the most detailed studies, the University of California analyzed the impacts—both costs and benefits—of nine different areas of federal regulations affecting their research activities. The areas of impact studied were: cash flow, cost recovery, financial management, health and safety, protection of the rights of human subjects, procurement of real property and of personnel other than members of the permanent payroll staff, property management, preparation of proposals, and time-and-effort reporting on the part of faculty members and other research personnel.

Ten other sets of regulations were identified but not analyzed in detail to determine their impacts: affirmative action, procedures to be followed in selecting and using consultants, cost sharing, environmental impact, the rights to patents and inventions, care and maintenance of laboratory animals, the use and protection of narcotics and dangerous drugs, the rights to data, requirements for technical reports, and travel approval. Very brief summaries of several of the analyses will illustrate the nature and degree of impact of government regulations on the conduct and cost of research.

Cash flow. The university lost $630,000 in interest in one year because it had to use its own working capital to pay expenses of projects for which the sponsoring federal agency would provide reimbursement only after evidence of expenditures had been submitted and reviewed. (Other grants or contracts, even some from the same agencies, were paid in advance.) [24]

Environmental health and safety regulations. These increased the difficulty of contract negotiations and required numerous extra reports, with little or no increase in protection over that afforded by state, local, and university regulations. [25]

Protection of human subjects. There was some real improvement in the protection of the rights of human subjects, at a cost of about $100,000 a year and some decrease in the scientific value of some types of research. [26]

Property management. These requirements produced a substantial burden of paperwork that meant little to the federal agencies because most of the property involved was later given to the university. [27]

Time-and-effort reporting. The cost here was an estimated $500,000 each year. [28]

Preparation of reports. Much additional work was made necessary by the nonstandardized requirements of federal agencies. [29]

These results in no way depreciate the great value of federal funds for research. Federal support has enabled universities to accomplish much that otherwise would not have been possible. Nor do these figures challenge the objectives that lie behind some of the regulations: affirmative action, protection of the rights of human subjects, and honesty in the handling of public funds, among others. What is clear, though, is that to secure the information, analyze the data, and prepare the reports that will convince government auditors that a university has complied with federal requirements is a very costly business. Just how costly nobody knows. Faculty do not keep the kind of records that would fully satisfy an ardent cost accountant or, in this case, that would allow a university to arrive with confidence at a close estimate of all the costs incurred in meeting a particular regulation. Estimates are necessary, and estimates can be challenged. And the government auditor impresses his superiors by finding costs to disallow. And thus the irritation and mistrust are compounded.

The University of California is only one of the major research institutions in the university world. Similar costs were being incurred by other universities. It would be hazardous to estimate the total national amount by extrapolation from one example. But it can still be cautiously concluded that federal regulations, in their multiplicity, their detail, their variety, and their nonstandardized forms all add up to a very substantial increase in administrative costs. Some of these costs become part of the university's indirect costs for which reimbursement can be sought in future grants and contracts and so become an added burden on the taxpayers. Some of the costs cannot be handled in this fashion, thus reducing the funds that are available for other purposes—purposes that to faculty members and university administrators nearly always seem more important than filling in another form to send to Washington.

Sharing the Responsibility for Decisions

Universities are public institutions doing public business. The solution to the problem of controls over their research activities is not to remove them from public and governmental influence but to secure agreement on the methods of sharing responsibility that will best accomplish two goals: One is to acquire the additional knowledge that will help solve major national problems. The other is to advance scientific competence and understanding as soundly and extensively as possible.

As government agencies and universities have worked toward both of these objectives, a substantial change has occurred in the balance of decision-making responsibility. Shortly after World War II it seemed appropriate for research scientists and engineers to have considerable responsibility for planning peacetime research: Their spectacular contributions to military affairs were still fresh in mind. The Office of Naval Research, the first federal agency to provide major support for academic research in the postwar period, made grants to enable scientists to explore their own ideas. Sooner or later, the Navy believed, a considerable portion of the resulting new knowledge would prove to be useful; when that time came, more tightly organized programs of applied research and development could be organized to bring those ideas into practical application.[30]

Similar trust marked much of the support given academic research by the other military services; and when NSF came into existence, its first director and several senior staff members moved over from the Office of Naval Research, bringing with them the values and procedures they had employed at ONR.

Those practices were consistent with the system of internal checks and controls that has been best described by Michael Polanyi in *The Republic of Science*.[31] Polanyi argued that in pure science (not in developmental work) internal scientific controls, acting through peer judgment and scientific consensus, served so effectively to guide scientists into those problems that should next be studied that any external interference with the system would retard scientific progress.

As time went on, though, some influential congressmen and government executives became increasingly skeptical that the internal controls over scientific research were working effectively, that peer review was unbiased and objective, and that scientists could be trusted to select the problems that most needed attention.[32] On this basis they have required two changes: first, more central planning of the fields and problems to be studied and of the details of procedures to be followed; and second, a closely related increase in efforts to make scientists more accountable, both nominally to the public interest and directly to staff members of federal agencies and to congressional committees. Increasingly, grantees have been required to demonstrate that they have conscientiously followed the rules and instructions prescribed by their federal supporters.

These processes of control and accountability can be described from quite different viewpoints. They may be viewed as instruments to make scientists more responsible and accountable to societal needs and values, or as ways of muscling in on what should be internal university responsibilities. However one views the changes, the agencies responsible for them have also been under pressure, for they are accountable to Congress and the President for the accomplishment of their missions and the use of their funds. They cannot delegate all decision making to their grantees.

At least in the academic world, though, it is widely believed that regulation has swung too far in the direction of centralized management of research, and that research and the universities are both threatened as a result. One danger is that objectives and policies adopted through appropriate political processes may become distorted. A national objective is typically defined in broad terms in congressional legislation or Presidential statements. It then becomes an agency responsibility, and staff members of the controlling agency may enforce their own interpretation of that objective as they begin to implement it. In practice, then, the national will may be significantly redefined by agency staff members. President Truman observed that "every President in history has been faced with this problem: how to prevent career men from circumventing Presidential policy." Sometimes policy is deliberately circumvented; sometimes it is simply reinterpreted.[33]

The second danger is that too much control from the center will reduce the effectiveness of the research effort. One example has been identified in a review of the behavioral and social science research funded by NSF. A committee of the National Research Council found basic research in these fields that had been supported through traditional NSF procedures to be "generally excellent," whereas work done under the centrally planned RANN program was "not impressive."[34]

A more illuminating example, and one that had little to do with universities, was provided by Project Hindsight, a study of the research and development events that led to substantial improvements in military weapons between 1945 and 1965. One of the significant conclusions of that study was that most of the new findings that led to important advances had not been foreseen when R&D contracts were given out. Instead, a new finding or a new opportunity developed during the course of the work. To follow up that new opportunity required a shift away from the originally planned program. To negotiate a change in the research contract would usually have introduced more delay than the investigators were willing to accept before learning whether the new possibility was in fact as promising as it initially appeared. To avoid that delay, many contractors used their own funds, shifted resources from other contracts, or in some other fashion "bootlegged" the research that actually turned out to be more effective in achieving objectives than were the original plans.[35]

This conclusion is no surprise to students of the history of science, who argue persuasively that scientific knowledge advances most rapidly when each scientist can conduct the research that seems most likely to lead to a significant forward step. Independence is a precious commodity, but there is an old-fashioned ring to this argument, reminiscent of the days when research was usually an individual affair and when the necessary tools and materials were available or could be obtained through individual effort. Now, with scientific equipment as expensive as it is, with resources limited, with a cooperative effort necessary in many research areas, and with growing interest in multidisciplinary efforts, individual decisions are no longer possible and group decisions have become necessary. Nevertheless, there remains the problem of determining where and by whom decisions can most knowledgeably be made. There can be no universal answer, but the purpose of federally funded programs ought to be as explicit as possible so that there can be full agreement by both investigators and central agency personnel on working objectives, and the details of research planning and management then can be left as fully as possible to the investigators.

Changes in Funding: The Effects on Science, Technology, and the Universities

This section traces three major consequences of the rapid and sustained rise and the subsequent leveling off or decline of funds for research and development: What have been the effects on the quantity and pace of scientific research? What have been the effects on the practical application of new scientific knowledge? What have been the effects on the nation's research universities, those that constitute a de facto national system for graduate education and the advancement of science? Two time periods are involved: the period of expansion, which lasted long enough and ended long enough ago that any major effects should by now be clear; and the period of curtailment, which began only in the latter part of the 1960s and may not yet be over, thus demanding more tentative judgments.

Effects on the Advancement of Science

When American political leaders decided at the end of World War II to expand the national R&D program they expected the following chain of results: More research would be conducted; more new knowledge would be acquired and published; the new knowledge would lead to further advances in the sciences and also to inventions, innovations, and other developments that would improve national health, welfare, and economy.

Those expectations were sound. Much more research has been conducted, and the progress of science has been spectacular. In geophysics, as one example, a deepened understanding of plate tectonics, analysis of a wide range of sea-bottom and ice cores, detailed study of the magnetosphere, manned and unmanned exploration of the moon and planets, and other types of studies have led to a much richer understanding of the structure and history of the earth, the history of the solar system, and the complexities of solar-terrestrial relationships. In astrophysics, the discoveries of pulsars and quasars are popular symbols both of new knowledge and of new puzzles concerning the dynamics of the cosmos. Achievements have been equally impressive in immunology, solid state physics, molecular biology, oceanography, and other fields. In short, new ideas, new laboratories, more powerful instruments, more extensive and accurate collections of basic data, and additional numbers of bright young scientists, all made possible by generous and continuing financial support, have advanced scientific understanding tremendously.

Now that research funds have stopped growing, and in some fields have declined, has scientific progress also faltered or started to decline? In the long run, that could be expected, but time lags are inevitable during expansion and also during retrenchment. In a period of expansion it takes years to train new scientists and bring them to full productivity. In a time of retrenchment, there is a momentum to the enterprise that keeps the production and application of new knowledge going even after financial support and new entrants have begun to decline. The delays involved are of variable length. To secure a grant, conduct an experiment, and publish the results requires from several months to several years. The lag between announcement of a new finding and its effects on later research may be only a few days or may continue for years. The culmination of new knowledge in an important invention may take only a brief period or may take years. And between conception and realization of an innovation there is an average lag of about seven years.[36]

Although there is yet no way of knowing how serious or long lasting will be the full effects of the changes in research support, some evidence of declining trends has been summarized in *Science Indicators, 1974*, the 1975 report of the National Science Board to the President and the Congress. It suggests that the national research effort has been losing momentum and in some respects has declined. The number of scientific papers published in the U.S. grew fairly steadily up to 1968 or later, but has since slowed down or stopped in 10 of the 13 fields analyzed. In those 10 fields, the peak year of publication was not 1973, the last year for which full data are available, but some earlier year: 1972 for the atmospheric sciences, 1971 for engineering, 1969 for oceanography, 1968 for physics, and from 1968 to 1972 for six other fields.

As funds for university research increased, so also did the percentage of the nation's research papers that were written by university faculty members. They were responsible for 60 percent of the national total in 1960 and for 75 percent in 1973. But 1973 was not the peak year for university contributions in 7 of the 13 fields of science that have been analyzed. University contributions to the national total peaked in 1972 for chemistry, 1970 for atmospheric sciences, 1969 for psychology, and 1964 for oceanography. Thus in some major fields not only has the production of new knowledge slowed or declined (one would hope only temporarily), but the fraction of that new knowledge coming from universities has also declined.

During the period of increasing research funds, American authors, chiefly from universities, wrote a large share of the total world production of scientific papers. For the seven fields shown in Table 2, this ranged in 1965 from nearly 24 percent in mathematics to just over 79 percent in psychology. Moreover, in terms of the number of citations issued for published papers, U.S. authors were proportionately more broadly represented than authors from any other major country in biology and biomedical research, in physics, and in the earth and space sciences; and they were tied with the United Kingdom in clinical medicine, with West Germany in chemistry, and with France in engineering. U.S. contributions to the world's scientific literature are not only great in quantity but also high in quality as judged by their colleagues around the world.

Today, the U.S. is still the leading source of scientific papers, but our scientists are publishing smaller percentages of research papers than they were a decade ago in chemistry, engineering, physics, psychology, and systematic biology. They have maintained their percentages in mathematics and molecular biology, but these two are not necessarily exceptions to the general trend. Molecular biology has not had financial difficulties as serious as those in other fields; and in mathematics the

Table 2

Percentage of World Scientific Literature
Written by U.S. Authors, Selected Fields,
Selected Years, 1965-1973*

	1965	1967	1969	1971	1972	1973
Chemistry	25.9%	24.5%	24.2%	23.9%	22.4%	21.2%
Engineering	49.9	48.8	48.3	49.7	44.6	43.7
Mathematics	23.9	23.9	26.9	27.8	29.3	23.6
Molecular biology	46.6	48.6	47.6	48.7	45.9	46.7
Physics	41.3	42.1	41.0	42.4	38.5	38.4
Psychology	79.3	79.2	76.6	76.5	74.4	74.4
Systematic biology	—	35.8	29.4	33.3	31.2	30.8

*For comparison, U.S. scientists were the first-named authors of 41.5 percent of the scientific papers listed in the 1967 volume of *Current Contents*, whose worldwide coverage of all fields of science and technology includes from 80 to 90 percent of the papers that are subsequently cited in other scientific publications (Derek J. de Solla Price, "Measuring the Size of Science," *Proceedings of the Israel Academy of Sciences and Humanities*, Vol. 9, No. 6, pp. 98-111, 1969).

Source: National Science Board, *Science Indicators, 1974*, Table 1-6.

U.S. percentage continued to increase after 1965, hit a peak in 1972, and then dropped sharply in 1973.

Some information on the time patterns involved in these recent declines can be obtained by comparing the peak year of funding for research in several fields with the peak year of research publications in those fields. Data for this purpose are available for astronomy, biology, chemistry, engineering, mathematics, physics, and psychology. In five of these seven fields, the peak year of federal funding for basic research came in 1970 or earlier. In four of the five fields (engineering, mathematics, physics, and psychology), the peak year of publication came from one to six years later. (Astronomy was an exception; its peak funding year was 1969, and it was still showing an increase in publications through 1973.) Similarly, in six of the seven fields the peak year of total funding for basic research in universities came in 1970 or earlier. In five of these six fields (astronomy, chemistry, engineering, mathematics, and physics), the peak year of publications by faculty members came from one to four years later. (The exception was biology, which had its funding peak in 1970 and was still showing an increase in publications through 1973.)

An increase in financial support could lead to resumption of the upward trends of earlier years, so perhaps the recent declines will be temporary. But as of now, the evidence suggests that a downturn in the publication of new scientific findings can be expected from one to perhaps four or five years after a downturn in funding. Overall, the funding changes since the late 1960s have been followed by a decrease in the absolute number of scientific publications, a decrease in the percentage coming from university faculty members, and a decreased relative contribution of the U.S. to the world's scientific literature. There is still much first-rate research, and important scientific advances will continue to be made, but the pace appears to have slowed down, both absolutely and in comparison with the rest of the scientific world.

Impact on Technology and Applied Science

Achievements in the practical application of new knowledge have also been spectacular. From 1950 to 1975 the average yield of corn increased from 38 to 87 bushels per acre, wheat from 17 to 31 bushels, and soybeans from 22 to 27 bushels. Death rates from rheumatic fever, uterine cancer, tuberculosis, chronic nephritis, and several other diseases declined markedly, while poliomyelitis and smallpox were essentially eradicated. In the same quarter century, integrated circuits, worldwide communication by satellites, lasers, highly sophisticated computers and their time-sharing use, and many other innovations found wide use in industry, commerce, education, communication, and entertainment. In addition to innovations that have already been achieved, research progress makes others seem probable: more accurate forecasts of weather, highly specific insecticides with minimal side effects, genetic improvement of plant and perhaps also animal strains. The art of measuring the contributions of research and development to economic growth is not precise, but several econometric analyses agree in estimating that in the U.S. the returns have been positive. Terleckyj's estimates are 25 to 30 percent a year of direct return on industrial investments in R&D, and an additional 30 to 80 percent in indirect returns, as, for example, the benefits accruing to a business concern using purchased or leased computers.[37]

Some social values have changed, and some of the harmful side effects of technological developments have become more widely recognized than they were two or three decades ago. But this does not negate the fact that the original strategy achieved much of what was intended. The advances in technology, medicine, and agriculture since 1950 have been major contributors to the health, the food supply, the economic welfare, and the leisure opportunities of our nation and beyond.

It is also true, though, that for practical applications as well as for pure science we should ask if the funding changes of recent years have resulted in any decline in the rate of new developments. *Science Indicators, 1974* again offers tentative evidence. The number of patents awarded to U.S. individuals and corporations rose somewhat irregularly from 1960 to 1971 and then fell. The number of patents awarded by other countries to U.S. citizens rose slightly and irregularly to 1972 and then in 1973 dropped by 13 percent, by far the largest annual change in any year since 1966 or earlier. These changes, like others, may be only temporary, but U.S. citizens have not in recent years had as many patents awarded as they did somewhat earlier.

In a special study of innovations introduced into the market in the 1953-73 period, 500 were selected by an international panel of experts as being the most significant in terms of their technological, social, and economic importance. Of these 500, 319 were introduced by U.S. companies. Whether there have been fewer such innovations or a lower percentage originating in the U.S. cannot yet be determined.

Inventions come from a variety of sources, and innovations typically come as the culmination and synthesis of several lines of research. One would not expect more than a portion of the research underlying patents and innovations to have taken place in university laboratories, but there is evidence that that portion has been increasing. During the period of expansion of research support, basic research contributed increasingly to the development of new processes and new products awarded patents. Between 1950 and 1961, 28 percent of the citations of research on which basic U.S. patents were grounded came from universities and other nonprofit institutions. From 1962 to 1974, 48 percent of such citations were for research conducted in universities and other nonprofit institutions. Clearly the large amount of university research has contributed with increasing frequency to the development of patentable ideas.

As further evidence, the Research Corporation, which manages patents that grow out of university research, reported a new high in royalties to universities in 1975, and added: "The distributions have grown nearly 300 percent from 1972 to 1975, and reflect spreading utilization of technology originating in university laboratories."[38]

When 277 major innovations that had been developed in the U.S. between 1953 and 1973 were ranked in terms of their novelty and impact, it was found that the more radical the innovation the more likely it was that basic research had been involved. Basic research contributed directly to 45 percent of those innovations that merely constituted improvements in existing technology, to 48 percent of those that represented major technological advances, and to 68 percent of those that were classified as "radical breakthroughs." Not only was basic research involved in these innovations, but the involvement was to a very substantial extent; of the citations of the technology underlying these 277 innovations, 50 percent were to applied research, 27 percent to basic research, and the remainder to other sources, such as the transfer of existing technology developed within the same company.[39]

Given this evidence, one would expect a decline of research funds to lead to a decline in research and a subsequent drop in research reports and applications. And indeed the scientific returns from university research began to decline a few years after the funds stopped growing. Because of the lags involved, it is too soon to know how soon or how great will be the effects on the practical applications of new knowledge, but there are already warning signs that they too may be declining.

Effects on the Universities as a National System

The great expansion of academic research was paralleled by increases in the number of graduate students, the number of doctoral programs, and the number of doctoral-granting institutions. In 1950 approximately 150 American institutions offered the doctorate in one or more fields. By 1968 the number had climbed to 278 and many more were hoping to join that group. As it turned out, the number of doctoral-granting universities increased only slightly after 1968, and one important consequence of the post-1967 changes in support for academic research is that the number of such institutions has not expanded nearly as much as was expected a decade ago.

Moreover, some of the smaller or newer universities have reconsidered their aspirations for big league status. In 1964 and again in 1971, Gross and Grambsch surveyed faculty members and administrative officers at 68 American universities to study the power structure in each, to determine the amount of emphasis given by each university to each of 47 listed university goals, and to determine the amount of emphasis the faculty members and administrative officers at each university thought should be given to each of these goals. Among the major findings, the authors reported that "within universities there has been an increased meeting of the minds on the proper goals of the university. Conflict has given way to substantial consensus." As a result,

> universities have become distinctly more stratified. The sets of goals exhibiting congruence across universities show distinct differences and clusterings. Goals and goal preferences are found to divide sharply in private as compared to public universities, in highly productive as compared to less productive universities, and in top prestige as compared to bottom prestige universities. This stratification has reached the point where one might more appropriately speak of it as fragmentation, for stratification does imply that the universities are part of the same system. If anything, some universities (most strikingly those of low prestige) appear to be seeking wholly new objectives which do not compete with those of the more prestigious universities. This tendency suggests a breakup of the system itself, with still further options for students of different interests and talents. The university system may then become less of a monolith, better adapted to the enormously diversified student body that now finds attendance at an institution of higher learning not simply an advantage but an obligation.[40]

Contributing to this stratification, or segmentation, some universities have lost ground in the competition for research funds; and some have abandoned efforts to climb into the big university class, while others have succeeded in making that move.

The changed positions of a number of individual universities have also produced some shifts in major characteristics of the whole university research system. There was a small shift from private to public universities; in 1963-65 the top 50 recipients of federal research funds included 24 public and 26 private universities, but by 1973-75 the balance had shifted to 28 public and 22 private. Geographically, New England and the Middle Atlantic states lost a bit to the West; their share of the top 50 universities dropped by 3 from 15 to 12, while the Rocky Mountain and Pacific Coast share went up from 12 to 15. Not surprisingly, there was a similar shift in total federal funds for academic research, with the Middle Atlantic and North Central states losing and the Mountain and Pacific states gaining several percentage points.

These changes in the distribution of research funds, and of the universities receiving the largest amounts of federal research support, have had the effect of increasing the geographic dispersion of what was already the most decentralized distribution of scientists in any country. In 1967, New York City was the address of only 5 percent of the first-named authors of scientific papers written by American scientists, but 5 percent was more than could be claimed by any other American city. Among other countries, only West Germany approached that level of dispersion, with 8 percent of its authors in Berlin. Others showed substantially higher concentrations: United Kingdom, 21 percent in London; U.S.S.R., 50 percent in Moscow; France, 26 percent in Paris; Japan, 33 percent in Tokyo; Canada, 14 percent in Ottawa.[41]

The upward and downward shifts in the relative amounts of federal funds received by a number of individual universities no doubt had numerous and sometimes highly individualistic explanations. The Massachusetts Institute of Technology, which year after year led all other universities by a large margin, fell into a competitive range in 1974 when the Draper Laboratory began to be financed separately rather than as part of MIT. The University of California, San Diego rose rapidly in relative position because a full-fledged university could be built easily on the foundation of the Scripps Institute of Oceanography.

A more detailed analysis of the size and number of significant changes in relative position, and information concerning some of the correlates of those changes, can be obtained by comparing four sets of data:

(1) *Market Shares of Research Funds in 1963-65.* Since 1963, NSF has annually reported the total amount of federal money for research that went to each college and university, or to each of the top 100. Combining the amounts for 1963, 1964, and 1965 for each university gives a measure of its research standing at a time well after the beginning of the period of rapid expansion but before that period came to an end.

(2) *Market Shares in 1973-75.* The most recent year for which institu-

tional data have been published is 1975. Combining the amounts channeled to each university for 1973, 1974, and 1975 provides a measure of its research standing at a time well after the rapid expansion ended.

(3) *Quality Ratings in 1963-65.* In 1964 the American Council on Education (ACE) asked large numbers of scholars in each of a number of disciplines to rate the quality of the graduate programs offered by American universities in their fields. The field-by-field results of this study are familiarly known as Cartter ratings.[42]

(4) *Quality Ratings in 1973-75.* In 1969 ACE again secured peer ratings of the quality of graduate programs in American universities. These Roose-Andersen[43] ratings are not matched by date with the 1973-75 market shares but probably can be used for that period since in most cases the quality of a university does not change rapidly. This is evidenced by a 1975 Educational Testing Service study that obtained peer ratings of graduate departments of chemistry, history, and psychology in 24 or 25 universities. Rank-difference correlations of the mean departmental ratings in 1975 with the comparable Roose-Andersen ratings of 1969 were .99 for chemistry, .99 for history, and .98 for psychology. Although changes of as many as four rank positions were found, peer ratings are obviously highly stable over a few years, and it therefore seems safe to use the 1969 Roose-Andersen ratings as good approximations of the quality of the scientific programs of universities in 1973-75.[44]

In both the Cartter and Roose-Andersen surveys departments were rated, not universities. For the purposes of this analysis, however, each university was given two institutional scores. One was the total weighted rating its departments received for the 17 fields in the biological sciences, physical sciences, and engineering that were rated in 1964. The other was the similar combined score for the ratings its departments received for the 20 fields of science and engineering that were rated in 1969. These scores will be referred to as Cartter and Roose-Andersen scores respectively. It should be emphasized, however, that the authors of both reports carefully refrained from assigning overall ratings to the universities involved, and it should also be emphasized that the scores used here are also not overall ratings. They take no account of the quality of work in the arts and humanities or the social sciences. They are used as indices of total institutional competence in scientific research and should not be interpreted as anything more than that.

(The association between any two of these four variables can be measured by the correlation coefficient known as gamma. The numerical value of gamma may be interpreted directly as the percentage of errors avoided in guessing the order of two universities on one variable if one knows their order on the other. If gamma is zero and institution A is known to be above institution B on one variable, then [disregarding ties] A is equally likely to be above or below B on the other; one can only guess at random. If gamma is .75 and A is above B on one variable, errors will be reduced by 75 percent by guessing that A is also higher than B on the other variable. If gamma is negative, one should guess that they are in opposite orders on the two variables.[45])

Comparisons among these four sets of data show the following relationships:

Constancy of Shares. For the 100 universities receiving the largest amount of federal support for R&D in 1963-65, gamma between those amounts and the 1973-75 shares was .88. Within the more restricted top 50 universities of 1963-65, gamma was .80. In general, the large, research-intensive universities of the early 1960s were still large, research-intensive universities a decade later. Yet the upward and downward movements of some universities had been significant, not only for themselves but also for some characteristics of the whole university system. (This point will be more fully discussed later.)

Constancy of Quality. Among the 100 universities that received the largest amount of federal support for research in 1963-65, peer judgments of quality showed even greater constancy. Gamma between Cartter and Roose-Andersen scores was .96.

Roose-Andersen scores should normally be higher than Cartter scores, partly because Roose and Andersen obtained ratings on more disciplines than did Cartter and partly because some departments had actually improved between 1964 and 1969. As a matter of fact, Roose-Andersen scores were higher than Cartter scores for most universities. There were a few exceptions. Some universities were not judged to be as good in the sciences in 1969 as they had been in 1964. Relative positions, however, were highly stable as shown by the gamma of .96.

Market Shares and Quality. The gamma between 1963-65 market shares and Cartter scores was .89, and the gamma between 1973-75 market shares and Roose-Andersen scores was .85. The close relationship between shares and quality is reassuring and strengthens the credibility of both. When NSF was established, Congress instructed it to make scientific merit the ruling guide in allocating its funds. The peer review system of NIH has the same objectives. Hagstrom's analysis of the characteristics of the university departments most closely related to their Cartter ratings showed two to be outstanding: the number of research articles published by members of the department in the 1961-66 period and the number of citations in 1966 to publications by members of the department. The high correlations between quality ratings and market shares support the conclusion that the federal agencies have agreed closely with the collective judgment of scientists as to which departments were most capable of quality research.[46]

Changes in Shares and Changes in Quality. In general, universities that went up in quality ratings also increased their market shares between the two time periods, and those that declined in quality ratings also declined in market shares, but the relationship was not as close as those cited above. Gamma for the top 100 universities between changes in market shares and changes in quality scores was .31.

1963-65 Shares and Changes in Shares. For the 100 universities receiving the largest shares in 1963-65, gamma between those shares and changes in shares between then and 1973-75 was -.11, which means that across the 100 universities there was very little relationship between the size of 1963-65 shares and the extent to which 1973-75 shares were larger or smaller. However, among the universities that received exceptionally large shares of research funds in 1963-65 there was a clear negative relationship: The more they received in 1963-65, the more likely it was that they received relatively less in 1973-75. For the 50 universities that received the largest shares in 1963-65 ($16 million or more) gamma between those shares and the changes in shares between the two periods was -.31.

The negative signs of these coefficients indicate that the larger universities were subject to a leveling tendency. In absolute terms, they received more research money in 1973-75 than they did 10 years earlier, but their relative shares were smaller in the later period. This leveling tendency can also be shown by an analysis of institutional concentration of federal research funds. Some 98 percent of all federal research funds obligated to all of the over 3,000 colleges and universities in the country go to the approximately 280 that grant the doctorate in at least one field, and most of the total goes to a much smaller group of universities. The distribution has, however, become less concentrated than it used to be, as is shown in Table 3.

In 1963, one third of all federal funds allocated to academic research went to only 10 universities. Concentration in the top 10 is still high, but their share has gradually declined from one third to one quarter. The top 20 universities, which received half the total in 1963, now get a little over 40 percent. And the top 100, which received 90 percent in 1963, now get about 85 percent. Note, however, that the only group that has really lost is the top 10. The next 10, or 40, or 90 changed very little in their percentages of the total.

Thus there has been a significant flattening at the top. The most research-intensive universities of the early 1960s—and in general those were the ones judged to be of highest quality—now get more research money than they did then, but their relative share is smaller. Egalitarianism and the tightening of financial support since 1967 appear to have disproportionately affected those universities most highly esteemed and most heavily engaged in research.

Table 3

Concentration of Federal Funds for R&D
in Universities Receiving the Largest Total Obligations, 1963-1975*

Year	Top 10	Top 20	Top 50	Top 100
1963	32.8%	49.5%	71.9%	89.5%
1964	30.8	47.1	71.6	88.9
1965	30.0	45.8	70.5	88.8
1966	29.6	45.4	69.9	88.7
1967	29.1	44.9	69.6	88.1
1968	27.7	43.1	67.4	86.7
1969	27.4	43.2	67.3	86.1
1970	27.8	43.3	67.6	86.1
1971	27.1	42.7	67.2	85.8
1972	27.4	42.8	67.0	85.3
1973	27.1	42.4	67.1	85.1
1974	27.3	42.8	67.2	85.7
1975	25.8	41.4	66.2	85.0

*The percentages shown for 1974 and 1975 differ from those reported by NSF. Many individual changes collectively account for the reduction in institutional concentration of federal R&D funds, and most are part of the process demonstrated above. However, one change was so large and so specific in decreasing funds not only to one university but to the whole university sector that it calls for special treatment: namely, the separation of the Draper Laboratory from Massachusetts Institute of Technology. In 1973 and earlier, when it was known as the Instrumentation Laboratory, it was funded through MIT. In 1974 and later, its federal support ($85.626 million in 1974 and $76.212 million in 1975) came directly to the Laboratory. In order to avoid such a large discontinuity, the 1974 and 1975 percentages have been computed as if the Draper Laboratory were still funded through MIT. (For another factor that calls for caution in interpreting time-series data see the footnote to Table 4.)

Source: National Science Foundation, *Federal Support to Universities, Colleges, and Selected Nonprofit Institutions,* annual reports.

Changes in Research Status

The gamma coefficients measuring the strength of association between shares and quality, changes of shares and changes in quality, and the size of 1963-65 shares and changes in shares indicate that two counterforces have been at work. On the one hand, there has been a tendency for changes in judged quality to be associated with changes of the same direction in size of market shares. On the other hand, there has been a leveling tendency: Universities that were leaders in securing federal research funds in the earlier period have received relatively (but not absolutely) less in more recent years. Similarly universities judged in 1964 to be of the highest scientific quality have generally lost some of their share of federal research funds; of the 25 with the highest Cartter scores, 16 had smaller percentage shares in 1973-75 than in 1963-65.

Stating these relationships between shares of research funds and peer judgments of the quality of graduate programs does not imply a causal relationship in either direction. One need not assume either that more favorable peer ratings produced larger research funds or that larger market shares produced more favorable peer ratings. It is more reasonable to assume that upward and downward shifts in both measures reflected changes in research competence; that these changes resulted from the combined effects of all those decisions that determined which faculty members and graduate students with which scientific interests and abilities were attracted to or retained by each university; and that both scientific colleagues elsewhere in the country and the judges of research proposals were sensitive to these differences. Both systems of judgment seem to have been working effectively.

How the shifts in the allocation of research funds affected a number of individual universities is summarized in Tables 4, 5, and 6. Table 4 concerns the 25 universities that received the largest amounts of federal research funds in 1963-65—over $30 million each in the three years. It identifies those whose market shares increased or decreased by more than 15 percent between 1963-65 and 1973-75, and also shows the rank order in each of the two periods. The listings are in decreasing order of percentage change in size of shares. Consistent with the leveling tendency described earlier, only 3 of these large universities increased their market shares by over 15 percent, while 11 showed decreases of that magnitude.

Table 5 shows similar information for a second tier of research universities—51 that received from $10 to $30 million of federal research funds in 1963-65. For this group, the cutoff score for listing is an increase or decrease of over 25 percent in market shares instead of the 15 percent used for the first group. Of these second-tier universities, 17 showed increases of greater than 25 percent, while 10 showed decreases of that magnitude.

Public and private universities show up quite differently in these two tables. Of the 20 (in Tables 4 and 5) that moved up substantially, 14 were public and 6 private. Of the 21 that moved down by comparable percentages, 7 were public and 14 private. All 4 of those that climbed into the top 10 were public.

Among universities that received less than $10 million of federal funds for research in 1963-65 there were some very large percentage changes in market shares. But the only ones that need be identified are the few appearing in Table 6 that increased their market shares by 70 percent or more and in so doing also climbed into the top 75 of 1973-75. To make room for these surging institutions, others had to drop to low-

48

Table 4

Changes in Market Shares and Ranks of Universities Receiving $30 Million or More of Federal Research Funds in 1963-1965

Institution	Percent change in market share 1963-65 to 1973-75	Rank 1963-65	Rank 1973-75
Shares Increased 15 Percent or More			
University of Texas System*	71%	16	2
University of Washington	66	17	3
University of Wisconsin	17	10	8
Shares Decreased 15 Percent or More*			
University of Michigan	-49%	2	13
Princeton University	-43	21	44
Columbia University	-38	3	9
Case-Western Reserve University	-36	20	38
University of Chicago	-34	8	18
New York University	-32	12	21
Ohio State University	-26	19	28
University of Pittsburgh	-25	23	37
University of Illinois System*	-24	9	11
University of California-Berkeley	-23	6	10
Harvard University	-17	5	7

Note: Ten other universities in this size class changed by less than 15 percent: California Institute of Technology, University of California-Los Angeles, Cornell, Johns Hopkins, Maryland*, Minnesota, Pennsylvania, Rochester, Stanford, and Yale. Massachusetts Institute of Technology increased by 15 percent if funds for the Draper Laboratory are included for 1974 and 1975, and decreased by 31 percent if they are not (see footnote to Table 3).

*Several cautions must be observed in considering dollar amounts, market shares, and ranks of individual universities:

(a) All figures are for three-year periods. Thus neither market shares nor ranks agree with those reported by NSF for any single year.

(b) Dollar amounts are for obligations received, not for expenditures. Although the correlation between obligations and expenditures is about .95 for a typical year, the two may differ substantially for a few universities, especially those whose obligations received were increasing or decreasing rapidly.

(c) Because NSF reports of obligations are based on data furnished by federal agencies—while expenditures are reported by universities—there is some small danger of discrepancies. For example, a university that includes a medical school or a research foundation may have obligations reported separately for that component while its expenditure reports are included in the report for the university as a whole.

(d) Some reporting units have changed materially between the two time periods compared. This is especially likely to arise in state universities. In several cases 1963-65 obligations were reported under only one institutional name, whereas 1973-75 obligations were reported separately for each of several components. For example, all research and development funds obligated to the University of Maryland in 1963-65 were combined in a single account; in 1973-75 there were four separate accounts—for branches in College Park, Baltimore, Baltimore County, and Eastern Shore. Comparable changes were identified for the universities of Alabama, Arkansas, Illinois, Indiana, Louisiana State, Massachusetts, Missouri, Nebraska, Oregon, Tennessee, and Texas. In all such cases listed here market shares are computed on the combined amounts of all of the 1973-75 components that were included in the single 1963-65 reporting unit. This means that the share shown for 1973-75 may be far larger than that reported by NSF for the central or parent campus. The greatest discrepancy is for the University of Texas. In 1963-65, the University had a market share of 1.61 percent of all federal R&D funds that went to academic institutions, a share that put it in the 16th rank among universities. In 1973-75, the University of Texas-Austin received 0.99 percent of federal R&D funds for universities, putting it in 28th rank. But when all of the University of Texas units and its several medical centers that had not been separately reported in 1963-65 but were separated in the 1973-75 reports were combined into a single total, the market share was 2.75 percent and the rank was number 2. Universities for which several units or branches have been combined in this analysis of market shares are identified with asterisks in Tables 4 and 5. For these institutions, the figures reported are meaningful in considering changes in market shares for the systems they represent, but the 1973-75 market shares and ranks shown in the tables are all higher than those for the central or parent campus alone.

Table 5

Changes in Market Shares and Ranks of Universities Receiving from $10 to $30 Million of Federal Research Funds in 1963-1965

Institution	Percent change in market share 1963-65 to 1973-75	Rank 1963-65	Rank 1973-75
Shares Increased 25 Percent or More			
University of California-San Diego	228%	35	6
University of California-San Francisco	122	44	19
Colorado State University	84	73	46
University of Alabama*	81	63	39
University of Hawaii	75	68	43
University of North Carolina-Chapel Hill	57	50	33
University of California-Davis	45	45	34
University of Utah	42	41	32
Washington University (St. Louis)	40	27	20
University of Miami	36	37	30
University of Southern California	35	30	22
Baylor University*	29	40	36
Michigan State University	29	49	42
Emory University	28	74	61
University of Colorado	26	32	25
University of Iowa	26	42	40
Vanderbilt University	26	56	51
Shares Decreased 25 Percent or More			
Polytechnic Institute of New York	-69%	70	115
Illinois Institute of Technology	-60	66	107
Syracuse University	-55	47	88
Denver University	-52	71	104
University of Oklahoma	-49	65	98
Tulane University	-43	39	73
Brown University	-41	43	77
Iowa State University	-40	61	86
Carnegie-Mellon University	-36	46	70
Wayne State University	-36	67	89

Note: There were 24 other universities in this size class that changed by less than 25 percent: Arizona, Duke, Florida, Florida State, George Washington, Indiana*, Kansas, Kentucky, Louisiana State*, Missouri*, New Mexico State, North Carolina at Raleigh, Northwestern, Oregon*, Oregon State, Pennsylvania State, Purdue, Rutgers, SUNY-Buffalo, Tennessee*, Texas A&M, Tufts, Virginia, and Yeshiva.

*See footnote to Table 4.

Table 6

Changes in Market Shares and Ranks
of Universities Receiving from $5 to $10 Million
of Federal Research Funds in 1963-1965
and Showing Increases of 70 Percent or More
by 1973-1975

Institution	Percent change in market share 1963-65 to 1973-75	Rank 1963-65	Rank 1973-75
University of Connecticut	104%	106	65
University of New Mexico	85	105	74
Boston University	83	83	55
Rockefeller University	78	84	56
Temple University	71	90	58
University of Alaska	70	92	60

er levels. Some of those showing major declines are identified in the lower panel of Table 5.

Gross and Grambsch[47] were earlier quoted as reporting that "within universities there has been an increased meeting of the minds on the proper goals of the university." They also noted that greater internal agreement has been leading to a greater stratification. In 1971 Gross and Grambsch found larger differences than in 1964 between the goals most emphasized by private and by public universities and also a greater difference between universities of high prestige and those of lesser prestige.

Some of the substantial declines in market shares support the Gross and Grambsch description. But it seems doubtful that the change of goals and the resulting increase in stratification have resulted solely from a happy meeting of minds of the faculty members and administrators involved. The *Chronicle of Higher Education* and other members of the educational press report much internal dissension in some troubled universities that have not met their research goals of a few years ago. And the Gross and Grambsch study showed greater agreement within universities on the amount of emphasis actually being given to different goals than on the relative emphasis faculty members and administrators thought should be accorded those goals. Financial reality forced some universities to emphasize somewhat different goals than those of a few years earlier, but that did not mean that there was always close agreement on what their goals should be.

Confirming evidence was found in reports of site visits to a number of universities that varied widely in size, control, location, and amount of research funds. The observations and records made by the site visitors were completely independent of the analysis in this paper, but some of those observations describe universities that are listed in Tables 4 and 5 as having lost substantially in market shares between 1963-65 and 1973-75. Extracts or summarizing statements from the site visit reports describe some of the problems being encountered in universities that have had to change the emphasis given to different goals:

> *University A* is struggling to maintain its research level: "In the process there is a tilting of proposals to elicit funds, the undertaking of some team and interdisciplinary research, not because this might be desirable in itself, but because it is responsive to research opportunities—strategies openly and freely admitted as facts of life.... The climate...varies from gloom to a very guarded and cautious optimism."
>
> *University B* "is clearly on the defensive. The mood is one of widespread and deep concern over the future of the university. There is an air not of surrender but of discouragement."
>
> *University C* "In practically every department we visited, available indicators suggested that research is in decline.... [The university] has prided itself on being a center of basic research.... Consequently, the shift to an applied emphasis violates the traditions which the university has sought to establish.... Most of the departments...are now at the point of simply dropping out of the national research effort."
>
> *University D* is "in considerable trouble and the science and engineering research capability in particular trouble. Much of this may be due to over expansion in the boom years and now the issue is one of return to reality.... It is almost with some relief that they have given up their high expectations, and they actually seem to feel more comfortable with a lower level of science activities in the institution."

Some of these universities were comparatively high and others were considerably lower in terms of 1963-65 market shares. Now all are sliding to lower positions, and some appear to be sliding right out of the group substantially involved in graduate education and research.

In contrast, some other universities that have had considerable success in the recent competition for research funds gave the site visitors reason to write very different types of notes and summaries, as a few examples will illustrate:

> *University E* "is one of the nation's great research facilities in its area of specialization...spirit and morale [are] excellent...chief complaints: the gradual fiscal squeeze, erratic federal policy, and sudden zigs and zags."
>
> *University F* is "a superb institution, a national asset," but it is having trouble because of inadequate basic funding from the state, which treats it according to the funding formula used for all state institutions. "Morale is still pretty good," but they are fearful for the future.
>
> *University G* "seems to be faced with the prospect of either going back to being essentially a teaching institution as it was in 1960 or of going on to a different style of research." The university is now penalized by the state for having generated more research support, because

> overhead has to be turned in to the state while the university has to provide from its previous state budget the services that justify overhead payments on the new grants. After the state budget is set, each new research grant aids the principal investigator involved but penalizes the university. It is now "a second tier institution wanting to play in the national research game" that can go either way, depending to a considerable extent on state policies and decisions.
>
> *University H* has "benefited substantially from the shift of funding patterns in the direction of applied research." They think of themselves "as a specialized applied science institution and resource for the nation" in which there is an increasing orientation of the traditional basic science departments toward applied science and the interests of their strong professional schools. There is trouble with state funding practices, but they are energetic and "optimistic about the future if they can solve the problems they face with the state."

Both sets of sketches help to illuminate the living reality behind the changes summarized in Tables 4, 5, and 6. For a time, when federal research funds were increasing rapidly, many universities expanded their research activities substantially. Now the movement has split in two directions: Some universities are continuing as major research institutions of high quality and high volume. Others are dropping out or dropping lower. Differentiation within the whole set of universities is increasing.

Those that are de-emphasizing research have opportunities to concentrate on undergraduate education, continuing education, and some types of public service, and through these means to be of much value to their regions and communities. Those that are emphasizing research and graduate education are in some ways living more dangerously. According to Gross and Grambsch:

> The costs associated with following the path of specialization in research and scholarly production are great. There are definite and predictable sets of goals which characterize universities of high and low productivity. High productivity means focusing on research and graduate study and placing less emphasis upon traditional goals such as producing well-rounded students, loyalty to the local institution, or satisfying the needs of persons in the local areas.[48]

In choosing this route, public universities are running into increasing difficulties in maintaining public support and in persuading their state legislatures and state coordinating councils of the need for the special support and facilities that enable them to make best use of research funds provided by the federal government and other outside sources. Yet that support is essential if they are to continue to be leading universities whose high competence in research and scholarship serves their own regions, the rest of the educational system, and the entire nation.

Future Trends

Universities have had a great deal of experience in adjusting to changing circumstances. David Henry's review of the challenges they have faced concludes that adjustment has been a prevailing way of life through the boom of the 1920s, the depression of the 1930s, World War II, the GI bulge, and the heady expansion of the 1950s and 1960s.[49] Now universities are again deep in the process of adjusting to new conditions. This time they face somewhat different and tighter constraints than in the preceding decades. More of their financial support is for specified, categorical purposes. State coordinating boards are exercising stronger controls over public universities; faculty unionization and greater faculty participation in institutional decision making are reducing flexibility in reallocating resources. Major adjustments within universities will be made, but with more internal dissension than confronted the adjustments during World War II and the subsequent expansion. How well any particular university adapts, and how it fares in competition with other universities, will depend partly upon the strength and effectiveness of its own efforts, partly upon how well its particular capabilities and advantages match the needs and preferences of funding sources, and partly on other factors that will be understood only in retrospect.

Federal Funds for Research. Funds for research will continue to increase, probably at a rate adequate to keep up with inflation. Funds for university research will include substantial amounts for basic research. But it is not likely that the targeted, applied, multidisciplinary, or socially oriented interests of most of the federal agencies that make grants or contracts for university research will soon be de-emphasized. National needs call for such studies, and universities can contribute effectively to some of them. Federal emphasis will be heavily on project grants and contracts. In 1968, NSF devoted 12.4 percent of its funds to institutional improvement and general support. By 1974 this category had dwindled to 1.6 percent. To expand it substantially would require reversal of the policy that the National Board on Graduate Education summarized in 1975:

> universities are viewed as one among many types of competing institutions that can provide useful information to mission-oriented federal agencies. Research results are a commodity that the agencies can purchase as necessary from universities or any other competent supplier.[50]

Changed Relationship Between Research and Graduate Education. Both on and off campus there are worries about educating an unnecessarily large number of young scientists and scholars. Students naturally are helping to adjust supply to a diminished market, but universities also have a responsibility to help bring about that adjustment. Thus either by design or of necessity there is likely to be some loosening of the relationship between faculty research and the education of additional graduate students. Increased use of postdoctoral appointments seems probable, and larger use of research institutes that are wholly or partly removed from traditional university departments is being attempted.

If substantially wider use is made of independent or semi-independent research institutes, two outcomes are likely. One is that the best of these institutes will also become teaching institutions at the doctoral or postdoctoral level—as the Rockefeller Institute for Medical Research did when it changed its name to Rockefeller University, and as the Carnegie Institution of Washington and the Rand Corporation also have done, albeit less obviously and without a change of name. The other is that those institutes that are expected to serve as national laboratories (large accelerators, astronomical observatories, oceanographic facilities, atmospheric or environmental laboratories, etc.) will have their research programs largely planned by university scientists. Robinson found that this is what happened in physics, one of the pioneering fields in the development of national laboratories.[51] If this happens, there will be excellent research opportunities for faculty members, graduate students, and postdoctoral students—all selected in rigorous competition. With keen competition for access to these well-equipped laboratories, a reduction in the number of universities able to offer graduate programs of high quality in these areas will probably follow.

Progress of Science and Technology. Universities and other research institutes and agencies will continue to make the U.S. a major scientific country. However, U.S. contributions to the world's scientific literature and scientific advancement may be relatively smaller than in the recent past. Such a change will have very serious implications for this country's future productivity.

In technology, there is growing concern that the U.S. has slipped enough that its contributions will not be as great in relation to the rest of the world as in recent decades. Whether the longer term will reverse this trend or witness further decline is an open question. Already, however, the signs of a downturn in relative position summarized in *Science Indicators, 1974* and supported by evidence from scientists and engineers able to compare foreign and U.S. progress in their own fields of special knowledge have become subjects of concern, formal discussion, and some action. As one step, the 1977 and 1978 Presidential budgets included real (constant dollar) increases for basic research and for technological development, a change made to rectify what the budget makers decided had been a too restrictive policy in recent years.

External Controls. Federal and state governments are both seeking greater control over university activities, but to a substantial extent they are working at cross purposes. State agencies are inclined to assess universities' performance primarily in terms of short-term goals, while the federal government treats them primarily as members of the R&D community. State governments concentrate their support on educational functions and leave most research support to the federal government. The federal government, in its turn, expects the states or private sources to provide the basic continuing support that enables universities to qualify for federal research funds. The federal government has been withdrawing about as rapidly as it can from earlier forms of institutional support, and either by requiring cost sharing or through policies that prohibit payment of full indirect costs it does not cover the full costs of the research that its grants are intended to support.

The different and partly conflicting interests of federal and state governments seem likely to continue. That fact offers a special opportunity to the legislature of any state with a public university of high quality (or to the supporters of any first-quality private university). If such a university, already receiving substantial amounts of federal research support, were provided with a modest amount of uncommitted, flexible support for, say, the next decade, that investment could give the university much leverage in assuring its continuation high in the national rankings in quality and research funding. The special fund could be used for start-up grants for young faculty members, to supplement the library budget, secure special equipment, or in other ways give the university an advantage over others. As always, the universities with the best facilities and the ablest faculty members and graduate students will be the strongest competitors for federal research funds. The flexible funds proposed would simply help secure and retain those advantages.

External Rules and Regulations. University administrators and faculty members are becoming increasingly angry and frustrated over the variety and detail of federal regulations and over the way in which many are imposed without apparent regard for their effects on universities and without adequate opportunity for the reconciliation of differences. External regulation will surely continue and may increase, but the long run interests of both parties call for a better balance between the public need for some types of control and the needs of the universities for flexibility in using their resources. As Sanford Lakoff argues elsewhere within this volume, both sides will be better served if the conflict over external controls is resolved into a better state of balance.

How the universities will fare will depend to a considerable extent on how well they can work together to achieve the agreements and conditions that are in their collective interest. As a step in this direction, the National Association of Independent Colleges and Universities was established in 1976 to create "a stronger national voice," and the Association of American Universities strengthened its Washington staff in order better to defend universities against increasing federal controls.

Continuing Competition. Tightness of funds, mounting costs, inflation, changes in student population and in job opportunities for graduates, and the resulting need to readjust many plans have caused great difficulties for most universities and have been traumatic for some. One pervasive consequence has been a shift in relations between the university as an institution and its faculty members. The changes include increased faculty-administration bickering over indirect costs and the use of funds received for their reimbursement, stronger links between faculty grantees and the staffs of federal agencies, the proliferation of small independent research institutes, increased bureaucratization of universities to cope with federal regulations and faculty opposition to the regulations, shifts in university structure as various federally financed centers and institutes are created, a tendency for some units —particularly medical schools—to act independently of the parent university, and increasing unionization and pressures for maintenance of the status quo in departments and programs.

Nevertheless, the effects on the system as a whole have not been all bad. The country does not need as many universities emphasizing research and graduate education as aspired to that status a decade ago, or perhaps as it has now. The present readjustment is forcing some that could not attain that status to change their goals and reassess their plans. It could be argued that the weaker institutions are simply being shaken out. There is, of course, irony in having a government that has protected various business enterprises against the rigors of free competition now treating universities on a sink-or-swim basis; but the process is leading toward diversity among institutions of higher education. If state legislatures are wise enough to encourage that trend instead of frustrating it, the result could be advantageous to the entire nation. If we can be confident that the right universities will survive the competition so that readjustment leads to an appropriately sized and nationally distributed system of strong research universities, that will be a desirable outcome.

Whether the right universities will in fact survive is a question for speculation, but not for answer. So far, the sorting-out process has favored public over private universities. The great private universities are still receiving large amounts of research support and are high in the quality hierarchy, even though some have slipped lower in market shares. But at the second level, the decline of private universities has been marked; some are no longer in major contention for research funds and others appear to be in a highly precarious position. Whether public universities will continue to increase their relative position will depend in part on decisions by state governments. Research is not the major interest of these bodies, and many of them are creating or responding to pressures for greater equalization among the state institutions of higher education. Over the next decade or two, major movements up or down among the leading public universities are likely to be heavily determined by their success or failure in persuading their state governments to support them as universities, instead of at the same level as other institutions in the state system.

The momentum of the system promises that the strongest universities, public or private, will generally be high in the ranks a decade or more from now, and that those that are declining are not likely to re-emerge as strong research universities. Yet the number of substantial upward and downward shifts in relative position between 1963-65 and 1973-75 indicates that comparable shifts may occur in the next decade.

Ben-David argued that it was competition among German universities that helped them attain preeminence over the less competitive French universities that had been scientific leaders at the beginning of the nineteenth century, and that it was competition among American universities that helped them attain preeminence in the twentieth century.[52] If the federal and state governments provide adequate support and avoid overly stringent regulations, competition can continue to be advantageous for the entire university system and thus for the country as a whole.

1. Illinois Institute of Technology Research Institute, *Technology in Retrospect and Critical Events in Science [TRACES]*, a report prepared for the National Science Foundation (Chicago: Illinois Institute of Technology, December 15, 1968); Battelle Memorial Institute, *Interactions of Science and Technology in the Innovative Process: Some Case Histories*, a report prepared for the National Science Foundation (Columbus, Ohio: Battelle Memorial Institute, March 19, 1973).

2. National Science Board, *Science Indicators, 1974—Report of the National Science Board, 1975* (Washington, D.C.: National Science Foundation, 1975).

3. Everyone who analyzes R&D trends in the U.S. is indebted to the NSF Division of Science Resources Studies. I have drawn heavily on NSF annual reports on R&D funds, several special series of reports dealing with federal funds for universities and colleges, and other reports on the research enterprise. I am also grateful for receiving some 1975 data in advance of general publication. Specific NSF reports are cited in a number of places, but I want to thank NSF for all data concerning expenditures not specifically identified as coming from some other source. NSF provides information on three categories of federal support: total federal support to institutions of higher education, support for academic science, and support for R&D. Figures used throughout this paper are from the third category: R&D in what are sometimes called "universities proper." These figures do not include R&D centers that are wholly financed by the federal government but managed by universities or consortia of universities. Neither do they include capital expenditures. They do include independently financed research activities of students, regular faculty members, and members of the research faculty in the biological, physical, and social sciences; in engineering; and in the medical fields. Unless specifically noted otherwise, figures are for combined categories of basic research, applied research, and development. To simplify wording, the text will usually refer to all these categories simply as academic research or university research. The relative sizes of the three components in recent years have been: basic research, 71 percent; applied research, 25 percent; and development, 4 percent.

4. National Science Board, op. cit.

5. National Science Foundation, *Young and Senior Science and Engineering Faculty, 1974: Support, Research Participation, and Tenure*, NSF 75-302 (Washington, D.C.: National Science Foundation, 1975); Frank J. Atelsek and Irene L. Gomberg, *Faculty Research: Level of Activity and Choice of Area*, Higher Education Panel Report No. 29

58

(Washington, D.C.: American Council on Education, January 1976).

6. National Science Foundation, Ibid.

7. Frank J. Atelsek and Irene L. Gomberg, op. cit.

8. John T. Kalberer, Jr., "Impact of the National Cancer Act on Grant Support," *Cancer Research*, Vol. 35, March 1975, pp. 473-481; National Institutes of Health, *Extramural Trends: FY 1967-76* (Washington, D.C.: National Institutes of Health, Division of Research Grants, Statistics and Analysis Branch, 1976).

9. National Science Foundation, *A Price Index for Deflation of Academic R&D Expenditures*, NSF 72-310 (Washington, D.C.: National Science Foundation, 1972); Malcolm B. Scully, *Chronicle of Higher Education*, October 6, 1975, p. 6. See also D. Kent Halstead, *Higher Education Prices and Price Indexes* (Washington, D.C.: Department of Health, Education, and Welfare, National Center for Education Statistics, 1975). Because of limitations in the applicability of the GNP price deflator to academic costs, the National Science Foundation has arranged with the American Council on Education to develop a new "market-basket" index of the costs of academic research.

10. William P. Jacobs, Letter, *Science*, Vol. 170, December 25, 1970, p. 1359.

11. Thane Gustafson, "The Controversy Over Peer Review," *Science*, Vol. 190, December 12, 1975, pp. 1060-1066. Gustafson reviews the attacks against peer review of research proposals and the evidence concerning the effectiveness of the peer review system. He concludes that the critics have not made their case and that "peer review groups have a good capacity for recognizing potential in a research proposal, and for recognizing outstanding achievement when they see it."

12. Dwight D. Eisenhower, *Executive Order 10521*, Office of the President, March 17, 1954; Lyndon B. Johnson, *Strengthening Academic Capability for Science Throughout the Nation*, Memorandum from the President to the Heads of Departments and Agencies, September 13, 1965.

13. Federal Interagency Committee on Education, *Federal Policy and Graduate Education* (Washington, D.C.: Department of Health, Education, and Welfare, June 1975).

14. National Science Foundation, *Young and Senior Science and Engineering Faculty, 1974*, op. cit.; National Science Board, *Science Indicators, 1974*, op. cit.

15. National Research Council, *Social and Behavioral Science Programs in the National Science Foundation* (Washington, D.C.: National Academy of Sciences, 1976); Carlos T. Kruytbosch, National Science Foundation, Personal Communication, March 16, 1976.

16. Thane Gustafson, op. cit.

17. Roland J. Liebert, "Research-Grant Getting and Productivity Among Scholars: Recent National Patterns of Competition and Favor," *The Journal of Higher Education*, Vol. 48, March/April 1977, pp. 164-192.

18. National Science Foundation, *Young and Senior Science and Engineering Faculty, 1974*, op. cit.

19. Martin Trow, "The Public and Private Lives of Universities," *Daedalus*, Vol. 104, Winter 1975, Vol. II, pp. 113-127.

20. Bruce L. R. Smith and D. C. Hague, eds., *The Dilemma of Accountability in Modern Government: Independence Versus Control* (New York: St. Martin's Press, 1971); Bruce L. R. Smith, ed., *The New Political Economy: The Public Use of the Private Sector* (New York: John Wiley and Sons, 1975).

21. John Walsh, "NIH: Demand Increases for Application of Research," *Science*, Vol. 153, July 8, 1966, pp. 149-152.

22. Barbara J. Culliton, "Health Manpower, The Feds Are Taking Over," *Science*, Vol. 191, February 6, 1976, pp. 446-450.

23. Don K. Price, *The Scientific Estate* (Cambridge, Mass.: The Belknap Press, 1965).

24. Wesley Hall, *Cash Flow* (Berkeley: University of California Research Management Improvement Project, December 1974).

25. Arthur B. Jebens and Earl Z. Irvin, *Environmental Health and Safety* (La Jolla: University of California Research Management Improvement Project, December 1974).

26. Eugene J. Millstein, *The DHEW Requirements for the Protection of Human Subjects: Analysis and Impacts at the University of California* (Berkeley: University of California Research Management Improvement Project, 1974).

27. Earl Z. Irvin and Arthur B. Jebens, *Property Management* (La Jolla: University of California Research Management Improvement Project, September 1974).

28. Arthur B. Jebens, *Time and Effort Reporting* (La Jolla: University of California Research Management Improvement Project, 1974).

29. Arthur B. Jebens, *Proposal Preparation, Negotiation, and Award* (La Jolla: University of California Research Management Improvement Project, 1974).

30. Harvey M. Sapolsky, *The Polaris System Development: Bureaucratic and Programmatic Success in Government* (Cambridge, Mass.: Harvard University Press, 1972). Describes a fine example of a tightly integrated, centrally managed, successful developmental program.

31. Michael Polanyi, "The Republic of Science," *Minerva*, Vol. 1, Autumn 1962, pp. 54-73.

32. Harvey Brooks, "The Federal Government and the Autonomy of Scholarship," in *Controversies and Decisions: The Social Sciences and Public Policy*, ed. Charles Frankel (New York: Russell Sage Foundation, 1976), pp. 235-257.

33. W. Henry Lambright, *Governing Science and Technology* (New York: Oxford University Press, 1976).

34. National Research Council, op. cit.

35. Chalmers W. Sherwin and R. S. Isenson, "Project Hindsight," *Science*, Vol. 156, June 23, 1967, pp. 1571-1577.

36. National Science Board, *Science Indicators, 1974*, op. cit.

37. Nestor E. Terleckyj, *State of Science and Research: Some New Indicators* (Washington, D.C.: National Planning Association, 1976).

38. Research Corporation, *Research and Invention*, Vol. 5, No. 1, Spring 1976, p. 4.

39. National Science Board, *Science Indicators, 1974*, op. cit.

40. Edward Gross and Paul V. Grambsch, *Changes in University Organization: 1964-71* (New York: McGraw-Hill, 1974), p. 205.

41. Derek J. de Solla Price, "Measuring the Size of Science," *Proceedings of the Israel Academy of Sciences and Humanities*, Vol. 9, No. 6, 1969, pp. 98-111.

42. Allan M. Cartter, *An Assessment of Quality in Graduate Education* (Washington, D.C.: American Council on Education, 1966).

43. Kenneth D. Roose and Charles J. Andersen, *A Rating of Graduate Programs* (Washington, D.C.: American Council on Education, 1970).

44. Mary Jo Clark, Rodney T. Hartnett, and Leonard L. Baird, *Assessing Dimensions of Quality in Doctoral Education: A Technical Report of a National Study in Three Fields* (Princeton, N.J.: Educational Testing Service, 1976).

45. Leo A. Goodman and William V. Kruskal, "Measures of Association for Cross Classification," *Journal of the American Statistical Association*, Vol. 49, December 1954, pp. 732-764.

46. Warren O. Hagstrom, "Inputs, Outputs, and the Prestige of American University Science Departments," *Sociology of Education*, Vol. 44, Fall 1971, pp. 375-397.

47. Edward Gross and Paul V. Grambsch, op. cit.

48. Ibid., p. 100.

49. David D. Henry, *Challenges Past: Challenges Present* (San Francisco: Jossey-Bass, 1975).

50. National Board on Graduate Education, *Outlook and Opportunity for Graduate Education: The Final Report, With Recommendations* (Washington, D.C.: National Academy of Sciences, 1975).

51. David Z. Robinson, "Will the University Decline as the Center for Scientific Research?" *Daedalus*, Vol. 102, No. 2, 1973, pp. 101-110.

52. Joseph Ben-David, "Scientific Productivity and Academic Organization in Nineteenth-Century Medicine," *American Sociological Review*, Vol. 25, No. 6, 1960, pp. 828-843.

The Changing Relationships: Universities and Other R&D Performers

Walter S. Baer

Historically, universities have been the "home of science,"[1] the principal site of basic research in the United States. But other institutions with roots tracing back to the nineteenth century have also played significant roles in scientific research: the Smithsonian Institution; the federal government laboratories in the U.S. Department of Agriculture (USDA); the Coast Survey and the Geological Survey; independent research centers, including the Franklin Institute and Arthur D. Little, Inc.; and industrial laboratories maintained by companies such as Du Pont and General Electric. Pluralism in the conduct of R&D has been a fundamental characteristic of the American research system.

Other papers in this volume document the problems universities have faced as a result of the decline (in constant dollars) in federal expenditures for R&D since the mid-1960s. But the scientists and research administrators in government laboratories, industry, and nonprofit institutes tell the same story: Research budgets are down; good researchers have been let go or turned away. For every university that has reached its tenure ceiling, there is an industrial, government, or nonprofit laboratory with a hiring freeze. Plans to build facilities, purchase equipment, and extend research into new areas have been deferred or canceled in every sector of the research community. Universities by no means have borne the burdens alone.

Yet it is still appropriate to ask whether universities have fared better or worse than other performers of R&D in the U.S. Have federal funds for basic research been transferred from universities to govern-

---

An abridged and edited version of this paper appeared in Volume I of *The State of Academic Science* (see Chapter III).

ment laboratories or industrial firms? Which federal agencies have encouraged or de-emphasized R&D at universities during the past decade? What has happened to industrial support of academic R&D and to the other links between universities and the private sector?

Any such discussion of these and related issues must begin with the observation that this country has a richly diverse mix of colleges and universities. This paper is principally concerned with the research relationships between universities and other institutions, and therefore it focuses on the universities that perform research rather than on those primarily engaged in teaching. Yet within the university research sector there are public and private institutions with different objectives and approaches. Many have large agricultural and engineering research programs that traditionally have been linked closely with government and industry. Dozens manage large contract research programs for the Department of Defense and other federal agencies; others avoid such commitments. Some universities enthusiastically pursue "relevance" in research; others consciously eschew it. A number of universities actively encourage faculty members to seek industrial consulting work; others frown on such activities. While it represents one of the system's greatest strengths, this heterogeneity ensures that any generalizations about university research relationships will have notable exceptions.

Other categories of research performers are equally diverse, displaying a similarly wide range of attitudes and capabilities. The industrial R&D sector includes firms tinkering with minor product improvements as well as institutions like the Bell Laboratories that alone support more basic research than do most universities. In this paper, we will use the categories of research performers defined by the National Science Foundation (NSF) in its publications on R&D resources: universities, federal in-house laboratories, federally funded research and development centers (FFRDCs) managed by universities, industrial firms (including FFRDCs managed by industrial firms), and a residual category of other performers including independent research institutes, hospitals, and state and local government agencies. More precise definitions of these sectors can be found in *Federal Funds for Research, Development, and Other Scientific Activities*, a series that is published annually by NSF.

The Traditional Relationships

American universities traditionally have sought and received support for scientific research from multiple sources, including federal and state government agencies, industrial firms, and private philanthrophy. The Hatch Act of 1887 authorized USDA support for an agricultural experiment station at each land-grant college, and university research in the fields of agriculture, geology, and meteorology has been closely tied to research carried out in federal government laboratories. Academic research in astronomy, on the other hand, initially received its support from philanthropic sources and has been linked with private, independent research institutions such as the Carnegie Institution of Washington. In the 1930s research in experimental biology was backed principally by the Rockefeller Foundation. [2]

The historical and still predominant role of the university in its interaction with industry has been as the supplier of trained manpower. Scientists in the United States have always had a practical bent, as de Tocqueville noted, and professors have been far more willing to work on applied problems than their European counterparts. [3] As organized industrial research grew in the first decades of the twentieth century, industry interest in university research grew apace. By the 1940s the use of university faculty as consultants, the support by industry of specific university research projects and graduate fellowships, and the sharing of specialized research equipment had become the traditional modes of industry/university interaction.

Federal Support of University R&D After 1945

Federal support of R&D during and after World War II produced decisive changes in university relationships with other funding sources and R&D institutions. In line with the recommendations presented by Vannevar Bush in *Science—the Endless Frontier*, federal agencies such as NSF, the Office of Naval Research, and the Atomic Energy Commission (AEC) were established with explicit mandates to fund research in universities and other nongovernment facilities. By the early 1950s, the federal government had become the principal patron of university research, displacing the role previously held by university endowments and state funds. By 1966 the federal government supported 74 percent of all university R&D (see Figure 1), and 77 percent of basic research (see Figure 2) at colleges and universities.

The growing federal share of university research support obviously meant that universities relied less and less on other sources of research funds. Although industrial support of university R&D more than doubled between 1953 and 1966, the fraction of total university R&D represented by these funds declined from 8 to 2 percent. Similarly, the share of university R&D supported by foundations and other nonprofit institutions declined from 11 percent in 1953 to 6 percent in 1966, although the dollar amounts increased by more than a factor of four during that period. Figure 2 shows a similar pattern for basic research. Although industry and private foundations had played significant roles in funding

64

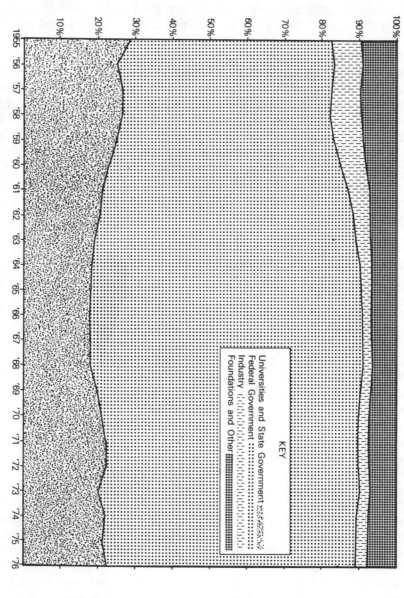

Figure 1

Sources of R&D Funds for Colleges and Universities, 1955-1976

KEY

Universities and State Government
Federal Government
Industry
Foundations and Other

Source: National Science Foundation, National Patterns of R&D Resources: Funds and Manpower in the Unites States, 1953-1976, NSF 76-310, Table B-1, pp. 20-21. Data for 1975 and 1976 are estimates.

Figure 2

Sources of Basic Research Funds for Colleges and Universities, 1955-1976

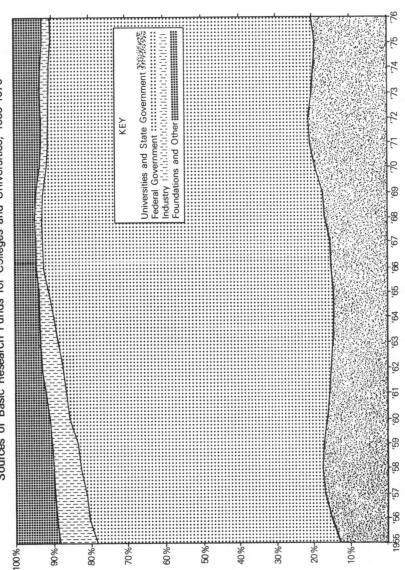

Source: National Science Foundation, *National Patterns of R&D Resources: Funds and Manpower in the United States, 1953-1976,* Table B-2, pp. 22-23. Data for 1975 and 1976 are estimates.

academic science prior to World War II, they together represented less than 10 percent of university research support by 1966.

Funds for Universities and Other R&D Performers

Figures 3 through 6 show the distribution by performer of federal and total spending for basic research and R&D respectively, as derived from statistics published by NSF.[4] It is easier to observe trends among performers by noting relative changes in shares of U.S. research spending than by comparing current or constant dollar amounts. Universities and colleges have steadily increased their percentage shares of spending in each research category. The year 1966 was the first in which the university sector reported spending more than half of all federal funds for basic research, up from 36 percent in 1955. When applied R&D is included, the university share of federal R&D spending is clearly smaller, but it increased from 5 to 9 percent between 1955 and 1966.

The rapid growth of federal funds for research also spawned new, research-based institutions. New government laboratories, industrial firms, and nonprofit research institutes were set up to perform government funded R&D, and a new class of FFRDCs was created to perform research exclusively or principally for a federal agency. Department of Defense (DOD) agencies, AEC—which became part of the Energy Research and Development Administration (ERDA)*—and the National Aeronautics and Space Administration (NASA) have relied extensively on FFRDCs for R&D in their specific mission areas.

Among the well-known FFRDCs managed by universities are the Los Alamos and Livermore Laboratories operated by the University of California for ERDA; the Applied Physics Laboratory operated by Johns Hopkins University for DOD; and the Jet Propulsion Laboratory operated by the California Institute of Technology for NASA. By the early 1950s the FFRDCs operated by universities had become the third largest recipient of federal funds for basic research, after universities and government laboratories. In 1966 university-administered FFRDCs accounted for 10 percent of federal spending for basic research and 5 percent of federal spending for all R&D.

The massive infusion of federal dollars since World War II thus created a complex pattern of U.S. research performers by 1966. The university sector, predominantly supported by federal funds, became the largest performer of basic research. Industry's share of basic research funds dwindled from more than one third (36 percent) in 1955 to less than one quarter (22 percent) in 1966. The university-administered

---

*In October 1977, the Department of Energy was created, absorbing ERDA. As this occurred subsequent to the writing of these papers, all references in this volume are to ERDA.—Eds.

Figure 3

Distribution of Federal Funds for Basic Research by Performer, 1955-1976

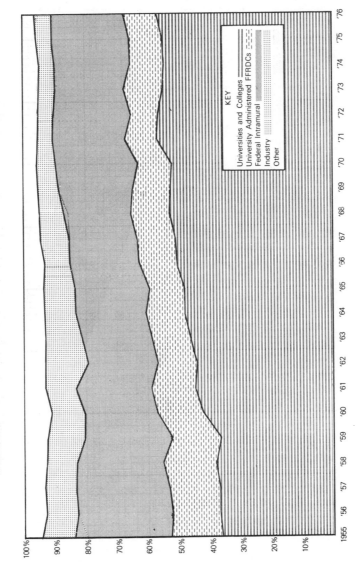

Source: Data contained in National Science Foundation, *National Patterns of R&D Resources: Funds and Manpower in the United States, 1953-1976,* NSF 76-310, Table B-2, pp. 22-23. Data for 1975 and 1976 in the original table are estimates.

Figure 4

Distribution of Total Funds for Basic Research by Performer, 1955-1976

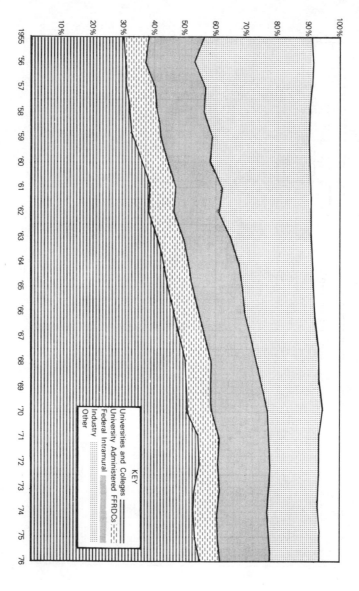

Source: National Science Foundation. (See Figure 3.)

Figure 5
Distribution of Federal R&D Funds by Performer, 1955-1976

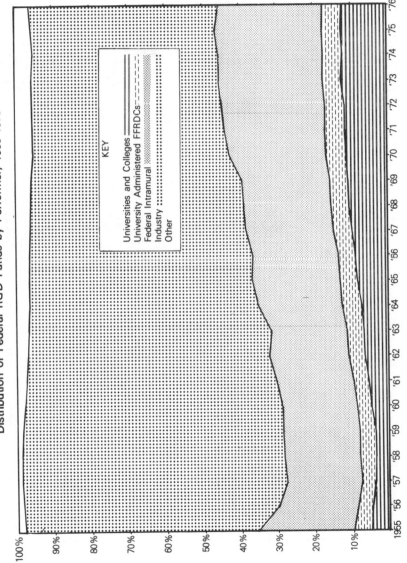

KEY

Universities and Colleges
University Administered FFRDCs
Federal Intramural
Industry
Other

Source: National Science Foundation. (See Figure 1.)

Figure 6
Distribution of Total R&D Funds by Performer, 1955-1976

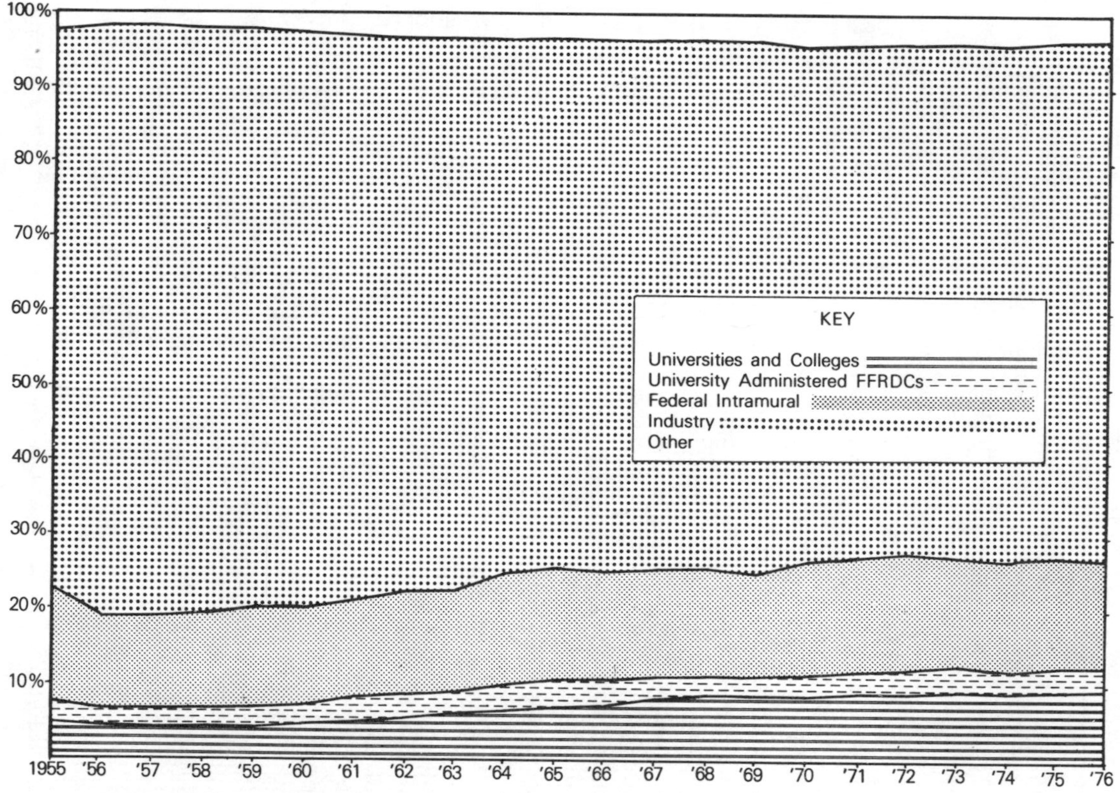
100%
90%
80%
70%
60%
50%
40%
30%
20%
10%
1955
'56
'57
'58
'59
'60
'61
'62
'63
'64
'65
'66
'67
'68
'69
'70
'71
'72
'73
'74
'75
'76
KEY
Universities and Colleges
University Administered FFRDCs
Federal Intramural
Industry
Other

Source: National Science Foundation. (See Figure 2.)

FFRDCs and federal in-house laboratories maintained their shares of funds for basic research during that period. And a large number of new institutions emerged in each sector. In the space of 20 years the national commitment to research created a very strong U.S. science and technology community, but it also meant an enormous number of institutional mouths to feed.

Changes in R&D Spending Since 1966

The relative impact of the slowdown in U.S. research funding since the mid-1960s can be seen in the changes in the percentage shares for each group of research performers (see Figures 3 through 6). Universities have continued to increase their share of federal and total funds for basic research since 1966. As of 1975 universities and colleges accounted for 53 percent of the total funds for basic research, compared with 46 percent in 1966 (Figure 4). To be sure, this increase was not as great as that of the preceding decade when the university share rose from 30 to 46 percent. Still, despite great fiscal pressures, universities managed to increase and consolidate their positions during the last decade as the predominant performers of basic research in the United States.

The increasing share of basic research performed by universities has come at the expense of industry. Total funds for basic research spent in industrial laboratories increased by less than 6 percent in current dollars between 1966 and 1975, resulting in a drop in the industrial sector's share from 22 percent in 1966 to 16 percent in 1975. Industry's decreasing share of basic research was due to both an absolute drop in funding from the federal government and a rise in industry's own funds for basic research that was too modest to keep pace with the national average. While total U.S. spending for basic research increased 45 percent in current dollars between 1966 and 1975, industrial firms themselves spent only 16 percent more. Moreover, the percentage of industry's own R&D funds devoted to basic research declined from 6.3 percent in 1966 to 3.6 percent in 1975. The implications for university/industry relations of industry's lower share of basic research spending are discussed in a later section. The federal intramural laboratories, university-administered FFRDCs, and other research performers have largely retained their shares of basic research spending—as percentages both of total funds and of federal funds—during the past decade.

In its share of total R&D funds since 1966 the university gain is much smaller (Figure 6), since universities typically perform less than 1 percent of the development function. The university share of total R&D spending grew from 8 to 9 percent during 1966-75, while its share of federal R&D spending increased from 9 to 11 percent. The federal in-house laboratories increased their share of federal R&D spending more significantly—from 23 to 29 percent—during this period. Both these increases again reflect a decline of industry's share of federal R&D funds.

University-affiliated FFRDCs by and large have maintained their share of spending for both R&D and basic research since 1966, despite the changes in the patterns of support for these centers that are described below. Similarly, the share represented by the independent research center and "other nonprofit institution" category have remained nearly constant.

The patterns of university research support have changed only moderately since 1966. With the slower growth of federal funds for university R&D, state government funds and university endowments have assumed more important roles. The federal government remains the principal funder of basic research in universities, but its share of support has slipped from 77 percent in 1966 to 70 percent in 1975.[5] A similar trend is seen in support for total university R&D. Industrial, foundation, and other support of university research has increased modestly since 1966, but together these sources constitute only 10 percent of the totals for university basic research or R&D.

Changes in Federal Agency Support Since 1966

The changes in federal support of research performers shown in Figures 3 and 5 reflect funding shifts by individual federal agencies. Table 1 presents the percentage shares of R&D support, by agency, for each performer category in 1966 and 1975. Similar data for basic research are presented in Table 2.[6]

The university share of R&D funding from the Department of Defense, for example, has fallen from 4 to 2 percent during the past decade. Since DOD remains the largest agency supporter of R&D, this seemingly small percentage change represents a large shift in resources. If universities had maintained the same share of Defense R&D during this period, they would have received about $200 million more in 1975, or nearly 10 percent more than the total federal funding for university R&D in that year. Table 2 shows a similar but smaller drop in the DOD share of basic research contracts awarded to universities. The shift of Defense R&D resources away from universities is a direct result of policy decisions made by Congress and the Department of Defense in the late 1960s, as discussed briefly below. Between 1966 and 1975 the DOD in-house laboratories were the chief beneficiaries of these shifts in allocation of R&D funds. Since 1975 DOD has changed its policy to increase the share of R&D funds for industry at the expense of the in-house laboratories.[7]

NASA also has decreased its dollar support of university R&D, from $117 million in 1966 to $83 million in 1975. This drop, however, reflects

Table 1

Changes in Federal Agency Support of R&D by Performer, 1966-1975

Department or Agency	R&D Obligations (millions of $) 1966	1975	Percent of Agency R&D Obligations									
			Universities 1966	1975	University-Affiliated FFRDCs 1966	1975	Federal Intramural 1966	1975	Industry[a] 1966	1975	Other 1966	1975
Defense	$7,023	$9,608	4%	2%	2%	2%	27%	29%	63%	64%	4%	3%
NASA	5,050	3,071	2	3	2	3	17	33	78	60	1	1
HEW	1,014	2,233	53	52	-	-	18	20	4	5	25	23
AEC	1,212	1,704	7	6	32	33	2	1	55	57	4	3
NSF	227	653	79	78	7	6	6	2	1	7	7	7
Interior	143	557	14	8	-	-	66	39	10	45	10	8
Agriculture	235	406	26	24	-	-	70	73	1	-	3	3
Transportation	172	397	1	6	b	1	24	18	73	55	2	20
EPA	b	343	b	6	-	-	b	25	b	59	b	10
Commerce	55	263	7	10	-	-	76	53	16	17	1	20
Others	173	362	18	10	-	-	43	49	17	13	22	28
TOTAL	$15,304	$19,597	9%	12%	4%	5%	21%	27%	61%	51%	5%	5%

a
Includes FFRDCs administered by industrial firms.

b
Agency did not exist in 1966.

Source: National Science Foundation, *Federal Funds for Research, Development, and Other Scientific Activities,* Vol. XVI, 1967, pp. 112-113; XXIII; XXIII Detailed Statistical Tables, 1974, pp. 16-17.

Table 2

Changes in Federal Agency Support of Basic Research by Performer, 1966-1975

Department or Agency	Basic Research Obligations (millions of $) 1966	1975	Percent of Obligations for Basic Research								
			Universities 1966	1975	University-Affiliated FFRDCs 1966	1975	Federal Intramural 1966	1975	Industry* 1966	1975	Other 1966	1975
Defense	$262	$257	50%	42%	1%	-	32%	41%	10%	13%	7%	4%
NASA	559	632	17	6	7	8	28	36	47	49	1	1
HEW	326	544	62	73	-	-	18	13	-	-	20	14
AEC	281	325	27	22	56	64	2	-	11	13	4	1
NSF	223	509	80	86	7	6	5	1	1	3	7	4
Interior	51	109	24	15	-	-	67	80	4	3	5	2
Agriculture	94	157	27	25	-	-	66	71	1	-	6	4
Others	48	66	16	26	-	-	78	68	4	2	2	4
TOTAL	$1,844	$2,599	40%	43%	12%	11%	24%	25%	18%	16%	6%	5%

*Includes FFRDCs administered by industrial firms.

Source: National Science Foundation, Federal Funds for Research, Development, and Other Scientific Activities, Vol. XVI, 1967, pp. 112-113; XXIII Detailed Statistical Tables, 1974, pp. 16-17.

the sharp cuts in NASA programs after the manned lunar landing, rather than a shift away from support of university R&D. Universities in fact received a larger share of NASA R&D spending in 1975 than in 1966, although a significantly smaller share of NASA funds for basic research. The end of the Apollo program principally resulted in the termination of many industrial contracts, with a shift of NASA R&D shares from industry to in-house NASA laboratories.

The three other principal patrons of university R&D—the Department of Health, Education, and Welfare (HEW), NSF, and AEC—have not significantly changed their percentages of R&D support flowing to universities during the past decade. HEW devotes a slightly larger share of its R&D funding to in-house research, but the university share declined only slightly from 53 to 52 percent. NSF, despite an increasing emphasis on applied research through the RANN program, devoted nearly the same share to university R&D in 1975 as it did in 1966. The principal impact of the RANN program on research performers appears to be the increased support of R&D performed in industry. Similar changes anticipated in energy R&D do not show up in the 1975 figures that pre-date the formation of ERDA.

The new emphasis on civilian R&D among other federal agencies (see Table 1) had not significantly affected university research support by 1975.[8] The Departments of Transportation, Commerce, Justice, and Labor, and the Environmental Protection Agency each increased the university components of their R&D programs. Because these programs are still small, however, they have had relatively little impact on the overall flow of federal R&D dollars to universities.

The most notable change in performer emphasis in the civilian R&D programs has been the increase in the shares of R&D support awarded to state and local government agencies, particularly in transportation, economic development, criminal justice, and air and water pollution control. According to NSF statistics, state and local governments received $228 million in federal research funds in 1975. The bulk of these funds was then awarded to other research performers, including universities; but its precise distribution remains undocumented. Spriestersbach et al., reported that for 10 selected universities, state funds for sponsored research increased 65 percent between 1970 and 1973.[9] This is undoubtedly a more rapid increase than that for the university sector as a whole, but it is clear that state governments are playing an increasingly important role in the funding of university research.

All in all, the increased university share of federal R&D support during the 1966-75 period has resulted more from increases in the R&D budgets in HEW and NSF, the two agencies that emphasize university R&D most, than from shifts of resources away from other research performers. In basic research, increased shares to universities from HEW and NSF have outweighed decreases from DOD, NASA, and AEC.

The university share of federal R&D support seems unlikely to increase in the next decade as it has in the past, particularly if the federal government places greater emphasis on R&D directed toward the civilian economy. Large R&D programs in energy, environmental protection, transportation, and other civilian sectors are more likely to increase industry's share of federal R&D expenditures. ERDA, for example, is committed to large-scale development and commercial demonstration of new energy technologies in partnership with industry. State and local governments may also be expected to increase their R&D spending as recipients of federal revenue sharing or direct R&D support, but some of these funds will in turn be spent in the university sector.

The major conclusion from an examination of funding patterns among research performers during the past 10 years is that universities have fared remarkably well. Fears that campus disorders and related university crises in the late 1960s and early 1970s would turn Congress away from supporting university research have, fortunately, not been realized.[10] The university sector has increased its share of total spending and its share of federal funds for R&D and basic research during the past decade. That trend is unlikely to continue into the future, not because of a diminished federal interest in university research but because new federal priorities will imply greater commitments to large-scale development and demonstration programs carried out by industry and other research performers.

Changing Relationships Between Universities and Other R&D Performers

Behind the financial statistics of the past 10 years stands the paradox of universities moving toward both greater cooperation and more competition with other research institutions. Since the demand for new research PhDs diminished in the late 1960s, colleges and universities have been urged to be more responsive to the direct manpower needs of industry and government. Many voices, within academe as well as industry, have called for universities to redress their neglect of industrial research problems. The call for "relevance" in university research also has implied a need for closer associations with government, industry, and the nonprofit sector in addressing problems perceived to be of national importance. But it is also clear that competition for research funds between universities and other research performers has become far more intense than it was when resources were growing handsomely in the 1950s and 1960s. The competition is seen in trends such as:

- Severed or loosened ties between universities and contract research centers

- Changes in university-administered FFRDCs
- Growth of project research institutes run by faculty
- University competition with FFRDCs and independent research centers for applied and interdisciplinary research funds
- University competition with government in-house laboratories

These trends will be reviewed below, followed by a discussion of university relationships with industrial firms.

University Contract Research Centers: Moving Classified Research Off Campus

University-administered contract research centers, nearly all of which performed some classified research sponsored by federal defense agencies, became caught up in the wave of antimilitary protests during the late 1960s. Like other aspects of academic administration, university treatment of classified research was never particularly tidy or consistent. Such projects were often the direct outgrowth of a faculty member's consulting for DOD or serving on a defense agency panel.

Administering classified research in an academic environment raised not only problems of security in restricted access facilities but also questions of how such work would relate to traditional scholarship. A common solution was to establish a separate laboratory or center for classified contracts. Some centers were included as integral units of the university, such as the Instrumentation Laboratory at the Massachusetts Institute of Technology (MIT) and the Willow Run Laboratories at the University of Michigan; some were established as FFRDCs, such as the MIT Lincoln Laboratory and Johns Hopkins's Applied Physics Laboratory; and some were incorporated as separate institutions accepting both government and private research contracts, for example, the Stanford Research Institute and the Cornell Aeronautical Laboratory. [11]

Two developments of the late 1960s promoted friction: Whatever their administrative arrangements with the sponsoring university, contract centers became one focus of student protests against the performance of classified research in an academic environment. Contract centers became targets of picketing, sit-ins, and increasingly more violent protests, including the bombing of the Army Mathematics Research Center at the University of Wisconsin in 1970. Moreover, passage of the Mansfield Amendment in 1969 implied that in the future academic contract research centers could do less basic research unrelated to defense missions. University and defense officials alike began to question the usefulness of close DOD/university ties and to reappraise relationships.

As a result, a number of universities decided to eliminate on-campus classified research, and in the process some cut loose from their contract research centers as well. Stanford University's severance of ties with the Stanford Research Institute (SRI) in 1970 was the largest and most publicized of these spinoffs. But there were others. A year earlier, the staff of the Stanford University Applied Electronics Laboratory transferred to SRI. In 1967 Columbia University converted its Electronics Research Laboratory to an independent, nonprofit institution renamed the Riverside Research Institute. The MIT Instrumentation Laboratory was separated from the university in 1973, renamed the Charles Stark Draper Laboratory, and reoriented from military guidance and control projects toward space, air transportation, and related civilian research.[12] The University of Michigan converted its Willow Run Laboratories in 1972 to an independent, nonprofit institute emphasizing environmental research. Only a few contract research centers with annual expenditures of $1 million or more, such as the Denver Research Institute, still operate as integral parts of the sponsoring universities.

A particularly interesting case is that of the Cornell Aeronautical Laboratory (CAL), which was operated as a division of Cornell University although located 100 miles away near Buffalo. CAL was not classified as an FFRDC, since it accepted contracts from private as well as government sponsors, but much of its research was classified by the Department of Defense. In 1969, after students protested against classified work at CAL, the University tried to sell the Laboratory to a private firm. However, the state of New York, supported by many of the CAL employees, successfully sued to stop the sale. Blocked in its attempt to sell the Laboratory, Cornell University agreed to its conversion to a profit-seeking subsidiary, now renamed Calspan.

University divestiture has generally enabled contract research centers to broaden their R&D interests and to diversify their base of contract support. The effect on universities has been a more explicit arm's length and potentially competitive relationship between faculty and the centers.[13]

Separation was a natural consequence of a center's growth and maturity, as much as it was a result of the classified research controversy. Universities took on the responsibility for creating defense-oriented research capabilities at a time when they could offer the unique talents and resources to do so. By the late 1960s, more than 20 years after the end of World War II, many of these centers had become large, relatively stable institutions with interests quite different from those of their academic sponsors. The advantages to a university of receiving management and overhead fees from contract research, as well as providing research opportunities and specialized facilities for faculty members, were often outweighed by the disadvantages of managing an organization whose objectives were increasingly divergent from the institution's principal missions of teaching and basic research. From the contract research center's standpoint, university affiliation brought prestige and greater access to faculty members and graduate students, but it also carried with it the disadvantages of dealing with a university administration that often constrained the center's prospects for growth. Consequently, the separation of the contract center from the university has often proved to be in the best interests of both institutions.

University-Administered FFRDCs

The conflicts over classified research also turned against university-administered FFRDCs sponsored by the Department of Defense. As shown in Table 3, five of the eight university-managed, defense-sponsored FFRDCs of 1966 had by 1975 been phased out or transferred to other sponsorship. Only the Applied Physics Laboratory operated by Johns Hopkins University, the Applied Research Laboratory managed

Table 3
University-Affiliated FFRDCs
1966-1975

FEDERAL AGENCY SPONSOR/FFRDC	UNIVERSITY ADMINISTRATOR	CHANGE IN FFRDC STATUS, 1966-1975
Energy Research and Development Administration		
Ames Laboratory	Iowa State University	
Argonne National Laboratory	University of Chicago and Argonne Universities Assoc.	
Brookhaven National Laboratory	Associated Universities, Inc.	
Cambridge Electron Accelerator	Harvard University	Phased Out 1973
Fermi National Accelerator Laboratory	University Research Associates	Established 1968
Lawrence Berkeley Laboratory	University of California	
Lawrence Livermore Laboratory	University of California	
Los Alamos Scientific Laboratory	University of California	
Oak Ridge Associated Laboratory	Oak Ridge Associated Universities	
Princeton-Pennsylvania Accelerator	Princeton University and the University of Pennsylvania	Phased Out 1971
Plasma Physics Laboratory	Princeton University	
Stanford Linear Accelerator Center	Stanford University	
Department of Defense		
Applied Physics Laboratory	Johns Hopkins University	
Applied Physics Laboratory	University of Washington	Phased Out 1974
Applied Research Laboratory	Pennsylvania State University	
Army Mathematics Research Center	University of Wisconsin	Phased Out 1970
Center for Naval Analyses	University of Rochester	Became University Administered 1968

University-Affiliated FFRDCs, 1966-1975

FEDERAL AGENCY SPONSOR/FFRDC	UNIVERSITY ADMINISTRATOR	CHANGE IN FFRDC STATUS, 1966-1975
Center for Research in Social Systems	American University	Phased Out 1970
Human Resources Research Organization	George Washington University	Changed to Nonprofit Administered 1969
Hudson Laboratory	Columbia University	Phased Out 1969
Lincoln Laboratory	Massachusetts Institute of Technology	

National Aeronautics and Space Administration

Jet Propulsion Laboratory	California Institute of Technology	
Space Radiation Effects Laboratory	College of William and Mary	

National Science Foundation

Cerro Tololo Inter-American Observatory	Association of Universities for Research in Astronomy, Inc.	
Kitt Peak National Observatory	Association of Universities for Research in Astronomy, Inc.	
National Astronomy and Ionospheric Center	Cornell University	Established 1970
National Center for Atmospheric Research	University Corporation for Atmospheric Research	
National Radio Astronomy Observatory	Associated Universities, Inc.	

Department of Health, Education, and Welfare

Center for the Advanced Study of Education Administration	University of Oregon	Phased Out 1972
Center for Research and Development in Educational Differences	Harvard University	Phased Out 1967
Center for Research and Development in Higher Education	University of California	Phased Out 1972
Center for Research and Development for Learning and Re-education	University of Wisconsin	Phased Out 1972
Center for the Study of the Evaluation of Instructional Programs	University of California	Phased Out 1972
Center for the Study of Social Organization of Schools and the Learning Process	Johns Hopkins University	Phased Out 1972
Coordination Center for the National Program in Early Childhood Education	University of Illinois	Phased Out 1970
Learning Research and Development Center	University of Pittsburgh	Phased Out 1972
Research and Development Center in Educational Stimulation	University of Georgia	Phased Out 1970
Research and Development Center in Teacher Education	University of Texas	Phased Out 1972
Stanford Center for Research and Development in Teaching	Stanford University	Phased Out 1972

by Pennsylvania State University, and MIT's Lincoln Laboratory remained university affiliated throughout this period.

For different reasons, the attempt by HEW to establish university-administered FFRDCs for educational research proved unsuccessful. These centers were created toward the end of the R&D boom period by an agency that, unlike Defense and ERDA, had little experience in contracting for mission-oriented research. Faced with growing stringency in research budgets, a change of administration, and congressional skepticism, HEW phased out its university-administered educational research FFRDCs or transferred them to other institutional managers in the early 1970s.

The university-affiliated FFRDCs supported by NASA and ERDA have more stable histories. NASA's Jet Propulsion Laboratory and the ERDA multiprogram national laboratories have partly diversified from space, atomic energy, and basic scientific research to applied work directed toward energy, the environment, and other national priorities. Five of the eight ERDA multiprogram FFRDCs—Argonne, Brookhaven, Lawrence Berkeley, Lawrence Livermore, and Los Alamos—are university administered, while two—Oak Ridge and Sandia—are managed by industrial firms, and one—Pacific Northwest—is operated by a nonprofit institution. With the formation of ERDA in 1975, these FFRDCs have been called on to broaden their efforts in support of energy development and demonstration programs. This will have the likely effect of moving the multiprogram national laboratories toward closer working relationships with industry, since industrial firms are intended to be the ultimate users of the energy technologies developed by ERDA. Whether strengthening such ties with industry will prove difficult for university-administered FFRDCs or require changes in their administrative structures remains to be seen.

The remaining university-administered FFRDCs supported by ERDA provide specialized research facilities for high energy physics, plasma physics, and other areas of nuclear science. However, the increasing costs of high energy accelerators resulted in the closing of some facilities (e.g., the Princeton-Penn Accelerator and the Cambridge Electron Accelerator) in order to free funds for the new Fermi National Accelerator Laboratory. The National Science Foundation also supports university-managed FFRDC facilities in astronomy and atmospheric science. One of these facilities, the National Astronomy and Ionospheric Center in Puerto Rico, was picked up from the Department of Defense in 1970 as a result of DOD's shifting some basic research support to civilian agencies after passage of the Mansfield Amendment.

The establishment of new national research centers seems possible in the future as more fields of science require large capital investments in research facilities with full-time staff to operate them. Frontier research in many fields may be conducted by user groups of scientists from different institutions sharing specialized facilities, as is done today in high energy physics, astronomy, and oceanography.[14] More biological and medical research will require special cell cultures or animals maintained in centralized laboratories. And social scientists see a parallel need to develop common data bases available to users from many institutions.[15] Although this trend toward sharing specialized research facilities already appears well established, available data are inadequate to document its full extent. In the future, some research centers now managed by a single university, and newly created national facilities for basic science, may be converted to the university-managed FFRDC category.

Project Research Institutes

Although the boundaries between university contract research centers and FFRDCs are ill defined, both differ from institutions incorporated to perform research on specific grants and contracts. Such "project institutes" are, in the words of Harold Orlans, a close observer of R&D policy, "the most motley and volatile type of institute...[created] most frequently as ventures of faculty who, dissatisfied with the constraints on projects administered by their institutions, may be adventurous in their spare time while retaining the security of tenure."[16] A project institute may be little more than the extension of a professor's consulting practice, perhaps incorporated to obtain higher consulting rates than those paid by government agencies. The center may, however, develop a sizable staff and become a permanent entity. The Center for Policy Research, a project research institute in New York City, noted in its review of its first five years of operation:

> While the Center initially sought part-time senior staff [professors who combine their university affiliation with summer work of limited consulting at the Center], in recent years, full-time researchers have been added.[17]

From a professor's point of view, a project institute can bring added income, flexibility to do work that the university might not approve, and freedom from paying university overhead while still maintaining access to facilities such as the university's library and computers. From the government agency's standpoint, contracting with a project institute can mean faster research results at lower cost. Some professors reportedly have been encouraged to submit proposals through a project institute rather than through their university in order to meet an agency's time and budget constraints.

Such project institutes seem to be an inevitable part of a dynamic research system with multiple funding sources and performers. As research performers, they are the most responsive to new policy directions and changing research priorities of government agencies. Their potential for abuse—overcommitted faculty or unreimbursed use of university facilities—is apparent but seems largely controllable by sensible university regulations.

Project institutes headed by part-time faculty members appear to be proliferating rapidly. However, no reliable data are available on their numbers, funding levels, or importance as research performers. Although recent interviews with federal officials, faculty members, and university administrators indicate that project institutes have in the last decade become larger and more clearly distinguishable research performers, a more coherent description of their size, status, and role in the U.S. research system must await a more systematic survey.

Government In-House Laboratories

Universities now face greater competition for research funds than they did a decade ago. The competition is principally among the universities themselves, though university administrators cite competitive pressures from nonprofit institutes and in-house government laboratories. Many believe that federal intramural research is taking an expanded share of government R&D dollars. As research budgets contract, the argument goes, federal agencies tend to favor their own in-house laboratories over universities and other R&D performers. Thus a 1975 Department of Defense study reported:

> We found that the in-house laboratory share of the DOD budget has increased by about 15 percent in the past six years. No compelling reason for increasing the laboratories' budget was found. To the contrary, there was some evidence of the laboratories being under strain to stay fully employed. Based on some Service studies and personal visits to most of the laboratories, it is believed that a modest reduction in the size of the in-house laboratories...could produce some savings and eliminate some excessive competition.[18]

Similarly, a 1975 ERDA report stated:

> There is the need, however, to address the beliefs, real or perceived, on the part of some members of industry and universities, that the [ERDA] laboratories do not make sufficient use of out-of-house research and development resources, are self-perpetuating, and, in fact, compete with them for limited federal research and development funds.[19]

Federal in-house laboratories have increased their share of federal R&D spending more than the university sector, but both have grown since 1966. In the distribution of federal spending for basic research, the university share has grown slightly faster than that of the intramural laboratories during the past decade. The largest relative gains for the federal intramural sector have come in the development category and at the expense of industrial firms.

However, the quality of federal in-house R&D is questioned more often than its quantity. As a recent National Academy of Sciences report (the Pound Report) noted with respect to the Department of Agriculture, few government agencies encourage peer review of their in-house research, which consequently may be below the standard of work performed at other institutions.[20] Maintaining high quality research is a perennial problem that receives more attention in times of financial stringency. Regular, high-level review of intramural agency R&D in relation to work in other institutions—perhaps by the recently created Office of Science and Technology Policy—seems advisable to encourage high quality research as well as to promote fair competition among research performers.

But it is in applied research that universities now face the most serious competition from other institutions. Most interdisciplinary and policy-oriented research falls into this category. Universities, with their tradition of departmental autonomy and incentive systems for exclusive disciplines, have not moved easily into interdisciplinary research activities. Once they have, universities have found themselves in competition with a number of research institutions—private consulting firms, independent nonprofit organizations, and FFRDCs—that specialize in this kind of work.[21] Consequently, it is not surprising that academic institutions received only 50 percent of the applied research funds awarded by the National Science Foundation in 1975, compared with 86 percent of NSF grant moneys for basic research.[22] Given the large number and variety of institutions that are capable of conducting applied research or policy-oriented research, it seems unlikely that universities will perform a significantly greater share of this work in the future.

University Relationships With Industry

The academic and industrial research communities have consistently held ambivalent attitudes toward each other. On the one hand, certain interactions were natural and desirable, e.g., university faculty consulting for industry, the hiring of university graduates by industry, firms sponsoring fellowships. Engineering faculty members have for many years received industrial support for research, worked in industrial laboratories during the summer, and sent graduate students to write dissertations in industry. Industrial firms have valued university contacts as windows to new developments as well as sources of expertise unavailable within the firm.[23] For many firms, a small investment in university research support or graduate student fellowships has been an effective means of extending their own research capabilities and obtaining advanced knowledge of new results. On the other hand, academics and industrialists traditionally have been suspicious of each other's motives and modes of operation. The professor's condescending attitude toward the commercial exploitation of knowledge and the businessman's disdain for ivory tower research are the familiar stereotypes that need to be overcome.

Recommendations on how to improve university/industry relationships through joint research projects or other collaborative efforts abound. Yet the obstacles to closer collaboration are very real. Discussions of the issue consistently cite differences in research objectives and in the time frame for obtaining and reporting results, differences regarding publication and patent policies, and mutual misunderstandings exacerbated by a lack of communication.[24] The publication and patent problem is a particularly difficult issue. Professors want freedom to publish their research results, but a company sponsoring a joint research project wants to benefit from the information before its competitors can. Telling an industrial research manager that his firm cannot have proprietary rights to research it sponsors at a university is as difficult as telling the university professor that he can only publish his results anonymously. Neither approach is likely to generate much enthusiasm for joint research projects.

Since these barriers to university/industry cooperation are hardly new, it is instructive to begin with an analysis of how the coupling problems have worsened in recent years. Although hard evidence is lacking,[25] there are reasons to believe that the links between universities and industry weakened in the two decades following World War II and approached their nadir in the early 1970s. The principal factors behind the decline appear to have been:

- the separation of academic research from perceived industrial needs;
- the decreased interest among PhDs and other graduates in industrial research; and
- the relative decline of basic research in industry.

Separation of Academic Research From Industrial Needs. The era of rapid growth of federal funds for academic research gave universities less incentive to maintain or strengthen their ties with industrial firms. Moreover, support from defense and space agencies drew university research, especially engineering, toward high technology and away from other industrial problems. Engineering faculty engaged in research on space vehicles or advanced radar systems found little in common with conventional industrial engineering. Defense and space research focused on *performance* improvements while other industrial R&D continued to emphasize *cost* improvements as well. There was no question that the former seemed the more interesting direction for university engineering faculty to pursue.

Some close working relationships developed between aerospace firms and university engineering departments in the 1950s and 1960s. Many new high technology firms were created as a result of academic research, and professors became their corporate directors or entrepreneurs. The high technology companies surrounding Harvard and MIT on Route 128 and the new electronics and instrument firms near Stanford became models for the rest of the nation. But because of the end of the Apollo program, the decline of defense support for university research, and the shift in national priorities, university engineering faculties often found themselves unfamiliar with the relevant industrial firms that had not ventured into high technology.

This situation was not prevalent in all engineering departments. Academic scientists researching certain topics—for example, exotic materials for space and defense applications—communicated with related manufacturing industries. But such efforts seemed more the exception than the rule during the 1950s and 1960s, especially at the most prestigious universities. Regional universities serving specialized clienteles were more successful in maintaining their established industrial ties.

Decreased Student Interest in Industrial Research. The availability of federal funds for academic research and the general expansion of higher education in the 1950s and 1960s also drew students away from careers in industrial research. With the prospects of faculty appointments (often with promises of early tenure) in growing departments or at "centers of excellence," new PhDs naturally opted for academia over industry. And many professors were delighted to train their best students for careers in academic research. In an expanding era it was all too easy to believe that only the second-rate student or worse need be relegated to industry, government, or nonresearch teaching positions.

To the corporate research manager outside the aerospace and high technology industries, university training seemed less and less applicable to industrial needs. A 1973 American Chemical Society report stated that "there is no doubt that the structure of many graduate programs in chemistry has been oriented, unconsciously if not consciously, toward careers in academic research. Since at most a few hundred faculty and postdoctoral positions in chemistry became vacant each year, the bulk of the annual 2,000 or more chemistry doctors are being unrealistically trained." [26] "Too many [candidates for employment] are overspecialized in [their disciplinary] training and are not interested in broadening their horizons," wrote the vice president of R&D at Koppers Company.[27] "Send us well-trained graduates, free of antibusiness bias," said the general manager of research at Standard Oil (Indiana).[28] While industrial research managers undoubtedly have registered similar complaints in earlier years, concern over the imbalance between academic training and industrial research needs seems to have reached a peak in the late sixties and early seventies. Student protests against large corporations (among other institutions) at that time also contributed to the perceived weakening of university relationships with industry.

Declining Basic Research in Industry. A third factor contributing to weakened links between universities and industry was industry's diminishing role in basic research. Industry's share of basic research spending declined steadily between 1955 and 1972, and the proportion of industry's own R&D funds spent on basic research dropped dramatically after 1966. Beyond these national statistics, discussions with individual corporate research managers confirm that industry's emphasis has shifted from basic to more applied research during the past decade. Inflation, an uncertain economy, and increased government regulation, among other factors, have led to corporate decisions to favor projects with short-term payoffs. In a widely quoted article entitled "The Breakdown of U.S. Innovation," *Business Week* reported: "...there is a growing sense that something has happened to American innovation...within a growing number of companies, such changes and pressures have led to a reappraisal of corporate goals and the emergence of what one top research scientist dubs 'the MBA syndrome,' a super-cautious, no-risk management unwilling to gamble on anything short of a sure thing." [29]

Industry's shift away from basic research made working relationships with universities more difficult. The key to effective links between universities and industry is face-to-face, scientist-to-scientist contact. As Robert Sproull has observed from his career in both university and industrial research administration: "The most effective impedence transformer between industry and the university has been and is the able, articulate industrial scientist or engineer who visits a university to give a seminar and talks informally with students in the lab." [30] Or as Jacob Goldman, chief scientist of Xerox Corporation, puts it: "Your admission ticket to the [basic research] club is to have something of your own to talk about." [31] As industry's commitment to basic research has declined, firms have generated fewer such admission tickets, and industrial scientists' links with their university counterparts have weakened.

International Comparisons

Despite these problems, the United States still appears to be superior in fostering relationships between universities and industrial firms, as perceived by other nations. The 1970 report of the United Kingdom Working Party on Universities and Industrial Research praises the "tradition of close collaboration between universities and industry" in the United States, citing federal research funding in universities and industry, university entrepreneurship (the Route 128 effect), and faculty consulting for industrial firms.[32] Comparative studies of the organization and financing of basic research in Europe and North America by the Organization for Economic Cooperation and Development (OECD) also points to this country's success in developing effective university/industry relationships.[33] The OECD review of the research systems in Germany, France, and the United Kingdom observes that "each [country] still looks with something approaching envy to the United States" in fostering strong industry/university links.[34]

Similarly, despite some concern on the part of university scientists, the site visits for this study found no evidence of any substantial "reverse brain drain" or migration of U.S. scientists and engineers to Europe. About a dozen instances were reported of faculty scientists leaving American universities for positions in European universities or research centers. There was no consistent pattern in these cases. Personal considerations often appeared to be a predominant factor, though inadequate research support was occasionally mentioned. Most postdoctoral fellows or assistant professors who spent time abroad returned to the United States, and many of them reported that conditions in European laboratories had not been as favorable as they had initially hoped. European science has, however, made notable strides in some fields. More information and assessment of potential migration trends of American scientists to Europe lies beyond the scope of this study.

Prospects for Closer University/Industry Cooperation

University/industry relations were relatively weak in the early 1970s, but since then efforts have been made to improve them. Recent speeches and congressional testimony by both government officials and industry executives call for increased support for university research to provide the foundation for future technological innovation and economic growth. The theme is well expressed by the past president of the Industrial Research Institute: "...as a start, there must be strong support by government and industry for a major commitment to undirected basic research at the universities.... Only if we can be assured of a strong, viable university structure in its own right do we then have the basis for the integration of some added university efforts into broad national missions."[35]

For their part, universities also are seeking to rediscover their ties to industry. Research interest in solving the critical problems relating to the civilian economy is a factor, but other more practical matters are certainly involved: the availability of government funds for applied and problem-oriented research; greater university interest in industrial research support to supplement a static or declining federal share; changes in graduate student employment expectations; and a recognition that continuing education for industry may become a major source of university support in the 1980s and beyond.[36] Whatever the mix of motives, university faculty and administrators seem considerably more interested in strengthening their research ties to the private sector than they were five years ago. This appears especially true in the most prestigious universities, at which anti-industry protests and attitudes were strongest in the late 1960s.

Consulting and staff exchanges (an industrial scientist serving as a visiting professor or a faculty member spending a summer or sabbatical in industry) are the most direct ways of linking academic and industrial research. They are probably also the most effective means of transferring knowledge between the two sectors. Beyond these direct links, however, universities and industry have attempted other means to encourage closer collaboration as listed in Table 4 and described briefly below.[37] These means can be characterized as efforts to organize collaborative research projects and to improve the overall environment for knowledge transfer. In the past five years, NSF, the Small Business Administration, and the Department of Commerce have supported sev-

---

Table 4
Examples of University/Industry Collaboration

Mechanisms to Encourage Collaborative Research

- Direct corporate funding of university research projects
- Cooperative (cost-sharing) research programs
- University/industry research consortia
- Joint industry/university laboratories

Mechanisms to Encourage Knowledge Transfer

- Consulting
- Technology licensing and technological brokers
- Extension services
- Industrial associates programs
- Industrial parks
- Innovation centers
- Small business institutes

---

eral projects directed toward these ends. A brief discussion of these efforts follows.

Direct Corporate Funding of University Research. Although universities have always sought unrestricted research grants and endowment funds from industry, some have been wary of accepting corporate grants for specific projects or fields of research that might confer proprietary advantages to the donor. Others, however, seek industrial support more aggressively and are active in the technology transfer process. As one example, Harvard University and the Monsanto Company announced in February 1975 that Monsanto had agreed to provide up to $23 million for a 12-year program of biological and medical research at Harvard. "In return," according to a newspaper account, "Monsanto will have the opportunity to develop and distribute any medical materials growing out of the research." [38] In fact, the company is given exclusive licenses for a period of time to inventions made in connection with the Monsanto-supported research.

According to Harvard and Monsanto officials, Monsanto and the University have created a special advisory board of individuals not connected with either institution to review plans for publication, dissemination of information, and use of discoveries made under the program. In particular, the board has authority to require sublicensing of an invention if it believes such a step is necessary in the public interest. This arrangement nonetheless represents a substantial step away from some university policies that do not permit a firm to hold proprietary rights to inventions arising from university research it supports.

Bilateral arrangements between a university and an industrial firm generally result in person-to-person interactions that favor technology transfer. The firm presumably supports the research in expectation of a net economic return. In the past, such industrial support has typically been on a project-by-project and year-by-year basis.[39] In hard times these projects are often the first to be cut off. In contrast, the Harvard-Monsanto arrangement represents a long-term, high-level commitment by the Company to support basic science in return for closer links to university research and some proprietary advantages.

Cooperative Research Programs. In some cases individual firms may be willing to pay for part of the cost of a university research project. If the project offers prospects of educational or social benefits (such as creating jobs), the remaining costs may be paid for by a government agency, a private foundation, or the university itself. Federal support for such cooperative research can also be justified in cases of market failure where individual firms cannot recoup the benefits from R&D and consequently conduct little research. These arguments were used in the early 1960s to support cooperative research between universities and textile firms under the short-lived Civilian Industrial Technology Program in the Department of Commerce. At present the National Science Foundation through its RANN program sponsors cooperative research programs at Carnegie-Mellon University, North Carolina State University, and MIT. (Another program operated by the MITRE Corporation under the RANN cooperative research program is actually a form of technology brokerage. See page 95.)

The Processing Research Institute (PRI) at Carnegie-Mellon University was funded by NSF in 1971 to develop a Master of Engineering program oriented toward the processing industries. Cooperative research projects supported by individual firms form an integral part of the PRI program. In the three and a half years between January 1972 and June 1975, 26 firms and industrial associations paid approximately $800,000 to support 34 separate research projects.[40] PRI provided another $500,000 in matching funds from its NSF grant. The sponsors of research projects at PRI were large industrial corporations heavily involved in R&D, including Du Pont, Exxon, Xerox, Westinghouse, Alcoa, and Ford. Few companies with annual sales below $100 million have participated.

The PRI program uses cooperative research projects to involve graduate students in problem-oriented research directly relevant to industrial needs. The program is not aimed at improving productivity in participating firms, nor is it addressed to any specific market failures. It is by no means clear, for example, that the federal contributions to PRI research projects do not simply substitute for the funds the companies would have spent on research anyway, albeit in their own laboratories and not at Carnegie-Mellon. Nevertheless, the PRI program represents a direct effort to use federal funds as a catalyst to reorient university engineering studies toward industrial interests.

Similarly, the RANN-funded Polymer Processing Program at MIT seems directed toward large firms in the plastics industry with substantial R&D capabilities. Although one of the principal goals of the program is "to recommend alterations in public policy which would result in increased R&D investments and efforts by small firms,"[41] the five initial industrial participants are large corporations with annual sales ranging from $40 million to over $10 billion. According to a preliminary evaluation, "a great deal of informal interaction exists between the program staff and industrial members...and a high degree of satisfaction with the program is indicated by member firms."[42]

In contrast, the RANN-sponsored cooperative research program at North Carolina State University is directed toward the U.S. furniture industry, which is highly fragmented and conducts little R&D. Six furniture manufacturing firms participate in research projects with the University. As might be expected, establishing effective links has been more difficult in this case because of the companies' limited R&D capability. The preliminary evaluation reports that the Furniture R&D Applications Institute "is not meeting the cost-sharing goal" and that "the depressed economy has had substantial negative impacts on the development of the program. Industrial members hesitate to implement innovative processes and change furniture design when their revenues are uncertain and decreasing."[43] Moreover, the evaluation notes that while "the Institute's establishment was announced in the trade publications, and presentations have been made to the National Association of Furniture Manufacturers...and the Forest Products Research Society,...no results have been observed from these efforts."[44]

While it is still too early to judge the final results of NSF's efforts to stimulate cooperative research, these three contrasting examples support the view that universities can more easily create research partnerships with large, technically sophisticated companies than with small firms.

University/Industry Research Consortia. Another emerging approach to strengthening university/industry ties is the creation of research consortia with well-defined applied research objectives. The Department of Defense successfully adopted this approach for developing certain kinds of military technology, such as coatings for refractory metals in supersonic aircraft.[45] A group of experts in the field defines the key research needs, solicits proposals from both university and industry groups, selects the best proposals for funding, and coordinates the reporting and publication of results. Informal meetings of members to discuss their ongoing work have been instrumental in the success of research consortia.

An example of such a consortium in a nonmilitary field is that organized by Clemson University to conduct research on fabric flammability with support from the Experimental Technology Incentives Program (ETIP) of the Department of Commerce. ETIP viewed the consortium as a vehicle to speed the commercialization process from laboratory research to demonstration to subsequent diffusion. The consortium includes three universities, a nonprofit laboratory, a government laboratory, and four private firms.[46] Although in operation for only two years, the consortium seems successful in linking university research to industrial needs and in stimulating additional industry R&D.

In general, research consortia made up of universities and industry appear most productive when they are directed toward the achievement of a specific goal. A federal agency or other sponsor is usually necessary to provide the rationale and the financial support. If the consortium is willing to set research priorities, bring the participants together to discuss and critique each other's work, and otherwise act as a strong research coordinator, it can serve to build effective ties between universities and industrial firms. ERDA has indicated interest in establishing university/industry consortia for research on energy problems.

Some states are also active in creating consortia of state and local government agencies, universities, and industrial firms to conduct research on issues of state concern. Michigan, for example, established in 1975 the Michigan Energy and Resource Research Association (MERRA), whose members include state government agencies, large industrial firms such as Dow Chemical and Detroit Edison, and major universities, including Michigan State University, Michigan Technological University, the University of Michigan, and Wayne State University. MERRA's stated purposes are to aid the creation of research consortia among its members, identify research projects and likely funding sources, and help obtain support for these projects.[47] MERRA has endorsed such projects as the study of *in situ* oil shale reporting, involving Dow Chemical and several Michigan universities, and the conversion of municipal waste to methane, involving a private engineering firm and researchers at Michigan State University and the University of Michigan. MERRA also has been actively seeking to have the new ERDA-sponsored Solar Energy Research Institute located in Michigan. Several other states reportedly are considering emulating the MERRA model to enhance their competitive positions for energy R&D funds.

A different model is the Gulf Universities Research Consortium (GURC) that brings together research groups from several universities to conduct environmental research sponsored by government and industry. The consortium is controlled by the universities, with industrial firms, nonprofit research institutions, and government agencies involved as research associates or affiliates. Although consortia of this type may be useful in promoting cooperation among universities and in obtaining research contracts, they seem less likely to build strong working relationships between universities and private-sector firms.

A Joint Industry/University Laboratory. Part-time use of specialized research equipment in universities by industry personnel, or vice versa, is not uncommon and may become more prevalent. University-managed contract research centers that engage in some research for industry are also widespread. Much more unusual, however, is the actual merger of university and industry laboratories into a single entity under joint control. One such example is the Fluid Dynamics and Energetics Laboratory of New York University (formerly the Aerospace Laboratory), which in 1973 was combined with the General Applied Science Laboratories (GASL), a for-profit company.

In 1973, New York University sold its University Heights campus and transferred most of the technical equipment, along with the faculty of the School of Engineering and Science, to the Polytechnic Institute of New York. But because the Institute already had sufficient facilities, the equipment and staff of the NYU Fluid Dynamics and Energetics Laboratory were merged with those of GASL. Although the physical facilities of the two laboratories have been combined, the professional staffs remain organizationally separate, and NYU and GASL use separate accounting systems for their operations. Complex legal and administrative issues remain, such as the disposition of government-furnished equipment and the cost apportionment of common services, but in principle these problems appear to be workable. A recent management study suggests that this arrangement can serve as a model for industry/university collaboration.[48] However, the NYU-GASL merger seems a forced marriage that, because of the basic differences between universities and for-profit organizations, is not likely to be replicated easily.

Encouraging University/Industry Knowledge Transfer

In addition to collaborative research, various approaches have been attempted to speed the transfer of knowledge from university research to industrial application. Government has provided the impetus for a number of such efforts in the past five years. The arrangements described below are by no means exhaustive; a more complete list is contained in the 1970 United Kingdom report of the Working Party on Universities and Industrial Research.[49]

Consulting. A traditional and effective means of knowledge transfer comes from consulting done by faculty for industry. Through consulting, university professors better understand industrial research needs and appreciate the problems of commercialization. However, few data exist in this area. A 1965 survey of University of California faculty members found that about 30 percent had done some consulting during that year, especially those in the fields of medicine, engineering, and social science.[50] A 1969 survey of about 2,500 business school faculty showed that 40 percent served as paid consultants to private firms. Of the responding faculty members in private universities, over half were consultants, compared with about one third in public universities. Moreover, the percentage of business school faculty employed as consultants to national corporations increased according to the prestige of the university, while no such variation was found for local consulting.[51] Finally, an American Council on Education survey during the 1972-73 academic year found that 48 percent of responding faculty members reported some paid outside consulting during the previous year.[52]

These data are too meager to suggest trends in academic consulting for industry. Frequent reports are heard about specific companies that have either abandoned or cut back on university consulting because of financial difficulties; on the other hand, some firms have begun using university consultants on a more systematic basis. Several corporations heavily involved in R&D, for example, have recently established technical advisory boards that include academic consultants to review their overall R&D strategies and programs.[53] No clear pattern of trends in consulting emerged from the site visits conducted for this study, except that faculty scientists, and particularly engineering faculty members, have shown a great interest in enhancing ties of all sorts with industry. To the extent that many faculty perceive consulting relationships as leading to further ties of potential mutual benefit, it seems probable that the time and effort devoted by faculty members to

seeking out and engaging in consulting activities have increased substantially in the past few years and will continue to increase. Better
data on faculty consulting to industry (perhaps as one of the NSF science indicators) would be helpful in observing trends in university/in-
dustry interactions.

Technology Licensing and Technological Brokers. A technological
broker linking those universities with particular research capabilities to
industrial firms with corresponding research needs is an appealing concept. Several types of brokers now exist: (1) university research foundations that license patents derived from university research;[54] (2) Research Corporation, Battelle Development Corporation, and other research corporations that license or otherwise commercially exploit inventions; and (3) private consulting firms, such as Dr. Dvorkovitz &
Associates, which specialize in technology brokerage between universities and industrial firms. Since 1973, Dr. Dvorkovitz & Associates has
sponsored an annual University/Industry Forum at which universities
can display their technologies for license. According to the firm, the
February 1976 meeting, called the "First World Fair for Technology
Exchange," drew more than 2,000 attendees. Although data on the extent of university technology licensing are unavailable, both universities and commercial firms seem to be showing increased interest.[55]

Federal agencies have in the past supported dissemination centers or
clearinghouses at universities to speed the flow of research results to
potential industry users, but their effectiveness as agents of technology
transfer remains in doubt.[56] More recently, NSF has funded a direct
brokerage experiment as part of its cooperative research program. The
New England Energy Development System (NEEDS) center, developed by the MITRE Corporation, is intended "to facilitate the flow of
technology between the New England electric utilities and those uni-
versities/nonprofit research groups capable of performing research
needed by the utilities."[57] The NEEDS center tries to match research
performers and utilities on individual projects, publishes summaries of
research results on specific topics, and conducts seminars for industry,
government, and university participants. However, it is not clear what
additional function a government-supported center serves for electric
utilities that not only have their own industry supported R&D programs through the Electric Power Research Institute, but also have
some established links with universities and other research performers. Without an identified market failure, a government-subsidized
technology broker may simply serve as a substitute for other linking
mechanisms provided by the private sector and the universities themselves.

Extension Services. The USDA Agricultural Extension Service,
which along with the Agricultural Experiment Stations is closely tied
to land-grant universities, is repeatedly cited as a model for knowledge

transfer in other fields. A 1963 report by Arthur D. Little, Inc., for example, recommended an extension service for the construction industry modeled after the agriculture experience.[58] Some of the ideas contained in the A.D. Little report were subsequently embodied in the Department of Commerce's Civilian Industrial Technology program, but this part of the CIT program was never approved by Congress. Other proposals in the past 10 years have called for extension services to aid local governments, vocational rehabilitation programs, marine activities, pollution control, and energy conservation.

In June 1976, Texas A&M University organized the Energy Advisory Service for Texas (EAST). As an extension service, its purpose is to provide "direct contact of energy technology specialists with energy-user groups. The specialists [will] work with manufacturers, builders, operators of buildings, and the general public to perform energy audits and to analyze the potential payoff of energy conservation strategies."[59] EAST receives support from the University's state funds, the Texas Governor's Energy Advisory Council, Public Technology Incorporated (a nonprofit organization financed largely by NSF to stimulate technology transfer for local public services), and ERDA. Independently, ERDA is now considering establishing energy conservation extension services throughout the United States.

Proponents of new extension services emphasize the value of decentralized operations, grassroots knowledge, and adaptation to local problems and needs. These characteristics of the Agricultural Extension Service are well linked to the decentralized and locally varying farming operations throughout the nation. In general, extension services seem most appropriate for fragmented markets where the cost of obtaining information about new developments is high. Energy conservation for residential and commercial buildings may be one such example. Extension services are expensive to operate, however, especially if they must be created anew for each application. Building on an existing agricultural extension service, as Texas A&M has done for energy conservation, seems a more sensible approach.

University Industrial Associates. A few universities successfully run Industrial Associates programs, in which member companies each contribute an annual fee—usually $15,000 to $25,000. The funds are used for general university purposes rather than specific research projects. In return, Industrial Associate members receive publications, attend special conferences and seminars, visit campuses, and meet individual faculty members. Industrial Associate members do not expect to receive proprietary information from their campus contacts, but they can use their favored status to exchange research results in fields they are actively pursuing and to receive intensive briefings in unfamiliar areas by a competent authority. Faculty consulting often grows out of an Industrial Associate contact, but that is an entirely separate arrangement.

Only a few of the nation's most prestigious academic institutions, such as MIT, Stanford, and the California Institute of Technology, have successfully run Industrial Associate programs. Several other universities that have attempted to institute them have failed to achieve the critical mass of corporate members needed to defray the costs of running the program.

Industrial Parks. Creating an industrial park near campus has been contemplated by many universities as a way of strengthening interactions with industry. Such a project is also financially attractive to universities with nearby available land. The most successful example is the Stanford Industrial Park, which has succeeded in attracting a large number of research-intensive companies and their spinoffs to locations near the Stanford campus. The increased opportunity for faculty consulting and entrepreneurship, industrial staff enrollment in university courses, and the use of industrial scientists as university lecturers stimulate technology transfer.

Other universities have emulated the Stanford project with varying degrees of success. The Research Triangle Park, developed with strong backing from the state of North Carolina, is associated with the University of North Carolina at Chapel Hill, North Carolina State University at Raleigh, and Duke University at Durham. The largest research-intensive company to locate in the Park is Burroughs-Wellcome, a major pharmaceutical company closely connected with the biochemistry research activities at the University of North Carolina. To augment the industrial Park, the three universities joined to establish the Research Triangle Institute (RTI) as an independent, nonprofit research organization. The Institute's board of governors includes state government officials, representatives from corporations located in the Research Triangle Park, as well as university officials. Many university faculty work on industry-sponsored research as consultants or part-time members at the Institute. The Institute has some research capabilities that the universities lack, and joint efforts between the Institute and university researchers to secure federal research funds are fairly common. The Institute also contributes a small annual payment to the universities for research support. The relationship between the Institute and the member universities generally has been good, although there are signs of increased competition within some departments as faculty scientists have moved into applied areas in an effort to maintain their levels of research support.

A university decision to pursue an industrial park development certainly will be based on criteria other than the fostering of university/industry research relationships. It will demand very strong political and financial commitments by the university and the local government. And it seems clear that only a limited number of universities can successfully follow the Stanford and RTI examples.

Innovation Centers. Another group of National Science Foundation experiments intended to foster productivity in U.S. industry are the three "innovation centers" supported at the University of Oregon, MIT, and Carnegie-Mellon University. The innovation centers provide college-credit courses intended to teach the skills necessary to move a new product from the laboratory to the marketplace. The centers also provide support for individual inventors. If successful, the innovation centers should strengthen the links between universities and the industrial firms that will manufacture and market the new products.

In June 1973, NSF awarded grants totaling $3 million to the three innovation centers for efforts over a period of five years. It is too early to assess their results in terms of encouraging stronger university/industry ties, but they have generated considerable enthusiasm on the part of students, faculty members, and industry executives. As one example, five students at the MIT Innovation Center developed new electronic games in response to the interest displayed in marketing them by a small local company. A marketing contract with the company was signed in April 1975. According to the Center's director, "By the middle of July orders for 400,000 units had been obtained from major retailers around the country. Since production began on November 28, 1975, the contractor has hired 70 new employees and created a pool of 100 additional people upon which to draw as production expands."[60] Overall, the NSF program director estimates that "during the first two years, the Centers contributed to the creation of 240 new jobs and $3.4 million in sales."[61]

University Business Development Centers. At least six federal agencies, including HEW, the Small Business Administration, NSF, the Economic Development Administration, the Office of Minority Business Enterprises, and the National Bureau of Standards, support programs at colleges and universities to assist small businesses. Generally, they offer management consulting and training in such fields as accounting, economics, contracting, and business law. The Small Business Administration has recently announced the formation of University Business Development Centers (UBDCs) that would coordinate these several agency efforts.

Most universities and colleges that participate in UBDC programs are urban, community-oriented institutions with little ongoing research. Consequently, while these small-business programs may stimulate technology transfer indirectly (by helping establish new firms that may then acquire technology from universities), their direct effect on university research links with industry appears to be minimal.

Conclusions

While this paper has been descriptive rather than normative, the discussion of research performers and their interactions leads to several judgmental conclusions. First, university strength in basic research seems undiminished despite the financial and institutional strains of the last decade. If anything, universities have strengthened their position as the predominant U.S. performer of basic research. Both the industrial and government sectors stress the importance of supporting university basic research as a foundation for mission-oriented applied research and development undertaken by other performers.

In applied research and development, universities face strong competition from industry, government laboratories, and nonprofit research institutes; and they have shown few comparative advantages in relation to these other performers. Concern for relevance in university research remains, but it has lost much of the strident sound it had in the late 1960s. And while national needs, technology transfer, and community service will continue to motivate or justify additional university research, these goals seem unlikely to overwhelm the traditional university objectives of fundamental research and education. The limitations of the multiversity have clearly been identified in the past decade.

In terms of research support, the federal government seems inevitably to remain the principal patron of university research. The roles of state and local governments appear likely to increase as more federal funds flow through them. Neither industry nor foundation support of university research shows signs of regaining the importance it held before 1955, although such support obviously can be important in many specific cases.[62]

The nation's growing concern for civilian problems and its own economic competitiveness focuses attention on university research links with the industrial firms. Both sectors have pledged to rectify their past neglect and to establish better university/industry relationships. However, the move to strengthen the links will encounter conceptual as well as practical difficulties. Universities and industrial firms have different objectives, different incentive schemes, and different approaches to research that will not be bridged by mere rhetoric.[63] Nor is it clear how closely the two sectors should be intertwined. The nation has profited from its set of diverse research institutions, and some competitive tension among the sectors seems more healthy than debilitating.

Still, there is much we can do to dispel the myths that have made university/industry relationships more difficult than they need be. Changing attitudes and expectations among university faculty, students, industrial scientists, and research administrators certainly seem helpful. And some additional government support may be useful in lubricating the pathways and experimenting with new ideas. But one must view present federal programs aimed at strengthening university/industry interactions as rather unstructured, unfocused, and uncoordinated. Some are meant to aid small businesses; some to improve productivity in R&D-lagging industries; some to spread research funds geographically and spur regional development; and some to tailor university engineering to the needs of large, technically sophisticated firms. Few seem directed toward identified market failures or government-induced obstacles to technology transfer. And most government programs seek to effect the links through the university supplier of research rather than the industrial producer of goods and services.

Such federal programs seem to suffer from the same difficulties observed on a much larger scale in government efforts to commercialize new technology directly: too much technology push, too little demand pull, and not enough concern with the incentive systems that influence the transfer of ideas from research to application.[64] Yet there are models that we know work. Perhaps federal programs should promote consulting and other exchanges of people between universities and industry, from which the transfer of knowledge may naturally follow. Perhaps more projects should focus on the industrial manufacturer or user of the technology rather than on the university supplier. The director of the Rockwell International Science Center puts the matter bluntly: "I have a basic thing about universities getting funds to solve hydrogen embrittlement problems when they don't have any."[65] And perhaps federal agencies should insist that proposals for collaborative research include a marketing or commercialization plan, as ETIP did in the fabric flammability program, rather than a dissemination plan. In any event, we need to develop better conceptual and evaluative frameworks for government programs to strengthen university relationships with industry.

Universities and private sector firms seem anxious to rediscover and reinforce the ties between them. Specific government programs may help cement these relationships, but their importance is by no means clear. Like other aspects of technology transfer, effective university/industry links depend most on the two partners' own incentives to promote the flow of people and ideas.

---

1. Dael Wolfle, *The Home of Science: The Role of the University* (New York: McGraw-Hill, 1972).

2. Ibid., pp. 22-32, 53-56, 93.

3. In the 1820s, for example, the builders of the Delaware and Hudson Canal reportedly sought consulting advice at Columbia University in developing their final engineering plans. See Arthur J. Alexander, "Cost Curves and Rate of Return on the Delaware and Hudson Canal 1831-1899," (processed).

4. National Science Foundation, *National Patterns of R&D Resources, 1953-1975*, NSF 75-307 (Washington, D.C.: National Science Foundation, 1975). These figures differ from those reported in the NSF annual series *Federal Funds for Research, Development, and Other Scientific Activities* in two principal ways. First they are based on actual expenditures of federal funds reported by the R&D performers, rather than on obligations reported by the federal funding agencies (except for federal intramural laboratories, where obligations are used in both series). The performers' expenditure data differ from agency obligations both in timing (expenditures occur later than obligations) and in the divisions among basic research, applied research, and development categories (e.g., industrial firms consistently report a lower ratio of basic to applied research performed with federal funds than do the agencies funding the research). Second, *National*

Patterns combines calendar year data for industry and nonprofit institutions with federal fiscal year data for universities and federal intramural laboratories, while *Federal Funds* uses fiscal year data for all performers.

5. Other components of federal support for colleges and universities, such as graduate student fellowships, have dropped far more dramatically during this period. See National Science Board, *Science Indicators—1974: Report of the National Science Board, 1975* (Washington, D.C.: National Science Foundation, 1975), pp. 137-138.

6. These figures are taken from the National Science Foundation series *Federal Funds for Research, Development, and Other Scientific Activities*, Vol. XVI, pp. 112-113; Vol. XXIII, pp. 16-17, 44-45. The performer share totals are not the same as those shown in Figures 3 and 5 because of the different data series used. See Footnote 4.

7. John L. Allen, "Statement on the Technology Base," Testimony before the Research and Development Subcommittee, Armed Services Committee, United States Senate, March 29, 1977.

8. National Science Foundation, *Science Indicators*, op. cit., pp. 40-43.

9. D. C. Spriestersbach, Margery E. Hoppin, and John McCrone, "University Research and the New Federalism," *Science*, October 25, 1974, pp. 324-327.

10. For example, see Rodney W. Nichols, "Mission-Oriented R&D," *Science*, April 2, 1971, pp. 29-37; and Harold Orlans, *The Nonprofit Research Institute: Its Origin, Operation, Problems, and Prospects* (New York: McGraw-Hill, 1972), p. 141.

11. For an excellent account of the rise of university contract research centers, see Harold Orlans, Ibid.

12. In the spirit of the nation's Bicentennial celebration three years hence, the Charles Stark Draper Laboratory issued its own Declaration of July 1, 1973: "When in the Course of Human Events it becomes necessary for two Institutions to revise the Bonds which have connected them,...it is entirely fitting that this Separation take place and it is likewise fitting for us to solemnly Publish and Declare that the Charles Stark Draper Laboratory is, and of Right ought to be, a free and independent institution, with full Power to contract Alliances, establish Commerce and do all other Acts and Things which Independent Laboratories may of right do...."

13. Harold Orlans, op. cit., pp. 126-132.

14. Albert Crewe and Frank Press, among others, have proposed that the federal government give greater emphasis to the support of national research facilities. See Albert V. Crewe, "Science on a Regional Scale," in *Science and the University*, Boyd R. Kennan, ed. (New York: Columbia University Press, 1966); and Frank Press, "New Arrangements for Science in the Universities," *Science*, July 18, 1975, p. 177.

15. A recent review committee of the National Academy of Sciences has called attention to the need for large-scale data bases in the social sciences. See *Social and Behavioral Science Programs in the National Science Foundation*, final report of the Committee on the Social Sciences in NSF (Washington, D.C.: National Academy of Sciences, 1976).

16. Harold Orlans, op. cit., pp. 42-43.

17. Nancy Castleman and Pamela Coty, *Center for Policy Research: The First Five Years, 1968-73* (New York: Center for Policy Research), p. 6.

18. J.L. Allen, et al., *The DOD Laboratory Utilization Study* (Washington, D.C.: U.S. Department of Defense, April 1975), pp. xiii-xiv.

19. *Report of the Field and Laboratory Utilization Study Group* (Washington, D.C.: U.S. Energy Research and Development Administration, December 1975), p. 32.

20. *Report of the Committee Advisory to the U.S. Department of Agriculture* (Washington, D.C.: National Academy of Sciences, 1973). Similar criticism is contained in Andre Mayer and Jean Mayer, "Agriculture, The Island Empire," *Daedalus*, Summer 1974, pp. 83-96.

21. For a comparative discussion of interdisciplinary research in universities, independent research centers, and government, see Jack M. Nilles, "Interdisciplinary Policy Research and the Universities"; W.S. Baer, "Interdisciplinary Policy Research in Independent Research Centers"; and P. Polishuk,"Problems in Interdisciplinary Policy Research and Management in Government,"*IEEE Transactions on Engineering Management*, May 1976, pp. 74-84, 92-100.

22. *Federal Funds for Research, Development and Other Scientific Activities*, Vol. XXIII, Detailed Statistical Tables (Washington, D.C.: National Science Foundation, 1974), p. 47, 67.

23. Or in the words of one industrial research manager, the director of the Rockwell International Science Center: "There are a lot of advantages...to working with universities.... One is the outstanding creative talents. That does not mean we do not have

them in industry; it just means our people get numb sooner." In T.L. Loucks, "University-Industry Joint Projects: An Industrial View," *Journal of the Society of Research Administrators*, Spring 1974, p. 35.

24. See, for example: United Kingdom Working Party on Universities and Industrial Research, *Industry, Science, and the Universities* (London: Confederation of British Industry, 1970), pp. 56-57, 88-89; and Joseph F. Libsch, "The Role of the Small, High Technology University," *Research Management*, May 1976, pp. 28-31. Most of the published literature on this topic consists of personal statements and calls for "better communications" between the two sectors; a thoughtful and perceptive exception is Rustum Roy, "University-Industry Interaction Patterns," *Science*, December 1, 1972, pp. 955-960. Additional efforts to develop an analytic framework for and quantitative data about U.S. university/industry interactions would seem highly useful.

25. Attempts to chart university/industry relationships by observing the number of ideas or events in the university sector that have led to industrial innovation seem of little help. The relative importance of the university-initiated ideas depends principally on the time frame used in the analysis as a comparison of the Hindsight and Traces studies indicates. The longer the time horizon, the more likely the innovation will have some university roots.

26. *Chemistry in the Economy* (Washington, D.C.: American Chemical Society, 1973), p. 445.

27. W.N. Maclay, "Science-Engineering Education for Industrial Research," *Research Management*, September 1974, p. 34.

28. P.C. White and C.C. Wallin, "What Industry Needs From Academia," *Research Management*, September 1974, p. 30.

29. *Business Week*, February 16, 1976, pp. 56-58.

30. R.L. Sproull, "The Industrial-Academic Interface: From the Academic Viewpoint," *Research Management*, May 1969, pp. 219-226.

31. J.E. Goldman, "The Need for Basic Research in Industry," *Physics Today*, December 1975, pp. 23-25.

32. United Kingdom Working Party on Universities and Industrial Research, *Industry, Science, and the Universities* (London: Confederation of British Industry, 1970), p. 108.

33. *The Research System* (Paris: Organization for Economic Cooperation and Development, Vol. 1: France, Germany, United Kingdom, 1972; Vol. 2: Belgium, Netherlands, Norway, Sweden, Switzerland, 1973; Vol. 3: Canada, United States, General Conclusions, 1974).

34. Ibid., Vol. 1, p. 249.

35. Herbert I. Fusfeld, "Industry/University R&D: New Approaches to Support and Working Relationships," *Research Management*, May 1976, p. 24.

36. R.A. Swalin, "Improving Interaction Between the University and the Technical Community," *Research Management*, May 1976, pp. 25-27.

37. Roy discusses several of these institutional mechanisms in more detail. See Rustum Roy, "University-Industry Interaction Patterns," *Science*, December 1, 1972, pp. 955-960.

38. "Monsanto, Harvard Join in Project," *St. Louis Post-Dispatch*, February 6, 1975, p. 18.

39. For example, note the approach described by Alcoa's vice president for science and technology: "The device used...is to tell a young industry researcher to visit the university which is doing the best work in his field, then provide him with a check, in Alcoa's case for $5,000, which the young industry representative can leave with the professor to help support a graduate student or to provide general support for the work, but to leave it only if he thinks the work being done is good and useful. Since most professors hope the industry representative will visit again next year with similar results, there is a real incentive to communicate and to establish a lasting relationship." In Eric A. Walker and Robert G. Hampel, "Improving Industrial R&D: University Relations," *Research Management*, September 1974, pp. 23-28.

40. *Fourth Annual Progress Report* (Pittsburgh: Processing Research Institute, Carnegie-Mellon University, June 1975).

41. Marcia L. Grad and Joseph Halpern, "Evaluation Status and Planning, Cooperative Research and Development Experiment," Report R 75-07, October 1975, p. 23. Prepared by the Denver Research Institute for the Experimental R&D Incentives Program of the National Science Foundation.

42. Ibid., p. 26.

43. Ibid., p. 18.
44. Ibid.
45. Rustum Roy, op. cit.
46. Richard A. Rettig, "The Use of Consortia for the Management of Research and Development: Some Initial Observations on the Clemson University ETIP Project" (Paper presented at the Clemson University Special Symposium on Flammability and Flame Retardation of Polyester/Cotton Blend Fabrics, Clemson, South Carolina, September 15-17, 1976).
47. *Merra '75 Annual Report* (Detroit: Michigan Energy and Resource Research Association, 1976).
48. John R. Ragazzini, "Management Study of a Merged Large-Scale Fluid Dynamics (and Energetics) Laboratory—A Joint University-Industry Venture" (New York: New York University, July 1976).
49. United Kingdom Working Party, op. cit., p. 112.
50. Dallas K. Perry, "Sample Survey of Faculty Supplementary Employment and Income During 1965: University of California and California State Colleges, Final Report," TM-L-2789 (Los Angeles: System Development Corporation, December 30, 1965).
51. Carlos E. Kruytbosch and David D. Palmer, "Academic Role Performance and Organizational Environment " (Mimeographed, 1976). University prestige determined by "peer-based prestige ratings of institutions," according to the authors.
52. Alan E. Bayer, "Teaching Faculty in Academe: 1972-73," *ACE Research Reports*, Vol. 8, No. 2 (Washington, D.C.: American Council on Education, August 1973).
53. Frank R. Bacon, Jr., and Thomas W. Butler, Jr., "The Technical Board," attachment to "Identifying Needs and Resources for Knowledge of Science" (Paper delivered by Thomas W. Butler, Jr., at the annual meeting of the American Association for the Advancement of Science, February 1976).
54. Raymond D. Daniels, Ralph C. Martin, Lawrence Eisenberg, Jay M. Lewallen, and Ronald A. Wright, "University-Connected Research Foundations, An Introduction," *SRA Journal*, Spring 1975, pp. 16-25.
55. Rebecca L. Rawls, "University Technology Licensing Set to Rise," *Chemical and Engineering News*, August 24, 1975, pp. 11-12.
56. Samuel I. Doctors, *The Role of Federal Agencies in Technology Transfer* (Cambridge, Mass.: MIT Press, 1969), pp. 92-127.
57. Marcia L. Grad and Joseph Halpern, op. cit., p. 29.
58. Dorothy Nelkin, *The Politics of Housing Innovation* (Ithaca, N.Y.: Cornell University Press, 1971), pp. 25-26.
59. Stephen Ritter, "The Energy Advisory Service for Texas" (Paper presented at the 1976 Summer Workshop on Energy Extension Services, Berkeley, California, July 1976, Mimeographed).
60. Y.T. Li, "Development of Future Innovators and Entrepreneurs" (Paper delivered at the annual meeting of the American Association for the Advancement of Science, February 1976).
61. Robert M. Colton and Gerald G. Udell, "The National Science Foundation Innovation Centers: An Experiment in Training Potential Entrepreneurs and Innovators," *Journal of Small Business Management*, April 1976, pp. 11-20.
62. P.H. Abelson, "Additional Sources of Financial and Political Support for Science," *Science*, April 20, 1973.
63. Perusal of the recent literature makes it easy to agree with the observation of one reviewer of the 1970 Confederation of British Industry report, "If the idea of collaboration between university and industry is buried underneath sufficient platitudes it will die of suffocation." D.C. Freshwater, "Industry, Science, and Universities," *Chemistry and Industry*, March 20, 1971, pp. 320-321.
64. See, for example, Robert Gilpin, "Technology, Economic Growth, and International Competitiveness," A Report Prepared for the Use of the Subcommittee on Economic Growth of the Joint Economic Committee, U.S. Congress, Washington, D.C., July 9, 1975; and Walter S. Baer, Leland L. Johnson, and Edward W. Merrow, *Analysis of Federally Funded Demonstration Projects: Executive Summary* (Santa Monica, California: The Rand Corporation), R-1925-DOC, April 1976.
65. T.L. Loucks, op. cit., p. 35.

Targeted Research:
An American Tradition

Carl M. York

Targeted research has played a significant role throughout the history of the United States, especially during the decade 1965 through 1975. During this period, a growing fraction of the federal research support for universities went into targeted programs, a trend that is a cause for concern among university administrators and researchers. The term "targeted research" distinguishes a specific pattern of research activities sponsored by the federal government. As used here it cuts across the familiar spectrum of basic research, applied research, and development, terms used for many years by the National Science Foundation (NSF) to classify federal obligations and expenditures. Targeted research has a shorter time span for results than the continuing programs of agencies with long-term missions, such as providing for the national defense or the general health and welfare of the people. It is similar to mission-oriented research in that the funding agency specifies the type of work to be done and solicits proposals on topics of limited scope. "Targeted" implies a directed attack on a clearly specified problem to be solved in a relatively short period of time.

Historical Review

In America's earliest years, research was oriented to the practical problems of dealing with a new frontier. The European explorers were sent by their monarchs to seek profitable trade routes or territories. The colonists who settled the New World sought the knowledge needed to subdue the wilderness. John Winthrop (1606-76) of Massachusetts, a member of the Royal Society of London, did pharmacological, chemical, and metallurgical research for very pragmatic reasons. [1]

As the hardships of survival receded before the maturing colonies, scientific research shifted to the promotion of continued development. In 1742, Benjamin Franklin founded the first permanent scientific society, the American Philosophical Society, which embodied all of the contemporary branches of science, including agriculture. It branched into entomology in response to the problem of insect damage to crops; it showed a similar practical orientation in its sponsorship of the first hospital and medical school in North America. The Society was aided financially by the Pennsylvania House of Representatives, which funded construction of an astronomical observatory and granted the Society tax-free land. Many specialized societies developed in the remaining years of the eighteenth century, primarily in medical and marine studies. Although their members were mostly of the upper classes, their interests were not altruistic: "The motivation of many of the colonial planters and merchants, who pursued science as an avocation, was plainly a utilitarian one." [2]

At the founding of the Republic during the Constitutional Convention in 1787, consideration was given to proposals for a national university, charters of incorporation for national societies similar to the colonial ones, and various methods of promoting advances in agriculture, commerce, trade, manufacture, and "useful" knowledge. However, these matters were not accepted as proper concerns of the national government and, being politically inexpedient, were not acted on. Still, as practical needs arose, funding of specific projects was granted in accordance with the provisions in the Constitution for acts necessary for "internal improvements" and "the general welfare."

The early emphasis on practical concerns was made explicit in a statement by William Smith, the provost of the University of Pennsylvania, in 1790: "The man who will...point out a new and profitable article of agriculture and commerce will deserve more from his fellow citizens than all the Latin and Greek scholars, or all the teachers of technical learning that ever existed, in any age or country." [3] Following this philosophy, West Point was established in 1802 for the purpose of developing military engineering, and in the process it produced many early researchers in practical concerns. In the following year, Lewis and Clark headed the first federally sponsored scientific expedition aimed at gathering geographical data and other knowledge about the continent. A precedent was set by the federal sponsorship as well as by the indication that certain scientific explorations were considered appropriate military concerns. Funding of civilian research was begun four years later with a coastal survey undertaken by the Swiss scientist Ferdinand Hassler in 1807 to encourage commercial interests. In 1818 the Missouri Expedition was organized under Major Stephen H. Long, in which a military escort was provided for civilian scientists. All of these were research projects with a specific, practical objective that legitimized the federal government's presence.

The Surgeon General's Office was established as part of the Army in 1818, and research on weather was begun because of its connection with health. The first government-sponsored research grant was made in the 1830s to the Franklin Institute in Philadelphia. In its orientation to a single, practical problem, it was similar to the federally funded expedition that had preceded it. A congressional resolution prompted the Secretary of the Treasury to request that the Institute (which already had established a committee on the subject) investigate the causes of boiler explosions. The result was a law in 1838 concerning boiler safety.

The concern that science be useful was evident in the establishment of the Naval Observatory and the Smithsonian Institution. In 1841 Congress refused to fund an astronomical observatory for the Navy, but the head of the Navy's Depot of Charts and Instruments obtained funds for studies of practical value to the Navy in hydrography, astronomy, magnetism, and meteorology. The result was an observatory in all but name.[4] The Smithsonian Institution, established in 1848, became the first national institution for research 17 years after its endowment by a private individual. It established noteworthy precedents in its method of funding research projects. Direct grants to investigators were approved by a committee of experts; and there were projects for which objectives were set before investigators were chosen.[5]

In the nineteenth century this country relied to a great extent on Europe for basic research, but during the 1850s the number of educational institutions in the U.S. offering science and engineering began to increase notably. The Civil War demonstrated the need for the further development and application of science and for an agency to provide the government with scientific advice. Congress responded by establishing the National Academy of Sciences (NAS) in 1863. The Academy was organized around specific questions, as well as areas of standing interest; and to ensure its autonomy, it was financed by private endowments. Another response to the need for more scientific research and education was the Morrill Act, or Land-Grant College Act, which allowed each state to have at least one college for instruction in "agriculture and the mechanic arts." It provided a form of direct federal government support without infringing upon the autonomy of the institutions. The Hatch Act of 1887, which provided for agricultural experiment stations in these land-grant colleges, allowed research in a limited, practical area of concern while preserving a measure of institutional autonomy.

In 1903 the government's almost exclusive concern with applied science was reinforced by the Committee of Government Scientific Work appointed by Theodore Roosevelt. The Committee concluded that science "on the part of government should be limited nearly to utilitarian purposes evidently for the general welfare." [6] Five years later, a committee of the National Academy of Sciences concurred. In order to deal with this philosophy, the Adams Act of 1906 was passed to prevent diversion of funds from original research in the agricultural experiment stations. To increase administrative control of these projects, the Department of Agriculture adopted the system of project review, which became an increasingly important element of the management of research support. [7]

World War I focused attention on the need for scientific advice within the government. The major response was the creation by Woodrow Wilson of the National Research Council (NRC), which was formed on a base provided by NAS to facilitate cooperation between various research sectors. Like the Academy, the Council was funded privately and remained autonomous. (Two other developments of the war were the Naval Consulting Board and Congress's Council of National Defense.) NRC functioned as a coordinator of projects necessary for the war effort, combining both basic and applied science with development. It continued to operate after the war, although at a much lower level, and provided a continuing flow of funds for basic research, which was perceived as more important than it had been earlier. Herbert Hoover, as Secretary of Commerce, often spoke of the need for basic research to facilitate technological development and promote the health of the economy.

In 1933 the Science Advisory Board (later superseded by the National Resources Committee) and the National Planning Board were established to coordinate and develop research policies. Although constrained financially, they managed to provide some funds for university research. A similar attempt in a different field was the special provision for funding of agricultural research passed by Congress in 1935. The establishment in 1937 of the National Cancer Institute provided for research in the field of health, defining health as a part of the "public welfare" and thus suitable for federal aid. The National Advisory Committee for Aeronautics also gave research grants to universities. The culmination of this trend was a report of the National Resources Science Committee, delivered to the President in 1938, entitled *Research— A National Resource*. Emphasizing the need for protection of research by the federal government, the report also discussed specific proposals for coordinating and upgrading research mechanisms. The war, however, delayed the impact of these proposals, though many were later put into effect.

As World War II approached, it spurred government actions on scientific affairs. The first was the establishment of the National Defense Research Committee, which conducted research on matters directly related to the war and weapons. It had more power than its counterpart of the preceding war—NRC—because it could enter into contracts with diverse groups and in fact did so on a large scale. As the need for a more powerful agency developed, the Office of Scientific Research and Development (OSRD) was established by executive order. OSRD was to oversee the research and production of advanced weapons, coordinate the scientific and technical affairs of the departments of the military and the National Advisory Committee for Aeronautics, and provide for medical research pertinent to military concerns. The Office served as a coordinating committee of experts, granting contracts to academic, industrial, and nonprofit laboratories, and in some cases establishing new facilities. The research was oriented to particular questions for particular ends, and it was carried out at various locations across the country, among them the Radiation Laboratory at MIT, the Applied Physics Laboratory at Johns Hopkins University, the Jet Propulsion Laboratory at the California Institute of Technology, and at Los Alamos, New Mexico; Oak Ridge, Tennessee; and Hanford, Washington.

The problem of project control was addressed in the late 1940s by Irwin Stewart, then deputy director of OSRD:

> The heart of the contract problem was to reconcile the need of the scientist for complete freedom with assurances that government funds would not be improperly expended.... The performance clause [of the contract] was a relatively simple provision. The contractor agreed to conduct studies and experimental investigations in connection with a given problem and to make a final report of his findings and conclusions...by a specified date. This clause was deliberately made flexible in order that the contractor would not be hampered in the details of the work he was to perform. The objective was stated in general terms; no attempt was made to dictate the method of handling the problem. [8]

In July 1945, as the war ended, staff members of OSRD completed a report entitled *Science, the Frontier*. It maintained that the federal government, in the interest of the national welfare, must assume responsibility for research and the researchers. The report proposed that a National Science Foundation be created to support basic research in academic as well as other institutions and to develop the necessary personnel base related to it. [9] The President's message to the Congress in September 1945 on reconversion dealt with this theme, although not this specific proposal. A report by the chairman of the President's Scientific Research Board submitted in August 1947, entitled *Science and Public Policy*, made recommendations similar to those of the earlier report. That same year a bill by Senator H. Alexander Smith passed Congress authorizing a National Science Foundation (NSF) patterned after the National Advisory Committee for Aeronautics. But it was vetoed by President Truman on the basis that it was too autonomous for the amount of money it would control and the important concerns it would oversee.[10]In 1950 these problems were resolved, and the Foundation was established to aid basic research and scientific education. The result was to ensure a higher level of support than was previously given during times of peace. [11]

A number of years before NSF began its operations, two agencies carried the momentum of basic research: the Atomic Energy Commission (AEC) and the Office of Naval Research (ONR). New developments in atomic research required special means of control, and in 1946 the AEC was established for that purpose. It functioned as an intermediary between the military and civilian interests and had a Joint Committee of Congress established for its affairs, the first such congressional committee for oversight of scientific research.

The military was also involved in other areas of basic research, having accepted the need for it as a preliminary step to future weapons development. Established by special legislation of Congress in 1946, the Office of Naval Research became prominent as a result of its support for research that went primarily to universities. Its programs provided greater freedom than ever before: Projects were proposed by researchers themselves, subject only to standards of quality and the general interest areas of ONR. Given the belated establishment of the National Science Foundation, ONR provided for a vital interest of the nation by funding basic research at that time. The other military services had a similar although lesser role in the funding of basic research. The Air Force Office of Scientific Research believed the need for academic basic research was important enough to continue it in 1954, contrary to a Bureau of the Budget decree, by concealing it under applied research for the B-58. [12]

In medicine, the National Institutes of Health (NIH) greatly expanded its role in funding research under the Public Health Service Act of 1944, authorizing grants to universities and other public and private institutions, as well as to individuals, for research projects recommended by advisory councils of its individual institutions. A major feature of the NIH grant process was its mandatory use of the peer-panel evaluation system, which was optional for other agencies. [13]

A turning point came in 1957 when the Russians launched Sputnik. Two new mission agencies were created in response to the threat this technical achievement symbolized. In July 1958 the National Aeronautics and Space Act established a civilian agency, NASA, to coordinate rocket and space technology. Later, in February 1959, the Advanced Research Projects Agency was formed within the Department of Defense (DOD) to coordinate missile research and other advanced defense-related technologies. With these new mission agencies as a base and broad public concern over whether the U.S. educational system was adequate to maintain world leadership in science and technology, the stage was set for a major expansion of higher education and its role in science research.

The period 1960 to 1965 saw an enormous spurt of growth in the federal funding of research activities in the nation's universities. The Seaborg Report called for a doubling of the number of research universities;[14] President Kennedy set a national goal of landing a man on the moon within the decade; and a spirit of unfettered growth and optimism pervaded the relationship between the federal agencies and the universities. It was this period of growth, this "post-Sputnik boom," that led to many of the difficulties encountered from 1965 to 1975.

Consider the data on federal funds for research and development in colleges and universities plotted in Figure 1. The sharp leveling of the curve between 1968 and 1969 was a clear signal that the period of growth was over. The change is even more dramatic if the effects of inflation are taken into account. This has been done by taking 1967 as the base year of comparison and calculating the lower dashed curve in terms of constant 1967 dollars. (This leveling off process after a period of exponential growth has been discussed by Price.[15]) The fact is that in 1968 the period of growth stopped and major readjustments took place between the federal agencies and the research universities.

Figure 1

Federally Provided Funds for R&D
in Colleges and Universities,
Current and Constant Dollars, 1965-1975

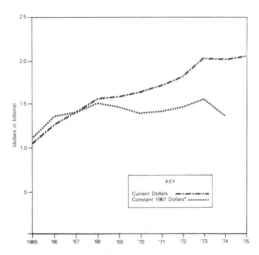

*Deflator calculated from National Science Board, *Science Indicators, 1974,* NSB 75-1, p. 174, Table 2-5.

Source: National Science Foundation, *National Patterns of R&D Resources,* NSF 75-307, pp. 21, 22, and 23. Data for 1974 and 1975 are estimates.

The Impact of the Decade 1965-1975
on the Universities

Money is only a symbol of the problems that have emerged between universities and the federal government. There are a number of characteristics of universities that should be borne in mind as we proceed to analyze the situation. The *raison d'être* of universities is to teach students, and this is the guiding principle of their organization. The faculty are organized in a hierarchical structure, which has as a base departments made up of teachers of a common discipline. Similar disciplines are grouped into divisions or colleges or schools, and these units in turn comprise the university. But the basic building blocks are the disciplines.

The primary function of the administrative structure that holds these disciplinary groups together is personnel management. The entire structure emphasizes excellence of scholarship, teaching, and research achievement *within a discipline* as the basis for appointment and promotion of faculty. Although many institutions say that other factors, such as public service, are used to determine promotions, very few young faculty members believe they can advance by this route. One other important aspect of academic life is the university calendar. The beginning of classes, midterm examinations, final examinations, and summer vacations are dominant features of campus life. Although there may be some flexibility, these calendar elements tend to be as rigid as the faculty compartmentalization by discipline.

With the increased availability of federal funds and the national emphasis on more and better universities, many changes in the structure of the campus research enterprise have been made. The experience of World War II led to a desire on the part of returning faculty for interdisciplinary units. The Fermi Institute at the University of Chicago dates from that period and typifies this type of organization. Faculty members continued to teach and hold their ranks in their departments. But they also held joint appointments for a fraction of their time to do research in the Institute. If the research projects were large, such as a cyclotron, other scientists and engineers were hired full time to help do the work. These researchers were usually not given faculty status, nor were they eligible for tenure. Thus a group of "second-class citizens" emerged around the "first-class faculty."

Usually these full-time researchers were paid from federal funds; so if the funds were cut off, they were out of a job. This posed no serious problem during the growth phase of funding, but by 1970 this practice led to substantial unemployment of scientists and engineers. In addition to relative insecurity about employment, the professional researcher at the university began to look toward the nonprofit research corporation as a better-paying source of potential employment. Wage differentials, lack of job security, and dependence of research projects on full-time staff created the major tensions within the university.

During the early 1960s the U.S. became concerned with its own leadership in science and technology and also with the question of civil rights for minorities. The Civil Rights Act of 1964 was a landmark in the expression of this concern and became a significant factor in the government/university relationship almost immediately. Every contract and grant proposal to a federal agency had to have an accompanying "statement of compliance" with this law. In subsequent years the expansion of this first step into full-scale affirmative action programs with full-time staff, major changes in the methods of personnel record keeping, faculty recruitment, and punitive actions by monitoring agencies for failure to comply symbolizes the intrusion of the federal government into the everyday affairs of universities.

As the federal bureaucracy increases its demands for more detailed procedures and record keeping, it is the university that must pay for the implementation. These costs can be passed back to the government in increased indirect overhead charges; but that usually means that in a grant or contract of a given amount, less money is available to the faculty member for research. If faculty members need to hire postdoctoral assistants, they find that complying with a complex and laborious set of regulations diverts their time and energy from their research. This diversion is a symbol of the growing burden on the individual faculty member, whose primary objective is to seek new knowledge.

The problems outlined above—a two-class personnel system; an inflexible, compartmentalized organizational structure; a rigid calendar for the teaching function; and an encroaching burden of administrative responsibilities on the individual faculty member—represent a formidable set of pressures on the universities and their faculties. When the mission agencies of government came to the universities requesting programs in nuclear physics for atomic energy; space sciences to support the space effort; clinical programs to fight cancer, heart attack, and stroke; environmental programs to purify our air and water; and energy programs to improve the efficiency of fossil fuel production and use—all of these problems of the university were brought into focus.

Consider another pressure that was created during this period: In the post-Sputnik era a number of federally funded fellowship and traineeship programs for predoctoral study were begun. The National Defense Education Act of 1958 inaugurated fellowships in the natural and social sciences and made provisions for institutional support funds. NASA introduced graduate traineeships for those interested in space-related science and engineering. NSF increased graduate fellowships in an ongoing program and introduced a traineeship program. The U.S. Public Health Service provided fellowship opportunities in health-related sciences. The history of this support pattern is shown in Figure 2.

Figure 2

Federally Supported Predoctoral
Fellowships and Traineeships, 1960-1971

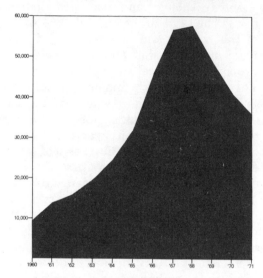

Source: C.M. York, *Science* Magazine, Vol. 172, May
14, 1971, p. 643. Figures for 1970 and 1971 are
estimates.

Life in the research universities centers around students, especially
graduate students, and the growth period of graduate student support
was easily implemented. Armed with traineeships, the departments recruited promising college seniors in their disciplines in the same en-
thusiastic way they were recruiting new faculty. Competition for the
best students was keen, and graduate students often moved from one
school to another. In 1969, the sharp drop in the number of awards was
noticed immediately, and the universities were hard pressed to adjust
to this new situation. For example, planning in most departments had
assumed a continuation of graduate student support. By 1969 these
plans had to be modified in a radical way, and a wave of concern swept
through the universities about the federal support picture.

A similar buildup and shutdown of federal funding occurred in the
area of construction of new buildings. Frequently the targeted programs of research required the university to provide all or part of any
new facilities needed to house new equipment or projects. Universities
often made major capital investments only to find the associated program funding lasting less than 10 years. There are now a number of
vacant or partially occupied buildings on campuses that once housed
busy cyclotrons or space laboratories, [16] and there has been no way for
many institutions to recover these unamortized capital costs.

The data on federal obligations to colleges and universities for R&D plant are given in Table 1. Again by 1969 the sharp drop in available funds was widely felt within the academic community. Again an extensive readjustment of plans that had been based on the assumption of continued federal support had to be carried out. To see more clearly how the drop-off in R&D plant funds was followed by a drop in program funds, consider the data plotted in Figures 3 and 4 for NASA's programs. After a relatively small R&D plant investment in the early 1960s, NASA's R&D programs increased in their levels of funding until 1968. Then in current dollar terms the curve flattened out for four years before beginning to drop. In constant 1967 dollars the curve began to drop in 1969 after peaking in 1968.

Table 1

Total Federal Obligations to Colleges and Universities for R&D Plant, 1963-1973 (dollars in millions)

1963	$105.9	1969	$54.5
1964	100.8	1970	44.8
1965	126.2	1971	29.9
1966	114.8	1972	36.9
1967	111.3	1973	43.3
1968	96.1		

Source: National Science Foundation, *Federal Support to Universities, Colleges and Selected Nonprofit Institutions, FY 1973*, NSF 75-304, Table B-1, p. 32.

Figure 3

Obligations by NASA to Universities and Colleges for R&D Program, Current and Constant Dollars, 1963-1973

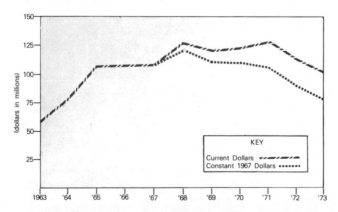

Source: National Science Foundation, *Federal Support to Universities, Colleges and Selected Nonprofit Institutions, FY 1973*, NSF 75-304, p. 32.

116

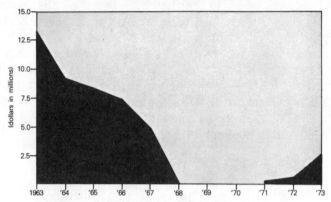

Figure 4

Obligations by NASA to Colleges and Universities
for R&D Plant, 1963-1973

Source: National Science Foundation, *Federal Support to Universities,
Colleges and Selected Nonprofit Institutions, FY 1973*, NSF 75-304,
p. 32.

Figure 5

Atomic Energy Commission Funds for Nuclear Research
in Universities and Colleges, for R&D Program,
Current and Constant Dollars, 1964-1974

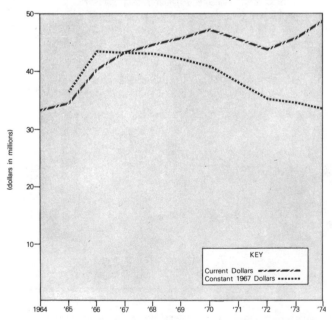

Source: Private communication, Dr. George Rogosa, Energy Research
and Development Administration, 1976.

A similar record can be found in the data for basic research in nuclear physics funded by the Atomic Energy Commission, [17] and in the corresponding data for R&D plant or capital expenditures. [18] The latter consisted of funds given to universities to buy cyclotrons and other modern accelerators. The data are plotted in Figures 5 and 6. The fact that this research is of a "basic" nature does not make it any less targeted, e.g., gaining a better understanding of the nucleus in order to further the development of atomic energy. As the national priorities in funding have shifted from nuclear power to fossil fuel development, there is a serious question about the magnitude of effort that should be maintained in nuclear research to fulfill its long-term mission.

From these specific cases, the pattern that emerges is that a mission agency will sometimes provide funds for buildings and facilities during the early years of its growth. Then the emphasis shifts to program funding and that curve may well peak and then decrease. If a university accepts a federally funded facility, it should clearly recognize that there is no guarantee of long-term programmatic support. In the past many

Figure 6

Atomic Energy Commission Funds for Nuclear Research
in Colleges and Universities, for R&D Plant,
1963-1968

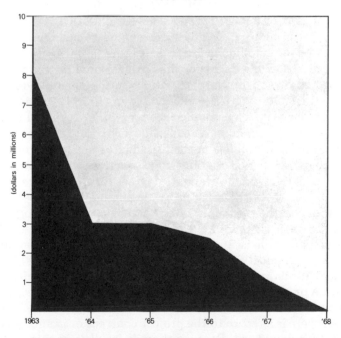

Source: Private communication, Dr. George Rogosa, Energy Research and Development Administration, 1976.

campus planners and administrators made decisions based on the assumption that funds were virtually assured for several decades. Because of this, complex internal readjustments have been required on many campuses.

There is no lack of evidence that the stresses on the universities have been of even broader scope than the examples discussed above. Student unrest on campuses started in 1964 and one theme of the demonstrations was the role of university research as a "tool of the military/industrial complex." The outcry against war-related or classified research did cause many institutions to review and modify their policies on these matters. The student complaint that professors were too busy doing research to teach has died down but not been clearly resolved. Faculties and administrators at the top research universities have taken the position that their research role is appropriate to the goals of the institution and must be balanced against teaching responsibilities. Curiously, faculties at four-year colleges have shied away from using teaching excellence as a basis for promotion and have tended to copy the publish-or-perish criterion of the graduate research universities. The individual faculty member is pressed to divide his or her time effectively between the classroom and federally supported research projects.

Another indication of the profound impact of federal policy shifts on the universities came in the late 1960s. While the unemployment level of scientists and engineers was substantial, graduate programs in the universities were continuing to produce new scientists and engineers at the highest rate in history. The data for engineers are the most complete and are given in Figures 7 and 8. Figure 7 illustrates that the steady flow of bachelor's degree or first professional degree recipients was not affected by substantial fluctuations in the unemployment rate shown in Figure 8. The sharp rise in unemployment in 1970 has been attributed to cutbacks in defense and space programs, a general economic downturn, and the beginning of a decline in recruiting for faculty.

The unemployment problem of their graduates has led many universities to review their degree offerings. The practical, moral issues of encouraging students to pursue graduate degrees for which there is no job market have been widely discussed by faculties all over the country. Many have urged their administrators to close certain programs or have exercised their right to limit admissions. Some professional societies, as widely diverse as the Modern Language Association and the American Astronomical Society, have taken similar stands.

The post-Sputnik growth in federal funding was accompanied by experimentation on the part of the funding agencies, which tried out new mechanisms for providing federal moneys to the universities. Currently, however, there is a return to the project contract or grant as virtually the only technique used. Because there is implicit in this method a clearly stated objective and a timetable for completion of a project, the

Figure 7

Bachelor's and First Professional Degree Recipients in Engineering, 1960-1972

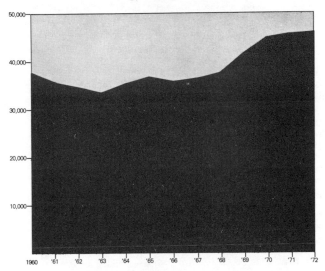

Source: National Science Board, *Science Indicators, 1974*, pp. 236-237.

Figure 8

Average Unemployment of First Professional Degree Recipients in Engineering, 1963-1974

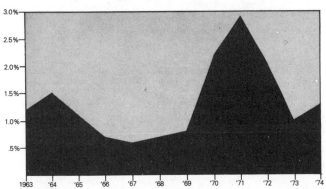

Source: National Science Board, *Science Indicators, 1974*, pp. 236-237.

idea that targeted research funding is increasing is widely held throughout the university research community. This perception is accurate and
can be documented by considering the data of Table 2. Here the percentage of federal funds expended by universities is broken down into

Table 2

Percentage of Federal Funds Expended by Universities for Basic Research, Applied Research, and Development, 1960-1975

	Basic Research	Applied Research	Development
1960	74%	22%	4%
1961	76	20	4
1962	78	18	4
1963	80	17	3
1964	84	14	2
1965	82	15	3
1966	80	15	5
1967	80	16	4
1968	80	16	4
1969	80	15	5
1970	79	16	5
1971	77	17	6
1972	77	18	5
1973	71	23	6
1974	75	22	3
1975	75	22	3

Source: National Science Foundation, *National Patterns of R&D Resources*, NSF 75-307, p. 21. Figures for 1974 and 1975 are estimates.

Table 3

Federal Obligations for R&D in Colleges and Universities, Distribution by Agency, 1963-1974

	HEW	DOD	NASA	AEC	NSF
1963	40.0%	26.5%	7.5%	8.5%	12.0%
1964	40.0	26.0	8.5	7.5	11.0
1965	39.5	24.5	9.0	7.0	11.5
1966	39.5	20.5	8.5	6.5	14.5
1967	43.5	19.5	8.0	6.5	13.0
1968	43.5	18.0	9.0	6.0	13.0
1969	44.0	18.5	8.5	6.0	12.0
1970	41.5	19.0	8.5	5.5	13.0
1971	43.5	15.0	8.0	5.0	13.0
1972	47.0	12.0	6.0	4.5	18.5
1973	48.0	11.5	5.5	4.5	19.5
1974	54.0	8.5	4.5	4.0	19.0

Source: National Science Foundation, *Federal Support to Universities, Colleges and Selected Nonprofit Institutions, FY 1974*, NSF 75-325. Detailed Statistical Tables, Appendix B, Table B-1.

basic research, applied research, and development. Without belaboring the fine distinctions between these categories, let us simply associate the notion of targeted or mission-related research with the combination of applied research and development. Then the data clearly indicate an increase over the past decade in the percentage of funds going to targeted research.

Another indication of this shift can be seen from the fraction of funds received by the universities from the various federal agencies. The mission agencies do fund substantial amounts of basic research that tends to be targeted toward the goals of the agency. Table 3 shows the percentage of funds supplied to the universities by the various agencies. The mission agencies—DOD, NASA, and AEC (now part of the Energy Research and Development Administration)—have markedly reduced their share of support over the past decade. However, HEW support for research, which primarily comes from the National Institutes of Health, has increased significantly. If we consider NSF to be the only nonmission agency, then a greater share of research support to universities is coming from the mission agencies, primarily in the life sciences. This conclusion is further supported by noting that 40 percent of the growth in NSF funding from 1971 to 1972 was the result of the RANN program (Research Applied to National Needs), which was developed in that period. The RANN program was an explicit break with NSF's traditional role as the primary source of basic research funds for universities and it significantly broadened the Foundation's role in targeted research.

By considering these data, we may conclude that targeted research in universities is in fact increasing. The relatively short duration of targeted programs has created significant administrative problems for universities and will continue to do so. Because of increased rules and regulations imposed by the federal government, there has been a serious erosion of the time and effort that faculty researchers can actually devote to their creative efforts. The net result of these factors is growing stress on those who do university research with federal support.

The Impact of the Decade on Federal Agencies

There is a tendency in academic circles to underestimate the federal agencies' efforts to meet the needs of the university research community. Before exploring the achievements of the agencies, consider the constraints on their operation. The federal agencies are line organizations of the executive branch of government, but they depend on the legislative branch for funds. The President and his administration operate on a four-year cycle and initiate new programs in response to problems as they are recognized. This orientation means that the action the administration takes to cope with a problem will most often be in the form of a targeted program. Not only can the President initiate programs, so can either house of Congress. Because the House of Representatives operates on a two-year cycle of reelection while the Senate functions on a six-year cycle, their reactions to problems often differ. Again, the agency assigned by Congress to solve a problem will tend to create a targeted program.

Given these pressures, it is impressive that the funding of long-term basic research in universities has been understood, accepted, and supported by the entire governmental structure as well as by the electorate. The assertion that there is widespread public support for science is based on a series of surveys commissioned by the National Science Board. In 1974, 75 percent of the public believed that science and technology had changed life for the better compared with 70 percent in 1972. In spite of periodic congressional attacks on specific programs of the various funding agencies, these criticisms cannot be construed as a general loss of support for the federally supported research effort. [19]

In addition to electoral cycles, there is another timing problem in the government/university relationship: the federal budget cycle. Every agency is simultaneously engaged in three different budgetary tasks. The first is to disburse funds under the appropriation for the purposes described in the legislation and under the constraints it prescribes. The second task is to defend the budgetary request for the following fiscal year and monitor its progress through the Congress. And the third is to prepare the budget to be submitted to Congress in the following year. This three-ring circus is almost never consistent with the timing of the academic world and places great pressures on the staffs of the agencies. There have been instances when program officers took grave personal risks and carried out intricate bureaucratic maneuvers to make sure fellowship programs were available for the rigid academic calendar despite a congressional delay in appropriating the funds. These efforts seldom receive proper public credit; however, it is axiomatic that if an agency's appropriation is delayed, the program officers will have enormous problems keeping their projects afloat. The highly motivated academic researcher tends to have little patience with these problems.

In the summer of 1976 the federal government shifted its budgetary calendar so that the fiscal year began on October 1 rather than July 1, as in the past, resulting in a three-month transition quarter between fiscal years 1976 and 1977. In fact, the purpose of the new procedure is to schedule the actions of Congress in passing appropriations in a more uniform way. The law now requires that Congress complete its passage of all final appropriation bills by September 25 so that every agency will have funding by the beginning of the new fiscal year on October 1.

In addition to dealing with the routine of program planning, funding cycles, and rapid shifts of policy, the agencies are required to enforce a host of legal restrictions that are peripheral to their primary mission. When a faculty member in the midst of a research project has his funds cut off because his university does not have an adequate affirmative action program, for example, frustration and tension tend to focus on the relationship between that faculty member and the program officer in the funding agency. Since HEW has the responsibility for civil rights enforcement, such interruptions often have interfered with the programs of other agencies. This and similar interferences of a faceless bureaucracy in the affairs of working partners have created malaise within the research community.

The increased demands for financial accountability by campus business offices heighten the atmosphere of distrust and unease in that community. It is not surprising that the site visit teams for this study found varied but almost universal signs of this tension on the campuses they visited. Unfortunately a great deal of the pressure must be borne by the program officers in the agencies. They watch their programs lose momentum and are helpless in the face of their responsibility to uphold the law and implement the regulations of their agency.

The role of enforcer that is placed on the program officer has an additional facet. Almost every one of these individuals holds a research PhD or has had professional experience in a research laboratory. Hence the officer is aware of the impact of his or her administrative actions on the research world. The converse is not true. The university researcher tends to have little or no interest in the world of the program officer. This lack of understanding places an additional strain on the focal point of federal/university relations: the program officer/researcher relationship. Many program officers believe that they are required to intervene in the internal affairs of the university in an improper manner when they enforce regulations that are unrelated to the research project at hand.

One of the most important federal programs undertaken in recent years is the Inter-Governmental Exchange Program, which gives faculty an opportunity to work in federal agencies for one-year periods. Under this program a faculty member from a state university is considered a state employee and can be sent to Washington to work in a federal agency. Most participants consider the experience invaluable in understanding the functioning of the federal government.

Consider next the effect on researchers when a new national goal is proclaimed. We have observed the post-Sputnik response of mobilizing an effort to land a man on the moon. This was followed by an environmental cleanup for "spaceship earth." Then there was a war on cancer; and the energy crisis appeared shortly afterward. With such clear problem definitions it is not surprising that the mobilization of effort should be organized in each case into a mission agency to carry it out. The new agencies that have been formed in response to these problems are always beset by internal organizational problems and by outside criticism for not producing perfect answers faster. The reaction is to transmit this pressure for performance to those who contract with the agencies—in many cases university researchers.

In the early 1960s, a basic philosophy pervaded the federal programs. To serve the needs of the country, it was necessary to educate ever larger numbers of highly trained scientists and engineers. The fact that this special training would draw on only the most intellectually gifted segment of the population and that their training at federal expense would create an elite group within the society was recognized, if not widely discussed. The decision was made to proceed with a number of programs designed to create this highly trained group because it was thought this approach would best serve the needs of the nation in meeting its defense goals.

The new programs focused on graduate traineeships as a principal technique for supplying technically trained manpower. Under the National Defense Education Act, HEW provided a broad program, NASA traineeships focused on space-related sciences, and NSF traineeships provided expanded coverage of science and engineering. Figure 2, page 114, illustrated the rapid growth and decline of these federally supported predoctoral fellows and trainees during the 1960-70 decade. The number has declined even more in subsequent years.

Other funding programs to broaden support for advanced science and engineering training were undertaken, and like the traineeship and fellowship programs, they too have been cut back. General support on a formula basis for colleges and universities was widely discussed during the 1960s, and legislation such as the Miller Bill was introduced into Congress. None of these bills was ever passed, and now such ideas are tainted by having been labeled "pork barrels for higher education." A more fundamental reason for failure of this kind of legislation is the fact that Congress has been, and is, wary of losing its control and oversight of such programs.

The use of institutional grants by NIH and NSF during the early and mid-1960s met a well-defined need. These funds were given directly to the college administration for on-campus research and were invaluable in providing locally administered discretionary funds to purchase new equipment or computer time or to provide other research assistance to individuals. Funding levels for these programs have declined, and the erosion of these locally managed funds has presented a serious problem to university administrators and weakened their ability to guide the direction of research in their institutions. This trend, coupled with a much more detailed control of budgeted expenditures by program officers in the federal agencies, once again demonstrates the intrusion of a federal agency into the operation of the university.

Special accounting procedures were introduced by the Bureau of the

Budget (now the Office of Management and Budget) for use by agencies in dealing with universities. In the early 1960s these procedures facilitated the working relationships that evolved during that period of growth. Although many changes have been made in the details of these procedures, one peculiar principle has remained: It is not possible for a university to recover the entire cost of a research project supported by the federal government. Over the years it has been argued in Congress and in the advisory groups of university administrators and federal representatives that research is a proper function of the universities and hence some cost of the project should be borne by the university. In these days of tight money and leveled enrollments, this principle of shared costs needs to be reviewed.

The Department of Defense tried several novel funding mechanisms during the early 1960s. The Advanced Research Projects Agency set up 12 interdisciplinary materials science research laboratories on campuses around the country. The scheme provided an umbrella grant to support the work of an interdisciplinary team of scientists and engineers on the campus for five years. Only general guidelines for the direction of the research were provided, and the results were monitored by the agency. After several years of operation, DOD's interests shifted and the work in these laboratories was no longer sufficiently relevant to the new mission of the agency. It was also clear that in many cases the outstanding researchers began to apply for funding from other agencies, and they were soon out from under the umbrella. Thus, the universities also changed the conditions of the original agreement; and although a majority of these laboratories are now funded by NSF, this funding mechanism is considered of limited value. Similar umbrella grants have been tried by other agencies, but they all have suffered similar problems.

A somewhat different form of institutional funding was introduced by the Ford Foundation in the 1950s and later adopted by federal agencies such as NASA. A new program would receive a grant for several years with the level of funding decreasing each year. The home institution agreed to increase its contribution to the program in each successive year to maintain the total funding level. Although this is an excellent way to start a new program, it has been difficult for many institutions to live up to their funding commitments. This mechanism is not used at present by federal agencies, but it has nonetheless left its mark on the research universities.

The rise and fall of these support programs forced major readjustments in the operating policies of the universities. Aggressive faculty and administrators fought the decline in funding by bringing political pressure to bear on their states' congressional delegations. These delegations, in turn, pressured the federal agencies and introduced the idea of geographic distribution of federal funds for higher education. This added constraint on the operation of federal agencies has contributed to the problems of the program officer in awarding grants and contracts.

It would be difficult to justify the existence of one outstanding research university in each state because of the great disparity in the states' size, population, and economic conditions. However, it is interesting to consider how research universities are distributed and how much public money goes into their programs. First, the several states can be grouped into the 10 regions used by the executive branch to administer many of its programs. Next assume that there are 40 top quality research universities in the country and that because of the various granting procedures used by the federal agencies these 40 institutions can be identified by the amount of federal funds they receive. An additional criterion for geographic distribution of federal funds could be the total federal funds that go to the states in a given region. Because some regions encourage the growth of their research universities with the infusion of state tax moneys, it is interesting to compare R&D funding by states in these regions. These data appear in Table 4a (the states in each region are listed in Table 4b). In 1973 the data indicate that every region had at least one of the top 40 fund recipients. The total R&D funding in a region does correlate somewhat with the number of institutions in the top 40. There is some correlation also with the amount of state funding. It is not surprising that the large population centers of the east coast (Regions I and II) and the west coast (Region IX) dominate the distribution of institutions and amounts of funding. The fact is that there is a reasonable geographic distribution of both top-ranked institutions and funds.

Table 4a

1973 Geographical Funding Patterns
by Federal Regions (dollars in millions)

Region	Number of Universities in Top 40	Federal Funding	State Funding
I	3	$271	$11
II	5	208	60
III	4	207	31
IV	3	172	26
V	9	314	38
VI	2	130	17
VII	2	79	6
VIII	2	72	11
IX	9	309	41
X	1	86	20

Source: National Science Foundation, *Federal Support to Universities, Colleges and Selected Nonprofit Institutions, FY 1973,* NSF 75-304.

Table 4b

States Included in Each Federal Region

Region I
Maine, New Hampshire, Vermont, Massachusetts,
Connecticut, Rhode Island

Region II
New York, Puerto Rico

Region III
Pennsylvania, New Jersey, Delaware, Maryland,
West Virginia, Virginia, Kentucky

Region IV
Tennessee, North Carolina, South Carolina, Georgia,
Alabama, Mississippi, Florida

Region V
Ohio, Indiana, Illinois, Michigan, Wisconsin, Minnesota

Region VI
Arkansas, Louisiana, Oklahoma, Texas, New Mexico

Region VII
Iowa, Missouri, Nebraska, Kansas

Region VIII
North Dakota, South Dakota, Montana, Utah,
Colorado, Wyoming

Region IX
California, Arizona, Nevada, Hawaii

Region X
Idaho, Washington, Oregon, Alaska

As federal funding has been eroded by inflation and by the increased number of universities requesting research funds, there has been a tendency for universities to focus their discontent on the agencies. In some cases the criticism may be deserved, but by and large the agencies carry out policy and are helpless to deal directly with shifts in national goals and policies.

Responding to Stress in the System

In the period of rapid growth in college enrollments and federal budgets for research, the universities responded enthusiastically. If a federal program required specialized training for students, faculty committees were organized to design appropriate curricula. As students signed up for the new courses of study, faculties were expanded and new buildings for classrooms and laboratories were planned. The federal agencies supplied construction funds to help build the needed facilities. More often than not these funds required a matching contribution from the state legislature or a private donor, and university administrators were eager brokers in the enterprise. New research institutes or departments were created to respond to the specialized needs of the funding agencies. The departmental base of faculty appointments was usually maintained, but new "border" disciplines emerged, such as computer science, operations research, molecular biology, and linguistics, to supplement the older departmental structures. Many of the developments were viewed by those faculty who had been trained in a liberal arts tradition as too focused or targeted in their objectives. However, the wave of expansion prevailed in most research institutions. In addition to expanded academic structures, the universities added the administrative staff required to purchase new equipment, hire research personnel, and enforce new federal regulations and the multitude of other details implicit in the expansion.

Now that the period of growth is over, it is more important than ever that the universities and federal agencies continue to work together to solve their mutual problems. These essential interactions can build on the network created during the expansion period. The federal agencies adopted many new techniques for dealing with the universities during the 1960s. The Office of Management and Budget set up a special set of guidelines to be used by the federal agencies. These have been reviewed and updated over the years and should continue to be modified as programs and funding levels change. Almost every agency draws on panels of experts from the academic community to advise it on program formulation, accounting procedures, selection of projects for funding, and so on. These interactions maintain a continuing flow of information between the universities and the agencies and help prevent crises.

As noted earlier, the agencies tried many new funding methods during the period of post-Sputnik growth. Although carefully designed and implemented, most of these have not withstood the tests of congressional scrutiny, economic recession, or decreased levels of funding. The project grant, or contract, historically has been the successful method for federal funding of research in universities and continues to be looked upon as the tried-and-true vehicle. In the past few years NSF has moved from a balance-wheel role in the funding picture to a lead-agency role for funding both basic and targeted research in the universities. In the current federal budgets this trend is being deliberately modified, and targeted research funds are being increased in the mission agencies. Meanwhile, NSF is returning to its former role providing for basic research areas that are not covered by the programs of the mission agencies, and the targeted programs sponsored by NSF are being phased down.

A Dynamic Balance

The interaction between the universities and the federal government underwent a remarkable period of growth followed by seven or eight years of transition to a steady-state level of funding. Not only has research funding leveled off but the post-World War II baby boom, which drove college enrollments up very sharply, is now moderating toward a peak in the early 1980s. Without continued growth in enrollments, state-supported schools, which are funded on a formula basis, can no longer justify expanded facilities and budgets. The transition to this steady state is not complete but is proceeding with a reasonable degree of mutual understanding between the universities and the federal agencies. The base of research in the United States has been significantly expanded and is now believed to be sufficient to educate the college-age population that is predicted for the next 15 years.

There is clearly a wide diversity in the federal agencies that provide R&D money to the universities. From NSF and the National Endowment for the Humanities, which look after basic research and fundamental scholarship, to the mission-oriented agencies of Defense; Health, Education, and Welfare; and Energy, which involve the universities in their assigned tasks, the system of funding is as diverse and flexible as it has ever been. It may not be as obvious that among the universities there is an equally broad spectrum. Smith and Karlesky have reported that two of the academic vice presidents of universities they interviewed gave the following answers when asked about their attitudes toward applied research:

> Vice president of Institution A: "This university is willing to do almost anything of benefit to the state."

> Vice president of Institution B: "The very brightest people are found in universities like this one; they should do the kind of fundamental work that only they can do and that eventually will help everyone." [20]

Clearly the federal agencies have a wide-ranging set of goals and there is an equally diverse set of university researchers who will help achieve those goals. Even those in the university community who push the hardest to permit their colleagues to pursue fundamental research problems do not go so far as to suggest that their institutions should ignore work related to national or state needs. The universities and the research communities will, and do, respond to national needs in as timely a way as possible. There is a widespread consensus that with that fundamental part of the relationship firmly in place, concern should now be directed toward long-range basic research.

To ensure that the basic research enterprise will flourish, one might ask what features are desirable in the agency/university relationship. Some members of the academic community have identified the need for balance between investigator-initiated research and sponsor-initiated research.[21] The latter is emphasized in a targeted program and places the burden for program design on the federal sponsor-manager rather than on the scientist in the laboratory. If the individual university investigator allows his research to be guided by his perception of the availability of funds rather than by what he personally believes to be of scientific interest and importance, then the future of the enterprise as a whole is certainly in jeopardy. Four desirable characteristics of a federal funding program for pure research can be stated from the academic point of view:

- Most proposals should be unsolicited.
- The support provided to the project should be of sufficient duration to permit time for completion of the work.
- Funds should be reasonably matched to the pressure of proposals and not distorted by the academic world's perception of their availability. In this way the nation's basic research program would be guided by the needs of science rather than political expediency.
- The funding mechanism should provide sufficient flexibility to rebudget funds from one category to another as changes in the program might demand. It should also provide for full cost recovery by the institution.

If these criteria are accepted as essential to the health of basic scientific research in the universities, then targeted research, as defined here, cannot promote a healthy atmosphere for performing basic research. The pressure on the mission agencies to produce results implies that they can never be relied on for the kind of basic research support described above. Here the reemerging role of the National Science Foundation as the agency to support research in fundamental areas of investigation is of great importance. The challenge for NSF is to reorient its operations to satisfy these criteria and at the same time to persuade the administration and Congress that it is providing adequate managerial control of public moneys. It is a formidable but crucial task if the overall balance of the system is to be maintained.

Conclusions

In tracing the history of federal support for research in the United States we have found that the universities have played an increasingly prominent role in fulfilling these national needs. A pervasive factor in the university/government relationship has been targeted research, which has formed the basis for a strong, dynamic, and apparently healthy relationship between two major elements of our society. Yet several concerns arise that could indicate future problems if current trends continue. The most important of these is the apparent increase in the proportion of targeted research over undirected or basic research in the universities, producing several kinds of problems:

Financial Problems

The substantial capital investment made by the federal government in new laboratories and facilities during the 1960s has not been continued. As a result, many facilities and a great deal of equipment are obsolete.

There are almost no discretionary funds available to university administrators of federal projects to explore new ideas or to smooth out funding interruptions.

Federal program managers and auditors have imposed costly, intricate reporting requirements on universities. These requirements force fundamental changes in internal management practices. Under present accounting procedures a university cannot recover the full cost of implementing such changes.

Personnel Problems

Senior investigators in universities are forced to spend their time on new, federally mandated bureaucratic procedures rather than on the research project at hand.

Young people hesitate to try innovative ideas because the path to success clearly lies in doing well-defined, targeted research.

The time limits of targeted research force the investigator to rely on full-time, professional researchers rather than on part-time graduate students, as in the past. This produces dual classes of faculty appointees and research appointees. In time, the pressure of this arrangement could change the historic relationship between graduate education and research.

Institutional Problems

The encroachment of federal regulations on the internal policies of universities poses both philosophic and practical problems. Could this encroachment eventually extend to the control of curriculum content? To a certain extent it has already done so in the case of some degree programs, such as nuclear engineering, and environmental studies. Can the contract or grant mechanism continue to maintain an arm's-length relationship between the universities and the federal government?

If the university cannot make any financial profit through

a project, or even recover the full costs involved, where will it find the resources to pursue its own institutional goals of scholarly excellence and freedom of investigation?

These issues cause the university administrator to view with concern the federal agencies' growing emphasis on targeted research. For the present system to maintain its health and vigor, it is essential that the research community continue to examine these issues and institute whatever measures are needed to maintain the dynamic balance between federal support and academic priorities.

1. United Nations Educational, Scientific, and Cultural Organization (UNESCO), *National Science Policies of the U.S.A.* (Paris: UNESCO, 1968), p. 9.

2. Richard H. Shryock, "American Indifference to Basic Science During the Nineteenth Century," in *The Sociology of Science*, eds. B. Barber and W. Hirsch (Glencoe: Free Press, 1962), p. 105.

3. G. Bell Whitfield, "The Scientific Environment of Philadelphia, 1775 and 1780," *Proceedings of the American Philosophical Society*, Vol. 92, No. 1 (Philadelphia, 1948), p. 11.

4. Daniel S. Greenberg, *The Politics of Pure Science* (New York: New American Library, 1967), p. 55.

5. UNESCO, op. cit., p. 13.

6. Greenberg, op. cit., p. 62.

7. UNESCO, op. cit., p. 15.

8. Stewart Irwin, *Organizing Scientific Research for War* (Boston: Little, Brown, 1948), p. 79.

9. UNESCO, op. cit., p. 22.

10. Greenberg, op. cit., p. 120.

11. UNESCO, op. cit., p. 23.

12. Nick A. Komons, *Science and the Air Force, A History of the Air Force Office of Scientific Research* (Arlington, Va.: Historical Division, Office of Aerospace Research, 1966), p. 128.

13. UNESCO, op. cit., p. 24.

14. G. T. Seaborg, "Scientific Progress, the Universities, and the Federal Government," Report of the President's Scientific Advisory Committee, Washington, D.C., November 15, 1960, p. 14.

15. Derek J. de Solla Price, *Little Science—Big Science* (New York: Columbia University Press, 1963).

16. William D. Matz, "Basic Research Funding: ERDA Deenergizes Nuclear Science," *Science*, Vol. 191, March 5, 1976, pp. 931-933.

17. "Nuclear Science: A Survey of Funding Facilities and Manpower" (Washington, D.C.: National Academy of Sciences, 1975).

18. Private communication from George Rogosa, Energy Research and Development Administration, 1976.

19. National Science Board, *Science Indicators—1974: Report of the National Science Board, 1975* (Washington, D.C.: National Science Foundation, 1975), p. 144.

20. Bruce L. R. Smith and Joseph J. Karlesky, *The State of Academic Science*, Vol. 1 (New Rochelle, N.Y.: Change Magazine Press, 1977), p. 36.

21. Private communication from Harvey Brooks, Harvard University, April 1976.

Effects of Recent Trends in Graduate Education on University Research Capability in Physics, Chemistry, and Mathematics

David W. Breneman

Any discussion of university research capability inevitably leads into graduate and particularly doctoral education, since the two are commonly described as joint products of the university. This analysis of recent statistical trends in physics, chemistry, and mathematics graduate programs is thus based on the assumption that the research capability of the university cannot be assessed adequately without considering the changes that are occurring in graduate education, as measured by trends in graduate enrollments, type and source of student support, PhD degrees awarded, and the length of time to completion of the degree. To describe more precisely the link between graduate education and faculty research productivity, statistical data are supplemented here with information from interviews with science faculty. The perspective taken throughout is that of an economist; academic departments in the three disciplines are viewed as productive units that utilize graduate students in various ways within each department's economy.

In addition to its direct production link with research, graduate education is also connected in an essential way to the long-run health of academic science. It is the process through which the current generation of scientists educates and develops its successors. Any break in that process is cause for concern, even if departments are successful in adjusting to immediate problems, such as those caused by declining graduate enrollments. The long-run problem of maintaining a continuous flow of young scientists into academic departments overshadows the more immediate adjustment problems confronting university science departments.

Statistical Trends

During the early 1970s, many observers feared that the adjustments of graduate schools to the cutbacks in federal support were producing an

134

undesirable shift of students and resources from stronger to weaker departments.[1] In a study sponsored by the National Board on Graduate Education this proposition was tested using National Science Foundation (NSF) data on graduate enrollments and student support for the six-year period Fiscal Year (FY) 1968-1973 for 14 science and engineering disciplines.[2] Data were organized by American Council on Education (ACE) quality ratings of graduate programs,[3] and the general findings did not support the view that redistribution of students and resources from stronger to weaker departments had occurred over this six-year period.[4] The years included in that study covered the transition from the rapid growth of the 1960s to the first years of the "new depression" in higher education; hence, it is desirable to update the data to determine whether definite trends have been established following the initial shocks of adjustment and transition. The present paper extends the time-series data of the earlier study by two years (FY 1974 and 1975) for the fields of physics, chemistry, and mathematics. The eight-year (FY 1968-75)[5] trends presented here provide essential information for the following discussion of graduate education and its relation to university research capability.

A word about methodology. As in the earlier study, the data for the tables and figures presented are from a subset of all doctoral-granting

Table 1

Full and Part-Time Fall Graduate Enrollments
in 168 Chemistry, 146 Physics,
and 120 Mathematics Departments, FY 1968-1975

	1968	1969	1970	1971	1972	1973	1974	1975
First-Year Full-Time								
Physics	2736	2609	2576	2154	1981	1808	1819	1904
Chemistry	3719	3433	3458	3191	2891	2656	2752	2947
Mathematics	3106	2918	2984	2883	2483	2276	1982	1973
Total Full-Time								
Physics	11043	11163	10681	10011	9210	8340	7788	7743
Chemistry	13546	13720	13194	12578	11998	11142	10703	10674
Mathematics	8958	8932	8493	8437	7770	7238	6664	6210
Total Part-Time								
Physics	2217	1630	1611	1456	1229	968	899	829
Chemistry	1515	1448	1760	1676	1356	1470	1491	1445
Mathematics	3190	2942	2777	2574	2280	2178	1975	2045

Source: National Science Foundation.

departments—those that completed the NSF surveys during each of the eight years.[6] The experiences of the same set of departments are thus reported for the FY 1968-1975 period. The data encompass 168 chemistry departments, 146 physics departments, and 120 mathematics departments, covering more than 90 percent of the departments in each discipline included in the ACE quality survey.[7]

Enrollments

Table 1 presents eight-year enrollment trends in these departments, including total full-time, first-year full-time, and part-time enrollments in each of the three disciplines. From FY 1968 to FY 1975, total full-time enrollments declined by 30 percent, 21 percent, and 31 percent, respectively, in these physics, chemistry, and mathematics departments. First-year enrollments also dropped substantially over the eight years, although the low point in both physics and chemistry was reached in FY 1973, with small gains in each successive year. If graduate students are indeed an essential part of the research production process, then it might be expected that this drop in enrollments would have had a noticeable impact on the research productivity of departments.

Apart from the question of research impact, the drop in graduate enrollments has been translated, after a several-year lag, into a drop in PhD production; Figure 1 charts the total number of PhD degrees awarded nationally in the three fields over the 15-year period, FY 1960-1975. PhD production peaked in chemistry in 1970, in physics in 1971, and in mathematics in 1972, reflecting enrollment declines that began in the middle 1960s. The fact that these enrollment declines have continued well into the 1970s means that PhD output will probably continue to fall until at least 1980.[8]

The next issue to be examined concerns the distribution of enrollments among departments of differing quality ratings. Figures 2, 3, and 4 display the percentage distribution of total full-time enrollments in the three disciplines over the eight years by ACE quality rating. Enrollments are grouped into three categories: higher rated departments with ACE ratings of 3.0-5.0; lesser rated departments, scoring 0.0-2.9; and nonrated departments, those that were too new to be included in the ACE survey. The numbers of departments in each rated category covered by the data are:

ACE Rating	Physics	Chemistry	Mathematics
3.0-5.0	29	37	24
0.0-2.9	80	85	69
Not rated	37	46	27
TOTAL	146	168	120

Figure 1

Annual Production of Chemistry, Physics, and Mathematics Doctorates, FY 1960-1975

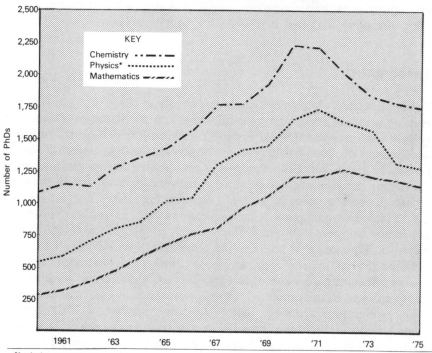

*Includes astronomy.

Source: National Academy of Sciences, *Doctorate Recipients From United States Universities, 1958-1966* (Washington, D.C.: National Academy of Sciences, 1967), p. 5. *Doctorate Recipients From United States Universities, 1967-1975,* Annual Publications.

Although changes in enrollment distribution have not been dramatic over the eight years, the higher rated (3.0-5.0) departments in physics and mathematics have slightly increased their shares of total enrollment, while the corresponding chemistry departments registered a modest drop of approximately 1.5 percent. Most of the shifts in enrollment distribution that have occurred since 1971 were among the rated departments; the nonrated group covered by these data have maintained a relatively stable share in recent years.

The proportion of enrollment in the very highest rated departments (4.0-5.0) is of particular interest. These data are displayed in Table 2. In each field, these departments slightly increased their percentage of total full-time enrollments.

Our final analysis of enrollment patterns concerns the trend in average enrollment per department by quality rating. The aggregated data

Figure 2

Distribution of Total Full-Time Enrollment
Among 146 Physics Departments,
by Quality Category, FY 1968-1975

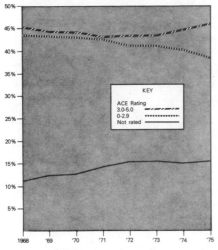

Source: National Science Foundation.

Figure 3

Distribution of Total Full-Time Enrollment
Among 168 Chemistry Departments,
by Quality Category, FY 1968-1975

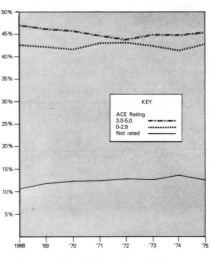

Source: National Science Foundation.

Figure 4

Distribution of Total Full-Time Enrollment
Among 120 Mathematics Departments,
by Quality Category, FY 1968-1975

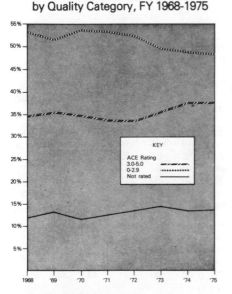

Source: National Science Foundation.

138

conceal the fact that departments differ significantly in size by quality category, as in Table 3. Each quality group has lost enrollment over the eight years, but the highest rated departments remain four to six times larger, on average, than the lowest rated departments. The data sug-

Table 2

Percentage of Total Full-Time Enrollment
in Highest-Rated Physics, Chemistry,
and Mathematics Departments, FY 1968-1975*

Year	1968	1969	1970	1971	1972	1973	1974	1975
Physics	19.1	18.4	18.7	18.5	18.4	19.1	20.3	20.8
Chemistry	17.4	17.3	17.5	17.1	16.8	17.1	17.7	18.1
Mathematics	13.6	13.0	12.9	13.4	13.4	14.8	15.3	15.9

*Departments rated 4.0-5.0. See Kenneth D. Roose and Charles J. Andersen. *A Rating of Graduate Programs*. Washington, D.C.: American Council on Education, 1970.

Source: National Science Foundation.

Table 3

Average Full-Time Enrollment in Physics, Chemistry,
and Mathematics Departments by Quality Rating, FY 1968-1975

ACE Rating	1968	1969	1970	1971	1972	1973	1974	1975
Physics								
4.0-5.0	211	206	200	185	169	159	158	161
3.0-3.9	152	153	144	130	121	107	100	103
2.0-2.9	84	85	81	72	64	58	53	49
0-1.9	37	37	35	36	32	29	26	26
Not rated	33	37	37	39	38	35	32	33
Chemistry								
4.0-5.0	214	215	210	196	183	173	172	175
3.0-3.9	154	152	144	133	125	119	112	110
2.0-2.9	91	92	87	85	82	75	70	74
0-1.9	46	46	44	44	42	37	35	35
Not rated	31	35	35	34	34	31	32	29
Mathematics								
4.0-5.0	152	145	137	141	130	134	128	123
3.0-3.9	118	124	115	108	99	94	93	85
2.0-2.9	85	82	83	79	74	66	55	52
0-1.9	50	49	46	49	41	36	38	34
Not rated	40	44	37	40	40	39	33	32

Source: National Science Foundation.

gest that many of the lowest rated departments have reached (or are approaching) an enrollment level so low that the continued existence of their doctoral programs must be in question. The higher rated departments have no apparent cause for concern in this area. (The minimum number of graduate students required to have a tenable doctoral program is not fixed, but when a department has only 30 students spread over five to six years of study, it is difficult to justify economically the necessary range of graduate seminars required for doctoral study.)

Graduate Student Support

Tables 4, 5, and 6 document the changes that have occurred over the eight years in the source and type of financial support available to grad-

Table 4

Source and Type of Graduate Student Support
in 146 Physics Departments, FY 1968-1975

Source/Number & Percent of Students	1968	1969	1970	1971	1972	1973	1974	1975
Federal Government	5983	5748	5304	4687	3929	3282	2840	2739
% of Total	54.2	51.5	49.7	46.8	42.7	39.4	36.5	35.4
Institution & State Government	3728	3978	4023	4091	3886	3885	3959	3953
% of Total	33.8	35.6	37.7	40.9	42.2	46.6	50.8	51.0
Self, Loans, Family	743	868	901	729	838	819	630	745
% of Total	6.7	7.8	8.4	7.3	9.1	9.8	8.1	9.6
Other	589	569	453	504	557	354	359	306
% of Total	5.3	5.1	4.2	5.0	6.0	4.2	4.6	4.0
TOTAL	11043	11163	10681	10011	9210	8340	7788	7743

Type/Number & Percent of Students	1968	1969	1970	1971	1972	1973	1974	1975
Fellowships & Traineeships	2772	2701	2311	1988	1589	1106	915	835
% of Total	25.1	24.2	21.6	19.9	17.3	13.3	11.7	10.8
Research Assistantships	4016	3899	3972	3604	3149	2860	2820	2734
% of Total	36.4	34.9	37.2	36.0	34.2	34.3	36.2	35.3
Teaching Assistantships	3062	3193	3182	3289	3233	3242	3194	3207
% of Total	27.7	28.6	29.8	32.9	35.1	38.8	41.1	41.4
Other	1193	1370	1216	1130	1239	1132	859	967
% of Total	10.8	12.3	11.4	11.2	13.4	13.6	11.0	12.5
TOTAL	11043	11163	10681	10011	9210	8340	7788	7743

Source: National Science Foundation.

Table 5

Source and Type of Graduate Student Support
in 168 Chemistry Departments, FY 1968-1975

Source/Number & Percent of Students	1968	1969	1970	1971	1972	1973	1974	1975
Federal Government	6108	5890	5251	4697	4125	3486	2822	2757
% of Total	45.1	42.9	39.8	37.3	34.3	31.3	26.4	25.8
Institution & State Government	5892	6210	6210	6281	6303	6354	6644	6431
% of Total	43.5	45.2	47.1	49.9	52.5	57.0	62.1	60.2
Self, Loans, Family	526	596	781	708	778	634	629	675
% of Total	3.9	4.3	5.9	5.6	6.5	5.7	5.9	6.3
Other	1020	1024	952	892	792	668	608	811
% of Total	7.5	7.5	7.2	7.1	6.6	6.0	5.7	7.6
TOTAL	13546	13720	13194	12578	11998	11142	10703	10674

Type/Number & Percent of Students	1968	1969	1970	1971	1972	1973	1974	1975
Fellowships & Traineeships	3846	3830	3236	2668	2286	1852	1547	1367
% of Total	28.4	27.9	24.5	21.2	19.1	16.6	14.4	12.8
Research Assistantships	3770	3617	3579	3374	3150	3028	2776	2852
% of Total	27.8	26.4	27.1	26.8	26.3	27.2	25.9	26.7
Teaching Assistantships	5170	5426	5353	5548	5503	5440	5596	5615
% of Total	38.2	39.5	40.6	44.1	45.9	48.8	52.3	52.6
Other	760	847	1026	988	1059	822	784	840
% of Total	5.6	6.2	7.8	7.9	8.8	7.4	7.3	7.9
TOTAL	13546	13720	13194	12578	11998	11142	10703	10674

Source: National Science Foundation.

uate students in the three disciplines. (The data record the number and percent of students receiving a particular type and source of support as their principal means of financing graduate study; data on dollar amounts are not available.) Substantial shifts in support patterns have occurred within each discipline, and noteworthy differences among the three fields are evident as well.

In all three fields, federal support for graduate students has dropped substantially, both in absolute terms and in relative importance.[9] In mathematics, the decline in federal support has been particularly sharp, reflecting not only the elimination of most fellowship and traineeship programs but also the small number of research assistantships in this field. The universities' own funds (including state government appropriations) have supported a roughly constant number of students over

Table 6

Source and Type of Graduate Student Support
in 120 Mathematics Departments, FY 1968-1975

Source/ Number & Percent of Students	1968	1969	1970	1971	1972	1973	1974	1975
Federal Government.	2564	2451	2144	1820	1331	921	595	353
% of Total	28.6	27.4	25.2	21.6	17.1	12.7	8.9	5.7
Institution & State Government	4420	4603	4570	4907	4560	4527	4597	4611
% of Total	49.4	51.6	53.8	58.1	58.8	62.5	69.1	74.3
Self, Loans, Family	1586	1597	1477	1431	1612	1583	1209	1041
% of Total	17.7	17.9	17.4	17.0	20.7	21.9	18.1	16.7
Other	388	281	302	279	267	207	263	205
% of Total	4.3	3.1	3.6	3.3	3.4	2.9	3.9	3.3
TOTAL	8958	8932	8493	8437	7770	7238	6664	6210

Type/Number & Percent of Students	1968	1969	1970	1971	1972	1973	1974	1975
Fellowships & Traineeships	2356	2364	2014	1721	1418	1049	895	656
% of Total	26.3	26.5	23.7	20.4	18.2	14.5	13.4	10.6
Research Assistantships	596	503	508	522	374	332	245	272
% of Total	6.7	5.6	6.0	6.2	4.8	4.6	3.7	4.4
Teaching Assistantships	3877	4028	3944	4281	4047	3965	4036	3939
% of Total	43.2	45.1	46.4	50.7	52.1	54.8	60.6	63.4
Other	2129	2037	2027	1913	1931	1892	1488	1343
% of Total	23.8	22.8	23.9	22.7	24.9	26.1	22.3	21.6
TOTAL	8958	8932	8493	8437	7770	7238	6664	6210

Source: National Science Foundation.

the eight years, but this means that local funds are now much more important in the total pattern of graduate student support, accounting for 51 percent, 60 percent, and 74 percent of the supported students in physics, chemistry, and mathematics, respectively, in FY 1975. The vast majority of this state and institutional support is provided in the form of teaching assistantships, which have increased both in number and importance as a type of support in all three fields.

It is interesting to note that there has been very little, if any, increase in the number of full-time graduate students in these three fields whose primary source of support is reported as self, loans, or family. Over 90 percent of the physics and chemistry students, and over 80 percent of the mathematics students, continue to receive financial support for graduate study from resources other than their own. Maintaining this high percentage of supported students has only been possible, however, because of the enrollment decline that has occurred; in fact, the decline in enrollments has paralleled the drop in federal support in each field.

The data in Tables 4, 5, and 6 on trends in type of support tell the following story: Fellowships and traineeships (which are largely federally funded) declined from over 25 percent to approximately 10 percent of graduate student support; research assistantships (also primarily federally funded) dropped in number also, but remained roughly constant as a proportion of total support; and teaching assistantships increased modestly in number but substantially in relative importance, accounting for 41 percent, 53 percent, and 63 percent of total support in physics, chemistry, and mathematics, respectively, by FY 1975.

The economic basis for graduate student support has clearly shifted away from federal support provided in the national interest toward local support dictated by the need to staff large numbers of undergraduate class and laboratory sections. If the projected undergraduate enrollment decline materializes in the 1980s, the number of teaching assistantships available can be expected to fall, leading, all else equal, to further declines in graduate enrollment. The field of mathematics would be particularly vulnerable to reduction in teaching assistantships since very few mathematics graduate students currently receive either fellowships or research assistantships (see Table 6).

Our next set of analyses concerns the distribution of graduate student support by rated quality of academic department. Figures 5, 6, and 7 display the total number of fellowships and traineeships by ACE quality grouping in each of the three fields over the eight-year period under investigation. The figures show that the very highest rated departments (4.0-5.0) have increased their proportion of the declining total number of fellowships and traineeships over time, a trend that is explained in part by the termination of such federal programs as the National Defense Education Act (NDEA) Title IV fellowships and NSF traineeships that were distributed to large numbers of institutions. The principal remaining federal fellowship program, NSF predoctoral fellowships, provides three-year portable fellowship awards directly to students, and the NSF fellows tend to enroll predominantly in the highest rated graduate programs. The result, as Figure 8 shows, has been a steady increase in the *proportion* of total fellowship support concentrated in the highest rated departments in each field.

Figures 9, 10, and 11 are analogous to Figure 8 in that they display the proportion of total research assistantships, teaching assistantships, and self-support in each field found in the highest rated departments (4.0-5.0) over the eight years. Figure 9 displays a fairly steady trend toward increasing concentration of research assistantships in the highest rated departments, while Figure 10 shows a dip in the proportion of teaching assistantships in 4.0-5.0 departments in FY 1972, but a return

Figure 5

Number of Fellowships and Traineeships
in 146 Physics Departments,
by Quality Category, FY 1968-1975

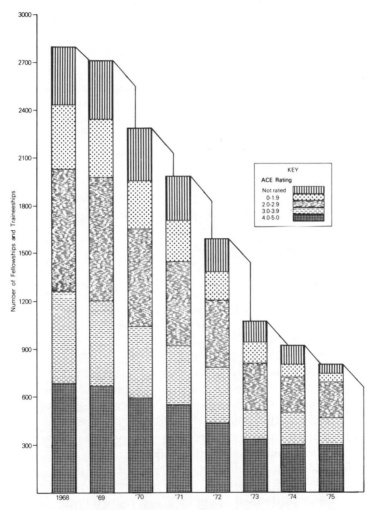

Source: National Science Foundation.

to 1968 levels by 1975. Figure 11 displays a jump in 1972 in the proportion of all self-supported students found in the highest rated departments, but by 1975 the proportions were generally back to 1968 levels.

It is worth noting that the forms of graduate student support dominated by the federal government—fellowships, traineeships, and research assistantships—have become increasingly concentrated in the highest rated departments even as the number of such awards has de-

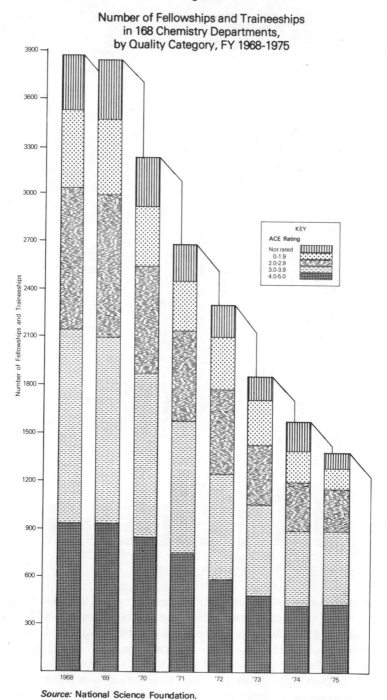

Figure 6

Number of Fellowships and Traineeships in 168 Chemistry Departments, by Quality Category, FY 1968-1975

Source: National Science Foundation.

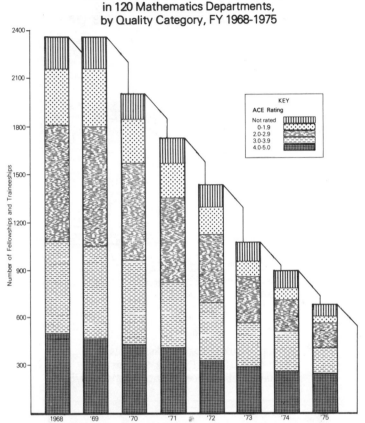

Figure 7

Number of Fellowships and Traineeships
in 120 Mathematics Departments,
by Quality Category, FY 1968-1975

Source: National Science Foundation.

clined, while the principal form of state support for graduate students—teaching assistantships—has not been similarly concentrated. The reason for this is that the bulk of the remaining federal money for graduate student support is allocated by competitive procedures that lead to concentration in higher rated programs, while state money for teaching assistantships is allocated largely on the basis of undergraduate enrollments, a measure not directly related to graduate program quality. Consequently, if federal support for graduate education continues to decline, with the states' contribution becoming relatively more important, the higher quality programs will undoubtedly face erosion in their competitive advantage for student support.

To summarize the changes that have occurred in graduate student support, the average department profiles for the highest rated (4.0-5.0) and lowest rated (0.0-1.9) departments in 1968 and 1975 are presented

Figure 8

Proportion of Total Fellowships and Traineeships
in 4.0-5.0 Rated Physics, Chemistry,
and Mathematics Departments, FY 1968-1975

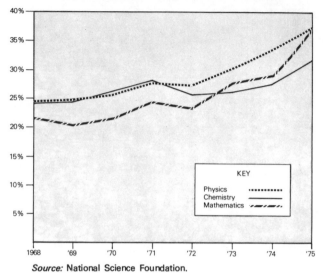

Source: National Science Foundation.

Figure 9

Proportion of Research Assistantships
in 4.0-5.0 Rated Physics, Chemistry,
and Mathematics Departments, FY 1968-1975

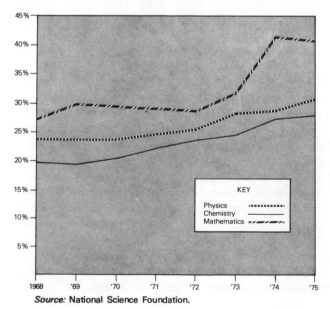

Source: National Science Foundation.

Figure 10

Proportion of Teaching Assistantships
in 4.0-5.0 Rated Physics, Chemistry,
and Mathematics Departments, FY 1968-1975

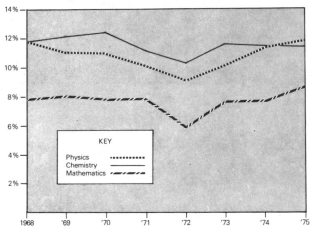

Source: National Science Foundation.

Figure 11

Proportion of Self-Supported Students
in 4.0-5.0 Rated Physics, Chemistry,
and Mathematics Departments, FY 1968-1975

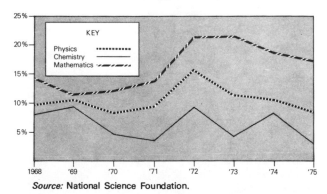

Source: National Science Foundation.

in Table 7. (Similar tables for departments rated 3.0-3.9, 2.0-2.9, and not rated are included in an appendix at the end of this article.) The data in Table 7 show that the average highest rated department in each field had lost roughly half of its 1968 fellowships and traineeships by 1975, that other types of support in the top ranked departments have been relatively stable, and that the enrollment decline in these departments, on the average, is roughly equal to the loss in number of fellowships. In

Table 7

Average Number of Graduate Students Receiving Support in the Highest and Lowest Rated Physics, Chemistry, and Mathematics Departments, FY 1968 and 1975

Type of Support	Highest ACE Rating 4.0-5.0		Lowest ACE Rating 0.0-1.9	
	1968	1975	1968	1975
Physics				
Fellowships & Traineeships	68	31	9	1
Research Assistantships	95	84	8	6
Teaching Assistantships	36	38	14	15
Other	11	8	5	4
TOTAL	210	161	36	26
Chemistry				
Fellowships & Traineeships	85	39	11	3
Research Assistantships	67	72	10	6
Teaching Assistantships	56	59	22	21
Other	6	5	3	5
TOTAL	214	175	46	35
Mathematics				
Fellowships & Traineeships	63	30	11	1
Research Assistantships	20	14	1	1
Teaching Assistantships	38	42	25	26
Other	32	37	12	6
TOTAL	153	123	49	34

Source: National Science Foundation.

the lower rated departments, however, virtually the only remaining form of support is the teaching assistantship, with fellowships, traineeships, and research assistantships virtually nonexistent by 1975. Seen in this light, state and institutional policies on financing teaching assistants become all important. These lower rated departments do not have the strength and flexibility of the high rated departments.

Length of Time to Degree

An important aspect of the PhD production process is the length of time required to earn the degree. One would expect that the major economic changes in the graduate environment in recent years, including cutbacks in federal support and the declining labor market for new PhDs, would have disrupted the process, resulting in lengthened time-to-degree statistics. Figure 12 records the median time to degree from the entry date of graduates over the 15-year period FY 1960-1974 for the three disciplines under study. The data are drawn from departments surveyed in 10 major universities: Stanford, Berkeley, Michigan, Yale, Harvard, Pennsylvania, Cornell, Chicago, Wisconsin, and Princeton.[10]

In physics the downward trend in time-to-degree from FY 1960 through 1969 was reversed during 1969-1974, ending at a level approximately six months above the 1969 low point. Chemistry follows roughly the same pattern, also increasing approximately one half year in time-to-degree from 1968 through 1974. Mathematics follows a less predictable pattern and has not shown a clear tendency in recent years to increase the length of time to a degree.

Figure 12

Median Time-to-Degree in Years,
From Date of First Graduate Enrollment, in Physics,
Chemistry, and Mathematics Departments, FY 1960-1974

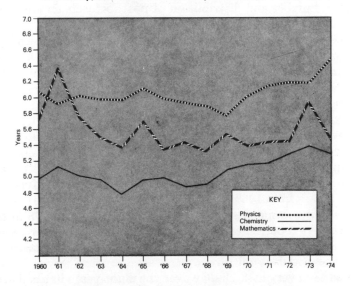

Source: National Academy of Sciences Doctorate Record File.

To some extent the increase in median time-to-degree since 1968 is a statistical artifact caused by enrollment declines that began in the middle 1960s;[11] however, most of the increase can be attributed to changing patterns of financial support, particularly the increased importance of teaching assistantships, and to the tendency of students to stretch out their programs because of the poor labor market in the 1970s. Nonetheless, Figure 12 does not describe a situation marked by major disruption in the production cycle of new doctorates; the modest increase in time-to-degree in physics and chemistry seems well within tolerable limits and suggests that departments are still producing PhDs with reasonable efficiency. It is also interesting to note the systematic tendency for the median time in physics to exceed that in mathematics, which in turn exceeds the time in chemistry. The reasons for these systematic differences will become clearer when we examine the role of the graduate student in the research activities of the three disciplines.

Postdoctoral Fellows

Although the focus here is on the relation of doctoral-level graduate education to research productivity in academic science departments, it is important as well to note trends in the number of postdoctoral fellows since these individuals also constitute an important labor pool for faculty research projects. In fact, postdoctoral fellows and graduate students can and do function in a complementary fashion on a research team or as substitutes for one another. Thus it is necessary to look at the trends in number and distribution of postdoctorals among departments during the period under discussion.

The NSF Surveys of Graduate Science Student Support and Postdoctorals asked for the number of postdoctorals and research associates in each surveyed department; these figures for the matched departments in the data set used here are reported in Table 8. A careful study of trends in postdoctoral education has not been undertaken since the 1969 report of the National Academy of Sciences,[12] and thus the following data are presented with minimum interpretation of changes that may have occurred in the nature of the postdoctoral position since 1969.

In looking first at the total number of postdoctoral appointments, it can be seen that both physics and chemistry reported approximately 10 percent increases from 1968 to 1975, while the number in mathematics (never very large) dropped substantially, falling to 55 in 1975 in these departments. As reported earlier, mathematics has far fewer research assistantships than either chemistry or physics, and this pattern is repeated at the postdoctoral level.

There has been very little change over the eight years in the distribution of postdoctorals among departments of differing quality ratings.

Table 8

Number and Distribution of Postdoctoral Fellows in 146 Physics, 168 Chemistry, and 120 Mathematics Departments by Quality Rating, FY 1968-1975

ACE Quality Rating	1968	1969	1970	1971	1972	1973	1974	1975
Physics								
4.0-5.0								
Number	318	309	318	332	329	342	313	315
% of Total	28.7	27.5	27.4	28.9	26.3	25.6	25.2	25.7
3.0-3.9								
Number	382	399	401	360	396	433	373	385
% of Total	34.6	35.5	34.6	31.4	31.7	32.3	30.0	31.3
2.0-2.9								
Number	291	283	302	292	347	351	355	329
% of Total	26.3	25.2	26.1	25.5	27.8	26.3	28.6	26.8
0.0-1.9								
Number	58	57	57	69	74	98	100	82
% of Total	5.2	5.1	4.9	6.0	5.9	7.3	8.1	6.7
Not rated								
Number	58	77	81	94	104	113	101	116
% of Total	5.2	6.8	7.0	8.2	8.3	8.5	8.1	9.5
TOTAL	1107	1125	1159	1147	1250	1337	1242	1227
Chemistry								
4.0-5.0								
Number	590	602	579	532	546	591	593	591
% of Total	30.2	28.0	26.3	24.8	24.1	25.1	25.5	26.1
3.0-3.9								
Number	707	763	758	730	747	773	709	679
% of Total	36.2	35.6	34.3	33.9	33.0	32.7	30.5	30.0
2.0-2.9								
Number	401	482	524	547	596	626	626	597
% of Total	20.5	22.4	23.8	25.5	26.3	26.6	27.0	26.4
0.0-1.9								
Number	116	137	159	173	190	195	197	209
% of Total	5.9	6.4	7.2	8.1	8.4	8.3	8.5	9.2
Not rated								
Number	140	163	185	166	186	171	197	188
% of Total	7.2	7.6	8.4	7.7	8.2	7.3	8.5	8.3
TOTAL	1954	2147	2205	2148	2265	2356	2322	2264
Mathematics								
4.0-5.0								
Number	119	107	103	84	75	57	48	30
% of Total	64.0	58.9	54.8	49.8	45.7	44.6	61.6	54.5
3.0-3.9								
Number	34	30	41	33	33	14	17	14
% of Total	18.3	16.5	21.8	19.5	20.1	10.9	21.8	25.5
2.0-2.9								
Number	16	35	34	36	42	19	9	9
% of Total	8.6	19.2	18.1	21.3	25.6	14.8	11.5	16.4
0.0-1.9								
Number	8	5	4	8	7	9	4	2
% of Total	4.3	2.7	2.1	4.7	4.3	7.0	5.1	3.6
Not rated								
Number	9	5	6	8	7	29	0	0
% of Total	4.8	2.7	3.2	4.7	4.3	22.7	0.0	0.0
TOTAL	186	182	188	169	164	128	78	55

Source: National Science Foundation.

The highest rated departments in physics and chemistry accounted for 25 to 30 percent of the postdoctorals each year, with the next highest rated group (3.0-3.9) accounting for another 30 + percent. Well over 50 percent of postdoctorals, therefore, are found in the leading 30 to 40 departments.

Graduate Education and Research Productivity

Having presented a statistical description of recent trends in physics, chemistry, and mathematics graduate education at the departmental level, we must now relate these trends to the major concern of this study—university research capability. This is done by drawing on information gained from numerous interviews with university faculty. During the interviews, the connections between graduate education and research output were discussed in detail, with particular emphasis on recent experiences. The author's own site visits were made in connection with two separate research projects. During the period October 1975 to March 1976, 10 universities were visited for interviews with mathematics and physics faculty (Harvard, Yale, Princeton, Pennsylvania, Cornell, Stanford, Berkeley, Wisconsin, Michigan, and Chicago). From March to June of 1974, chemistry department chairmen in 14 universities were interviewed (Wisconsin, Tennessee, Cincinnati, Kansas State, Tufts, Catholic, Berkeley, Pittsburgh, Tulane, Arizona, Stanford, the State University of New York at Buffalo, Cornell, and Northern Colorado). In addition, written summaries of the 30 university site visits conducted for the Smith/Karlesky study provided further background information (see the preface to Volume I).

One limitation must be noted: Constraints of time and resources made it impossible to measure objectively, or evaluate qualitatively, the actual flow of research activity emanating from the various departments. (There are difficult methodological problems in this area as well that should not be underestimated.) Consequently, I have had to rely on faculty evaluations of trends in the quantity and quality of research output produced by department members. Lacking objective data, I have relied similarly on faculty judgments about changes in graduate student quality.

The Joint Product Concept

In much of the recent discussion about graduate education, it has become fashionable to refer to graduate education and research as "joint products," a term borrowed from economics. This concept needs to be clarified before the specific interview findings are presented.

The standard example of joint products is wool and mutton, the two separately marketable products of the single activity—sheep raising. They are jointly produced not merely for economic reasons but simply because the one cannot physically be produced without the other. It should be evident that graduate education and research are not joint products in this same sense; research can be carried out in the absence of graduate education (or of graduate students), as the existence of non-university research centers demonstrates. On the other hand, it is not possible to have graduate education (or at least doctoral-level education) without research, since the PhD degree is, by definition, a research degree. Consequently, it is accurate to view PhDs and research as the joint products of graduate education.

The purpose of this discussion is to argue that a reduction in graduate enrollments (and hence in PhD production) need not entail a reduction in faculty research output. In this sense, it is misleading to apply the joint product concept to graduate education and research. Research activity can be maintained when graduate enrollment falls because other forms of labor input can be substituted for graduate students, for example, postdoctorals or technicians. But it may not be possible economically to maintain the level of research output, either because the services of technicians or postdoctorals are more expensive than those of graduate students or because faculty may be forced to reallocate their own efforts toward undergraduate teaching. However, such economic factors are a matter for empirical investigation, not for the *a priori* reasoning that would be acceptable in the case of truly joint products.

Although we have argued that research can be produced in the absence of graduate education, this is, of course, only true in the short run, since graduate education is the only method we have currently for training the next generation of high-level research personnel. We could shut down the graduate schools tomorrow and continue to produce research for a number of years, but the necessary knowledge required for a research career cannot be learned exclusively on the job. In this more fundamental sense, research and graduate education are mutually dependent.

Site Visit Findings

On the basis of faculty interviews, it is clear that the role of the graduate student differs significantly among the three disciplines studied here, both in relation to faculty research and to the budgetary demands of the departments. Chemistry departments rank first in their dependence on graduate students for efficient operation, followed by physics and then by mathematics. Because the functions performed by graduate students vary among the disciplines, departments have responded in different ways to the hard times of recent years. These differential responses are revealed in the statistics presented earlier.

Chemistry departments rely heavily upon graduate teaching assistants to staff the numerous laboratory sections of undergraduate chemistry courses; for instance, the marked increase in premedical and other life science majors in the 1970s has expanded the service load of chemistry departments substantially, putting a premium on the teaching services of graduate students. In addition, chemistry graduate students are valued members of faculty-led research groups, not only learning from participation but actually doing much of the research. They are valued, therefore, for their labor input as both teaching and research assistants. Although some substitution has been possible (e.g., postdoctorals), every department visited wanted to increase the number of graduate students and none had intentionally cut back enrollments.

This behavior stands in marked contrast to that found in physics and mathematics departments. As the data on student support show, physics departments also make extensive use of graduate students in teaching and research positions. There are definite differences, however, when compared with chemistry departments. Since physics courses are a much smaller component of the premedical curriculum, the service teaching load for undergraduates is not as extensive; hence, most physics departments have felt less pressure to maintain graduate enrollments as a source of teaching assistants. Similarly, there is less dependence in physics than in chemistry on graduate student labor on sponsored research projects. The time scale of research is a principal reason for this difference in the two fields; a typical physics experiment may require one to three years to prepare and execute, while chemistry experiments are often set up and completed in a much shorter time, with several experiments often undertaken simultaneously.

While graduate students in physics acquire valuable skills and experience from participating in research projects, they are not as critical a labor input as in chemistry. In fact, several physics professors expressed the view that the typical graduate student was more often a liability than an asset in the laboratory, if viewed strictly in terms of research production. Postdoctorals, however, are a different matter and are viewed in physics as much more essential and valuable relative to predoctoral students than is true in chemistry.

The different relative values placed on graduate students helps to explain why many physics departments initiated enrollment cutbacks in the early 1970s, while most chemistry departments maintained active recruiting efforts. Chemistry faculty report that a drop in graduate enrollments lowers research output, while physics faculty do not make the same claim, at least for the declines that have occurred thus far. (The major exception to this statement would be in those small and generally lower rated physics departments where the continued existence of a doctoral program is threatened.) In the larger and stronger physics departments, enrollments were scaled back largely in response to both the declining market demand for PhDs and the reduction in federal fellowship support; faculty interviewed in those departments stated that research activity did not suffer from reduced enrollments because the number of postdoctoral fellows remained stable and because the average quality of graduate students improved in the 1970s.

In mathematics, graduate students do not function as a source of labor on faculty research projects in numbers at all comparable to those in physics or chemistry, reflecting in large measure the differences in research procedure between laboratory and nonlaboratory disciplines. Graduate students are vital to the research environment, however, primarily through their effect on the allocation of faculty time. As the student support data show, large numbers of mathematics graduate students serve as teaching assistants, thereby releasing faculty from the time-consuming activities of teaching small undergraduate sections and grading undergraduate work. Graduate students also provide enrollments for graduate seminars that allow faculty to cover advanced material often near the research frontier; faculty members commonly referred in interviews to the importance of these seminars as a source of new research ideas. Similarly, graduate students are often a source of intellectual stimulus to faculty and on occasion may follow through on a line of investigation suggested by a faculty member.

One striking feature of the mathematics research environment that was mentioned repeatedly in the interviews was the need to have colleagues with whom to discuss ideas and problems. Whereas the stereotype of the mathematician at work is that of the lonely thinker, needing only paper, pencil, and solitude, the reality seems to be quite the reverse. There is simply a need to talk and to interact steadily with individuals capable of understanding the material under investigation; hence, the heavy stress in most departments on budgetary support for visiting scholars and for travel to conferences. Mathematics graduate students fit into this process in the role of junior colleagues who contribute importantly to the research environment, even though they may not work directly on a faculty research project as chemistry or physics graduate students do.

Given this description of the functions performed by mathematics graduate students, it is possible to understand why many of the larger departments were willing to cut enrollments in the 1970s as student support money fell and as the labor market worsened. So long as enough mathematics graduate students are available to meet the demand for teaching assistants and to justify economically a sufficient number of graduate seminars, faculty needs will be met. A 25 percent reduction in graduate enrollments in the larger departments has been absorbed with no reported loss in research activity or output.

With regard to changes in graduate student quality in recent years, faculty reports again differ by discipline. In physics and mathematics, faculty at the universities visited reported that the quality of graduate students enrolled was very high, fully the equivalent of the quality present during the 1960s. (In several departments, faculty noted that foreign students currently are setting the quality standard.) A common view is that the intellectually marginal students have been discouraged from pursuing graduate study by the poor job market prospects, by reduced financial support, and by reduced numbers of acceptances by graduate departments; the result is, if anything, an increase in the average quality of graduate students, at least in the leading departments. (One physics professor did mention, however, that some of the marginal students drawn into physics during the last two decades have provided real value to the profession in ways other than contributions to research, and he worried that their loss might weaken the outreach of physics into other areas of society.)

By contrast, chemistry departments reported greater concern over average student quality, in part because most departments have not scaled back acceptances significantly in the face of declining applications. In order to enroll the number of students desired by the faculty, admission standards in many departments have been lowered relative to the 1960s, and the competition for students is intense. Nonetheless, it does not appear that a serious erosion of graduate student quality has occurred, at least within the higher rated departments.

The slight increase in postdoctorals in physics and chemistry departments reported earlier provides a misleading sense of stability, if the universities visited are representative of national trends. Underlying the apparent stability is a substantial reduction in federal sources of support, and a marked and largely offsetting increase in the number of foreign postdoctorals supported by foreign government funds. In a number of the departments visited, faculty reported that in the absence of foreign support the department would have had only half the number of postdoctorals in 1975. Even at the predoctoral level, several faculty mentioned the growing importance in recent years of foreign students and foreign sources of financial support.

There were scattered comments during the interviews about severe supply/demand imbalances in particular subfields of the disciplines. For example, in high energy particle physics, the supply of young PhDs is apparently so large relative to the number of professional positions available that competition has become excessive and unproductive — individuals begin early on the time-consuming search for a job and are constantly watching the competition. On the basis of a limited number of interviews, however, it is unwise to attempt generalizations. The subjects of subfield specialization and postdoctoral education are both in need of further investigation.

Conclusions

Current research productivity in physics, chemistry, and mathematics departments has not been seriously undermined by the changes that have occurred in graduate education over the period FY 1968-1975. There are nuances and qualifications to this general conclusion, but it stands as the basic finding of this study. A much more serious problem involving graduate education does, however, threaten the health of academic science: the difficulty of maintaining a flow of younger scientists into increasingly tenured-in, nonexpanding science departments. Many faculty referred to this prospective lack of academic openings for new PhDs in the next decade—either through expansion or replacement—as the major human resource problem facing their own departments and the discipline at large. In this final section, the qualifications to this study's basic finding regarding the relationships of graduate education to research output are noted, along with the dimensions of the more serious, long-range problem of faculty age structure.

Qualifications to the Findings

The first qualification involves the concern expressed in some of the chemistry departments visited that declining graduate enrollment was reducing faculty research output. This observation occurred most often in smaller and lower rated departments and was generally linked to the related problem of reduced federal research support. There is a definite syndrome of decline visible in weaker departments: Reduced research support there leads to fewer graduate students, which in turn puts pressure on faculty to write more proposals, do more student recruiting, and take on more undergraduate teaching. As faculty time is splintered into these maintenance efforts, overall effectiveness usually suffers, and research support falls still further, setting off another round of decline. This pattern may not be as noticeable in physics and mathematics departments as it is in chemistry, because declining graduate enrollments have been more easily absorbed in these disciplines; however, site visit reports from the more than 30 universities visited as a part of the Smith/Karlesky project indicate that the weaker departments in all science fields are experiencing problems with an intensity not felt in the higher rated departments. An earlier study of graduate school adjustments to the "new depression" in higher education[13] reached this same conclusion, and two years of additional data and more recent interviews have reinforced the findings of that study.

As a second qualification it must be remembered that the majority of the statistical tables and cross-tabulations presented here involve comparative trends in departments of different quality ratings. This type of comparative or relative analysis is valid and useful for many of the questions addressed, but it should not be mistaken for an analysis of absolute change. Evaluation of resource allocation in higher education remains subject to the limitations imposed by the absence of well-defined and acceptable output (or outcome) measures. Third, this paper is focused principally on the effects that changes in graduate education have had upon faculty research productivity, and other, more obvious factors have not been addressed, such as changes in research support, except as these affected graduate support and enrollments.

Finally, the ACE ratings of graduate program quality used in the study are now over seven years old, and some shifting has undoubtedly occurred in the relative standing of the various departments. Although it is highly unlikely that the basic findings reported here would be changed by an updated rating of departments, the analysis suffers from the absence of a more current rating of departments.

The Serious Human Resource Problem

The serious threat to a vital and productive research capacity in the universities lies not in the domain of graduate education per se but rather in the limited number of openings for younger faculty that many science departments will have during the next 10 to 15 years. The rapid expansion in higher education from the late 1950s through the 1960s left many science departments with large numbers of relatively young, tenured professors, and these departments now face the prospect of a decade or more with very limited expansion or replacement demand for new PhDs. This prospect is a major source of concern in many departments, since the younger faculty are often the most creative and energetic members of a department.

In numerous interviews, faculty members expressed their concern that the absence of new blood would be stultifying. As one physics professor put it, "I know what everyone in this department thinks about the research subjects that interest me, and the thought of having no new colleagues to talk with is chilling." Faculty members in a large university mathematics department were so concerned about the lack of new faculty positions that they convinced the dean to let them trade 25 graduate teaching assistantships for three new assistant professor positions. As a third case in point, one of the nation's premier physics departments has only 2 nontenured professors in a total of 60 positions, and virtually no retirements slated for a decade. These examples suggest that the faculty age structure will be a critical factor in the health of academic science through the 1980s. Although the available data on this topic are sparse, they generally support the concerns expressed in interviews.

In an unpublished paper, Lee Grodzins presented data from matched science departments demonstrating the faculty age shift that occurred between 1968 and 1974.[14] The data for the three fields of interest to this paper are reproduced in Table 9. The figures document a substantial decline in the number of younger faculty members, and a corresponding increase in faculty seven or more years beyond the doctorate.

Allan Cartter's book prepared for the Carnegie Commission is the most recent and comprehensive analysis of the academic labor market. The book should be read in its entirety by those concerned with the human resources of universities, for only a few of Cartter's more salient findings can be noted here. On the projected faculty age structure, Cartter writes:

> Under these conditions [a set of plausible assumptions about student-faculty ratios, retirement policies, etc.] the median age of full-time college teachers would rise from age 43 in 1972 to 45 in 1980, and to 49 in 1990. Teachers 35 and under would decline from 25 percent in 1972 to 12.5 percent by 1990, while those over 60 would rise from 7.6 percent to 14.8 percent.[15]

A major explanation for this shift in age distribution is the limited number of academic openings for new faculty that Cartter projects through the 1980s; his basic projection based on replacement and growth needs calls for total hiring during the decade of the 1980s of 43,500 new faculty, an average of 4,350 per year. (Annual PhD output from U.S. universities in each of the last four years has been approximately 33,000.) By comparison, during the decade of the 1960s, 257,500 new faculty members were employed by colleges and universities.[16] Although Cartter is the first to point out the various factors that may alter his projections, there is no denying that a remarkable shift in the academic labor market will occur in the 1980s and 1990s that will make the problems of the early 1970s seem trivial by comparison.

It is beyond the scope of this paper to discuss policies that might provide greater employment flexibility for university science departments

Table 9

Composition of Faculty in Matched Doctorate-Level Science and Engineering Departments, 1968 and 1974

Field	Number of Departments	Total Faculty 1968	Total Faculty 1974	Percent Change 1968-74	Faculty by Years Since Receipt of PhD — 7 years or less 1968	7 years or less 1974	more than 7 years 1968	more than 7 years 1974	Ratio >7 years to < 7 years 1968	Ratio >7 years to < 7 years 1974
Physics	77	2162	2190	1.3%	826	400	1262	1759	1.5	4.4
Mathematics	69	2651	2849	7.5%	1242	989	1167	1746	0.9	1.7
Chemistry	103	2387	2555	7.0%	805	526	1522	1995	1.9	3.8

Source: Lee Grodzins (see footnote 14) based on National Science Foundation data.

160

during the next decade and a half. One information requirement is obvious as a starting point, however, and that is data on the age distribution and tenure status of faculty by academic department. At a minimum we need to know how many of our leading science departments are heavily tenured and face a 10- to 15-year period with few retirements. If the number of such departments is large, then an important and creative role will clearly exist for federal agencies, such as the National Science Foundation and the National Institutes of Health, and for private foundations concerned with the health of academic science, to help university administrators find new ways to employ young faculty. During the 1950s and 1960s federal agencies and private foundations provided millions of dollars for the education of graduate students; in the 1980s, the human resource focus must shift to the junior faculty level.

APPENDIX

Table A

Average Number of Graduate Students Receiving Support
in Physics Departments by Quality Rating, FY 1968 and 1975*

| | ACE Quality Ratings | | | | | |
| | 3.0-3.9 | | 2.0-2.9 | | Not rated | |
	1968	1975	1968	1975	1968	1975
TYPE OF SUPPORT						
Fellowships & Traineeships	30	9	19	5	10	3
Research Assistantships	72	46	28	13	8	8
Teaching Assistantships	34	33	26	25	12	17
Other	17	15	11	7	3	5
TOTAL	153	103	84	50	33	33
SOURCE OF SUPPORT						
Federal Government	91	46	44	13	13	8
Institutional & Local	43	42	28	29	14	21
Self, Loans & Family	10	12	7	6	2	3
Other	10	3	5	2	1	1
TOTAL	154	103	84	50	30	33

*For departments rated 4.0-5.0 and 0.0-1.9, see Table 7, page 148.
Source: National Science Foundation.

Table B

Average Number of Graduate Students Receiving Support in Chemistry Departments by Quality Rating, FY 1968 and 1975*

| | ACE Quality Ratings | | | | | |
	3.0-3.9 1968 1975		2.0-2.9 1968 1975		Not rated 1968 1975	
TYPE OF SUPPORT						
Fellowships & Traineeships	46	18	22	6	7	2
Research Assistantships	52	34	23	16	6	5
Teaching Assistantships	50	52	40	45	15	19
Other	5	7	6	6	3	3
TOTAL	153	111	91	73	31	29
SOURCE OF SUPPORT						
Federal Government	78	32	36	15	10	4
Institutional & Local	61	58	43	50	16	21
Self, Loans & Family	3	7	2	5	3	2
Other	12	14	8	4	2	2
TOTAL	154	111	89	74	31	29

*For departments rated 4.0-5.0 and 0.0-1.9, see Table 7, page 148.
Source: National Science Foundation.

Table C

Average Number of Graduate Students Receiving Support in Mathematics Departments by Quality Rating, FY 1968 and 1975*

| | ACE Quality Ratings | | | | | |
	3.0-3.9 1968 1975		2.0-2.9 1968 1975		Not rated 1968 1975	
TYPE OF SUPPORT						
Fellowships & Traineeships	37	10	19	4	2	2
Research Assistantships	10	2	4	2	1	1
Teaching Assistantships	46	53	42	34	17	23
Other	24	20	19	10	13	5
TOTAL	117	85	84	50	33	31
SOURCE OF SUPPORT						
Federal	38	3	23	2	8	1
Institutional & Local	53	61	48	40	20	26
Self, Loans & Family	23	18	13	8	9	4
Other	2	3	2	1	4	0
TOTAL	116	85	86	51	41	31

*For departments rated 4.0-5.0 and 0.0-1.9, see Table 7, page 148.
Source: National Science Foundation.

1. The reasons for such a shift are discussed in David W. Breneman, *Graduate School Adjustments to the "New Depression" in Higher Education* (Washington, D.C.: National Academy of Sciences, 1975), p. 13.

2. National Science Foundation, *Survey of Graduate Science Student Support and Postdoctorals* (Washington, D.C.: National Science Foundation, Annual Series), Special Tabulations.

3. Kenneth D. Roose and Charles J. Andersen, *A Rating of Graduate Programs* (Washington, D.C.: American Council on Education, 1970).

4. Findings of the study are summarized in Breneman, op. cit., pp. 76-78.

5. FY 1968-1975 refers to data for academic years 1967/68 through 1974/75.

6. Departmental data for FY 1968 through FY 1972 were provided by NSF for this analysis on magnetic tapes representing data furnished by doctoral institutions in their applications for NSF graduate traineeships. For each of the subsequent years, NSF provided data tapes from the *Survey of Graduate Science Student Support and Postdoctorals*, a survey conducted by the Division of Science Resources Studies beginning in fall 1972, which utilizes virtually the same format as the former application for traineeships. For the eight-year trend sequences shown in this report, only those departments that replied consistently to both of the series referred to above have been examined.

7. The data cover 109 of 113 rated physics departments, 122 of 124 rated chemistry departments, and 93 of 102 rated mathematics departments. The numbers of nonrated departments included in the data are: physics, 37; chemistry, 46; and mathematics, 27. In FY 1975 the matched departments enrolled 89 percent of the total full-time students in physics, 94 percent in chemistry, and 86 percent in mathematics. See National Science Foundation, *Graduate Science Education: Student Support and Postdoctorals*, Fall 1974, Appendix III, Detailed Statistical Tables, (NSF 75-322). For more thorough discussion of data coverage, see Breneman, op. cit., pp. 91-96.

8. For a more detailed discussion of the dynamics of PhD production, see Richard B. Freeman and David W. Breneman, *Forecasting the PhD Labor Market: Pitfalls for Policy* (Washington, D.C.: National Academy of Sciences, 1974).

9. GI Bill support provided by the Veteran's Administration is not reported separately in these figures, although NSF has tried, unsuccessfully, to collect such information. The NSF surveys are filled out by department chairmen who in many instances do not know whether a student receives GI Bill benefits; nor does the Veteran's Administration maintain data on graduate student support in detailed fashion. The GI Bill is rarely the major source of support and most likely appears in the data under "self-support."

10. Data are from the National Academy of Sciences *Surveys of Earned Doctorates*.

11. It can be demonstrated that even in the absence of any change in the distribution of time-to-degree among students in a department, the median will fall (with a lag) as the department expands and will rise (also with a lag) as the department contracts.

12. National Academy of Sciences, *The Invisible University* (Washington, D.C.: National Academy of Sciences, 1969). A new study of postdoctorates is being started at the Academy.

13. David W. Breneman, *Graduate School Adjustments*, op. cit.

14. Lee Grodzins, "Changes in the Distribution of Physics Faculties in the United States, 1959 to 1975" (Cambridge, Mass.: Massachusetts Institute of Technology, May 1976). Mimeographed.

15. Allan M. Cartter, *Ph.D.'s and the Academic Labor Market* (New York: McGraw-Hill, 1976), p. 172.

16. Ibid., p. 123. It should be noted that many faculty hired during the 1960s did not have the doctorate.

Accountability and the Research Universities

Sanford A. Lakoff

A striking change of mood has come over academic administrators contemplating the role of the federal government as a patron of science and higher education. A decade ago, when the federal component of academic research budgets was even more significant than it is now, having climbed to 77 percent of the total,[1] the mood was generally one of satisfaction and relief. Most experienced university presidents and deans probably would have agreed with J.C. Furnas that although the federal government conceivably could have used its financial leverage to undermine or abridge the autonomy of institutions of higher learning, in fact "it has not turned out to be the terrible, dictating ogre that many anticipated."[2]

Now, however, administrators are plainly troubled about the relationship with their public patrons, both at the federal and state levels. Above all, they are concerned with the increasing burden involved in complying with regulations and reporting requirements. Harvard University President Derek Bok has noted that "compliance with federal regulations consumed over 60,000 hours of faculty time in 1974-75 alone."[3] Earl Cheit of the University of California, noting the rising volume of requests for data and reports from both federal and state agencies, charges that as a result the universities have been consigned to nothing less than a "new purgatory right here on earth."[4]

More broadly, the administrators have expressed concern over what they regard as the increasing tendency for federal and state governments to intrude into sensitive areas traditionally left to the universities. "Within the last eight years," Bok observed in a 1976 report to the Harvard Overseers, "the government has begun to exert its influence in new ways to encourage colleges and universities to conform to a

variety of public policies." He cited a similar concern voiced by King-
man Brewster, then president of Yale, who was even more explicit in
warning of "a growing tendency for the central government to use the
spending power to prescribe educational policies." The government's
attitude, according to Brewster, could be summed up as, "Now that I
have bought the button, I have a right to design the coat."[5]

What has prompted this dramatic change of attitude toward government patronage of research and higher education? Bok points out that
while support increased, there was little inclination on the part of the
recipients to complain about the terms upon which it was given:

> Deans and presidents understood that there could be no turning back,
> for distinguished medical schools and science departments simply
> could not exist without government support. Although universities
> lost some of their independence in the process, few educators were
> troubled so long as appropriations rose year after year with so few
> tangible ill effects.[6]

Even in these years, however, growing support for the expansion of
academic research did not reflect an official, firm, or permanent commitment to science or higher education; it was rather an effort to support activities that were deemed important to the national interest,
especially military security. Although only a small fraction of this support came from the military agencies, it was tacitly understood that
the rationale for public spending was the contribution of basic research
and higher education, especially in the physical sciences, to long-term
national security. A standard tactic for preventing cutbacks was to
compare data on U.S. research expenditures and numbers of qualified
scientists and engineers with the figures for the nation's Cold War an-
tagonist, the Soviet Union. Fellowships for higher education were provided under the National Defense Education Act.

From time to time, and especially when controversy over the war in
Vietnam erupted on the campuses, this national security rationale for
the growth of support caused problems for the universities. On the
whole, however, public funding could be defended quite plausibly because academic autonomy was left essentially intact. Since the funds
came from a variety of agencies, it was hard for any one to exert undue
influence. Most of the research supported by the military agencies was
unclassified, and any classified research could be relegated to
off-campus facilities.[7] Deciding whether to seek security clearance in
order to perform military research or to apply for a government fellowship or loan was up to individuals; it did not interfere with the internal
management of the university.

The government agencies, moreover, perhaps as much out of inex-
perience in dealing with academics and their institutions as out of lib-
erality and respect, generally adopted procedures less stringent than
those applied to profit-making contractors. Scientists played an im-

portant role in the allocation process by advising on priorities and reviewing proposals, and universities enjoyed wide latitude in the administration of research grants. Most of the agency program officers were scientists strongly committed to academic values and likely to return to a university after a stint in government; they therefore had every incentive to cultivate good rapport with their clients.

In recent years, however, both administrators and researchers have come to believe that the terms of public support constrict and interfere with academic autonomy, impose economic burdens on the institution, and threaten to lower the quality of basic research by following publicly determined priorities rather than allowing researchers to chart their own courses. Much of the flexibility has been removed from grant procedures, and new federally mandated programs have added significantly to the universities' operating costs. Beginning with the Mansfield Amendment, which restricted the military agencies' research contracts to proposals directly related to the agency mission, more and more research support has come to be targeted for specific objectives, such as the Apollo landing, the war on cancer, or the pursuit of energy independence. The result is that in order to secure support, researchers must trim their sails to the changing winds of political fashion, instead of using their energies to exploit opportunities opened up by advances in each field of research.

General grants to institutions—those not earmarked for specific projects but intended to enable the universities to correct imbalances and support pioneering ventures—have been cut back severely. Certain government agencies, notably the Department of Health, Education, and Welfare (HEW), have threatened to withhold research support unless universities comply with federal regulations (as interpreted by the agencies) related to admissions and employment procedures. These agencies also have the power to order that all forms of federal support be withheld from universities deemed to be in violation of any of these regulations. In the case of institutions receiving too little federal support to make such a threat credible, the Internal Revenue Service lately has begun to review fund-raising materials to determine whether the institutions' policies warrant continuation of their tax-exempt status. The use by the National Science Foundation (NSF) and the National Institutes of Health (NIH), the two leading sources of support for basic research, of the system of confidential peer review—the system by which scientists regulate the distribution of support in terms of standards of merit internal to science—is under attack because it is said to be elitist in promoting the interest of a self-perpetuating clique and because it allows scientists to escape political regulation.

Following the lead of the federal agencies, state agencies have also increased the stringency of their regulations. The Buckley Amendment to the federal Freedom of Information Act gave applicants for admission to universities the right to inspect previously confidential letters of recommendation. In 1975 the California legislature passed a bill that would have given a similar right to candidates for faculty appointments and promotions. (The bill was vetoed by the governor after strenuous opposition by the president of the University of California.) In addition, in order to contain the rising costs of education, the state legislatures have sharply limited the expansion of research-oriented institutions in favor of less expensive forms of postsecondary education, thus inducing virtually all the state-supported universities to alter the direction of their educational programs.

For the universities these developments portend an ominous erosion of the tradition of academic freedom, at least as this tradition implies the right of the "republic of science" to set its own standards and administer its own affairs. For the government the virtue of respecting academic freedom must be balanced against the need to assure that public functions paid for even in part by tax revenues are performed in accordance with publicly established standards and objectives. A conflict of goals is inherent in the relationship between government and the universities, as it has always been inherent in the relationship of private patrons with artists and scientists. The need to protect the legitimate interests of both parties has been recognized virtually from the outset. In 1964, while the mood of academic administrators was still sanguine, the Committee on Science and Public Policy of the National Academy of Sciences (NAS) posed the essential dilemma in a report to the membership:

> Can freedom of scientific inquiry and accountability be reconciled?...
> What are the policies by which accountable support can effectively advance scientific inquiry in the common interest? How can inaccurate conceptions of both *the necessary freedom for scientific research* and *the accountability of funds* be prevented from stifling the fruits of research—a potent resource of our society not only for today but for the future?[8]

The dilemma, even in the best of circumstances, will never be wholly resolved. Certain of the tensions it produces, however, can probably be minimized by examining the changing character and context of the problem and considering ways of alleviating it. Such an analysis must take account of the new scope and dimensions of the quest for accountability, the impact of the most significant changes in the system, and the constructive alternatives that could be adopted both by the government and the universities.

The New Scope of Accountability

If in principle the problem of assuring accountability is hardly new, in

practice it has lately grown more ramified and far reaching. The principle is fundamental to all constitutional forms of government—systems, in other words, in which it is presupposed (as the political philosopher John Locke put it) that authority is ultimately a "fiduciary" instrument of the popular will. Since all authority is presumed to flow from the people, all those upon whom it is conferred must be responsible to the people for the performance of the duties entrusted to them.[9]
In the first instance, then, the principle of accountability applies to government officials and agencies; the celebrated checks and balances built into the American Constitution were intended to minimize the danger that any official or agency could succeed in overstepping an assigned sphere or usurping a power reserved to the states or the individual citizen.

Neither Locke nor the framers of the Constitution, however, could have anticipated the ironic turn of events in which the requirements of accountability have come to apply not only to those in government but also to major social institutions outside the governmental system. They assumed—understandably, given the character of both society and government in the seventeenth and eighteenth centuries—that government could be sharply distinguished from society, and that it was the government, because of its monopoly of coercive authority, that was to be held accountable to society. Today, in countries that preserve a separation between government and society, accountability is an issue for both sectors, and nowhere is this more evident than in the collaboration of the federal government with industry and the universities in scientific research and its applications.

This collaboration was first described sympathetically as an example of "federalism by contract"[10]and later, more suspiciously, as the rise of the "contract state."[11] The first characterization suggests that on the whole the "research partnership" is a benign development, inasmuch as it extends the constitutional principle of federalism from the system of coordinate sovereignties to the relationship between the public and the private sectors. Instead of expanding the scope of government to include all major efforts to pursue and apply scientific knowledge, the government underwrites research and development by nongovernmental institutions, thus reinforcing the pluralistic character of the social structure. Research is conducted, moreover, where it will have immediate benefits, in the one case for higher education, in the other for economic innovation. The more suspicious characterization suggests that as a result of the collaboration, public funds are used to subsidize profit-making activities while the critical independence of the university is compromised; in this view the mobilization of higher education's scientific capabilities for public purposes frequently has meant the improvement of the military arsenal.

In either case, the effect of the collaboration clearly has been to extend accountability beyond the sphere of government to institutions formerly exempted from such scrutiny. This problem has at least three separate but intertwined dimensions. These are the traditional need to hold government responsible and the new need to assure the accountability of private industry and that of the universities for the performance of public functions. The progression from the first to the second two is logical enough, and inescapable given two assumptions: (1) that the institutions of society, however independent they may be structurally, perform public functions using public money, and (2) that they impinge by their actions upon the rights of individuals—rights that the government is obliged to protect. Although this extension raises problems of a philosophical nature, we must content ourselves with an attempt to identify their practical manifestations.

Accountability in Government, Industry, and the Universities

In the case of government, accountability is assured by a variety of techniques. An elected official is required to stand for reelection, at which time his or her record presumably will be scrutinized by the voters. The "dislocability" of the elected official, as Jeremy Bentham put it, is one important security of fidelity to duty. Legal and judicial sanctions, including impeachment while in office and punishment afterward, are also available. Executive agencies can be held accountable by the legislature, directly through the exercise of the legislative power itself, which is used to develop rules governing administrative conduct and to appropriate support, and indirectly through the use of its investigative authority.

Agencies whose activities are shrouded from public view, such as those that gather intelligence concerning foreign affairs, may require the development of special oversight mechanisms. The party system, the press, public opinion, and ultimately the inner check of conscience or of the values inculcated by the political culture also serve to assure the responsibility of the governors to the governed. From time to time, none of these techniques or barriers will prevent a particular abuse or even a pattern of abuse, but only if the entire social fabric is riddled with corruption and demoralization will such abuses persist, and in these circumstances no system of accountability can prevail.

Certain of these checks against abuses, notably the use of legal sanctions and investigative power, are also applicable to extragovernmental institutions, but some, such as the electoral check, are clearly inapplicable. Other means are more appropriate. The auditing of contractual performance is one such technique. A less formal but still potent sanction is the threat of a loss of future business in the event of inadequate performance or impropriety. This loses much of its force, however, whenever the mutuality of interest between the agency and the contractor becomes too intense; the relationship is transformed into one of mutual dependency instead of dealings between a customer and one of a number of potential suppliers.

The tendency for the military services to form such relationships with large corporations sometimes heavily dependent upon military procurement contracts may lead to collusion in which the larger public interest is confused with the narrow interests of the agency and the contractor. In such cases, the agency's efforts to assure accountability are apt to be feeble, unless reinforced by fear of public criticism. Similarly, the tendency of managers to move from public to private employment and in so doing to skirt conflict-of-interest regulations is apt to make them less than zealous in the enforcement of accountability.

Managers of private corporations are also responsible to shareholders. If these are publicly owned corporations, their activities are subject to review by agencies not bound by mutual interest and wholly committed, in theory at least, to the job of regulating them in the public interest. The politics of influence and appointment, however, can sometimes make of regulators agents and advocates rather than controllers. Regular immersion in the problems of industry, however desirable for moderating the effect of bureaucratic rigidity, may evoke a sympathy that inhibits the strict enforcement of legal standards.

In the case of research support, the effort to assure accountability in industry and the universities encounters a common obstacle. In both cases, the uncertain character of research (and to a lesser extent of development) poses a special problem. Since the path of successful performance is often by definition obscure, contractual terms must be kept flexible. As a rule, there is less uncertainty in industrial research, where applications are the focus of activity, but contractors are still apt to have enough leeway to engage in questionable practices. Contractors have been known to submit low bids in order to obtain contracts with the intention of exceeding the estimates by claiming later that unforeseen difficulties require additional funding. Given the diversity and sophistication of modern high-technology development, in some cases even the most scrupulous government auditor may not be able to find fault with such procedures, especially since in many cases the initial error may be honest. In some cases, program officers and company officials have such a strong common interest in seeing a program undertaken that they will deceive higher authorities about costs.

In the case of university research, assuring accountability requires a still different set of approaches and raises other problems. In the first phase of governmental support, much was made of the distinction between the "purchase" of research, as in the case of a government agency interested in procuring an item of hardware from an industrial firm, and the "sponsorship" of research, in which a government agency undertook to support academic research of a fundamental nature in an area broadly relevant to agency concerns. The contract was said to be the instrument best suited to purchased research, since it was possible to specify the outcome expected and to set yardsticks by which to measure performance.

The grant, originally developed by private philanthropic agencies, was thought to be best adapted to university research since it was not considered possible or desirable to restrict scientists to some rigid, predetermined objective. Instead, the aim was to provide funds for university research on terms that seemed most likely to assure the success of the project. In particular, NSF sought to assure researchers that they were expected to use their best scientific judgment and merely asked — "plaintively," as one commentator noted — to be kept advised in case of changes in research direction:

> The Foundation has no desire to inhibit the intellectual curiosity and research initiative of the principal investigator; however, on such occasions when either new and promising leads or fruitless lines of inquiry do occur, which may lead to major deviations from original research objectives, the Foundation would appreciate being informed of such deviations.[12]

Over time, the original distinction between purchased and sponsored research and between the contract and the grant has largely disappeared. Certain agencies support university research through contracts, others through grants. When contracts are used, however, they are apt to be more flexible than industrial contracts, and grants are much less flexible than they once were.[13] "Over the years," an experienced research administrator has noted, "the regulations of the federal granting agencies as expressed in their grant manuals have multiplied manyfold. Contract requirements have also increased somewhat, but to nothing like the same extent as grant manuals."[14]

Nevertheless, it continues to be acknowledged, explicitly and implicitly, that the standards of accountability applicable to university research must be different from those applied in the case of industry. The rationale behind this is based on a number of elements:

(1) Universities, unlike industrial firms, are exclusively committed to public-interest goals. Like government, but less broadly, their mandate is to promote the general welfare. Since they are not designed to generate profit for their sponsors, they are not susceptible to the same inherent temptation to use public funds for private purposes.

(2) Since most academic research tends to be fundamental or basic, it results primarily in openly published scientific papers aimed at advancing knowledge and available to all, rather than in proprietary technology that is apt to be of special benefit only to the developers.

(3) Inasmuch as the quality of scientific work is subject to appraisal by the research community, unlike industrial development, account-

ability is assured by a process internal to science without the need or advisability of external review by government officials apt not to have the requisite level of competence.

(4) Since research is in essence mental work, it is not readily adaptable to such conventional accounting techniques as time-and-effort reporting. For this reason, even when such reporting is required, it is at least tacitly understood that such measurements are to be taken only as rough and informal guides to faithful performance.

(5) The best scientific work requires that the investigator be free not only to chart his own course at the outset but to alter the course as work proceeds. To require that the researcher not deviate from some predetermined research outline would be to impose an altogether inappropriate condition and actually to mandate inefficiency in many cases.

(6) Because it must venture well beyond the boundaries of what is already known, the most creative scientific work is constantly exposed to the risk of failure. To measure the value of such research by the standards of immediate success is therefore to inhibit the search for great breakthroughs and instead to encourage an avoidance of risk, which could be fatal to the possibility of major achievements.

(7) A scientist's reputation, and therefore his ability to secure appointments as well as further support, depends upon the judgment of his peers, who referee his research findings when they are submitted for publication and who alone can evaluate their significance and influence. This gives the strongest incentives to use available resources wisely.

These considerations help account for the relative looseness that so far has characterized the accountability system imposed upon academic researchers. On the whole, the government agencies that have supported research have taken them into account in monitoring performance and in awarding support. They have relied heavily on peer review and the advice of other researchers in the same or a closely related field in assigning priorities in research support; they have given researchers latitude in defining and redefining their objectives; and they have learned to accept the notion that basic research may not lead to any certain results within the scope of a particular project, but that even failure can be a contribution to the advance of science.

At the same time there have always been misgivings within government over the idea that anyone, even a prestigious scientist, can escape public review or that any institution, including a university, can be trusted to do as it likes with the taxpayers' money. Lately these misgivings have become more explicit, with effects that threaten to override the recognition of the special character of academic research. To compound the problem, government agencies have broadened the concept of accountability so as to make the support of research contingent on compliance with social policies related only peripherally, if at all, to the performance of research.

Accountability and Accounting

Certain of the misgivings have a basis in truth. The university, because it is an organization, and the researcher, because he is a fallible mortal, can both make mistakes and sometimes even succumb to the temptation of irresponsibility. Simply because the university is not a profit-making institution does not assure that it will manage its funds properly; indeed, it may seek to avoid bankruptcy or lesser financial embarrassment by shifting support from an area for which it was intended to another where the need is considered more acute. Not surprisingly, accounting irregularities and worse have occasionally been discovered.

In an investigation of the Health Professions Student Assistance Program, for example, the General Accounting Office (GAO) found a number of instances of blatant mismanagement. At one medical school, a student's allowable budget included $600 for the feeding of a spouse's horses; at another, a request was approved for a loan of $1,000 to enable a student to pay for a girl friend's abortion; [15] in the entire sample studied, 63 percent of the aid recipients came from families with incomes above the low income ceiling, thus defeating one of the primary purposes of the legislation. [16]

These examples indicate that in the absence of federal guidelines (for which GAO blamed HEW), irregularities are as apt to occur in institutions of higher education as in profit-making firms. Indeed, since profit-making firms are compelled to accept stringent audits to conform to government regulations and to satisfy shareholders, whereas a university often operates with less outside restraint, the tendency for loose administration may be more of a problem in the universities.

This tendency toward careless management has also shown up, although only in a few isolated instances, in the administration of research support. In another inquiry GAO found that many research institutions did not maintain records of equipment inventories, thus making it impossible to discover whether a piece of needed equipment was actually on hand. Again, since NIH provided no guidelines concerning record keeping, the universities often took no pains to maintain records. The GAO investigators also found examples of wasteful administration. A researcher at one university acquired a new spectrophotometer costing about $5,000 for use on a project. He was apparently unaware that his university owned a comparable unit that had not been used in three years. At another institution, an ultracentrifuge went unused over two years when five ultracentrifuges said by GAO to be comparable were purchased at a cost of $7,300 each. None of these universities had records suitable for institutionwide screening of available equipment. [17] In some instances the investigators found that researchers had come to regard equipment acquired through government-sponsored projects as virtually their own property. One had an ultramicrotome that had not been used in almost five years; he admitted that he had not informed anyone of the availability of the equipment because "the machine was purchased on my grant for my use."[18]

From time to time other glaring instances come to light, including one case where a leading institution had to cancel an energy research project after discovering that the funds allocated had been used improperly, and another where a leading cell researcher was compelled to resign after his university discovered that he had used federally supported research as a vehicle for creating a personal business. And government auditors register other complaints about the administration of federal funds:

> There are such allegations as inadequate documentation of costs, claiming reimbursement for more than 100 percent of a faculty member's salary, retroactive transfers of costs from one grant or contract to another without documented justification, and treatment of student aid as reimbursable salaries and wages.[19]

It may be that such episodes are rare and that universities and university researchers do a good job of policing themselves, but government auditors and congressmen may be forgiven for wondering whether many more instances would come to light if more investigations were made. As the GAO reports point out, however, the universities are not necessarily at fault, inasmuch as it is the responsibility of the federal agencies to set guidelines. Nor, as the reports also note, is it necessarily true that all the problems uncovered can be remedied by new procedures. From an accountant's point of view, it may seem eminently sensible for researchers to share equipment, but the researchers themselves often point out that the same basic equipment may need to be modified for different functions and that when equipment is shared by too many users, only one of whom is responsible for maintaining it, the results are apt to be frustrating to all concerned.[20] GAO's strictures, furthermore, do not consider the costs that universities must bear for improved inventory management.

Accountability translates into accounting in another contentious area: the degree to which the federal government ought to reimburse universities for indirect or overhead costs associated with the performance of federally sponsored research. At the outset, the federal government provided research funds to universities on terms markedly different from those governing relations with industry. Whereas industrial firms were eligible for reimbursement of full audited costs, universities were permitted to recover only a fraction of their indirect costs. The theory was that since research was a regular function of universities, some of the university's own budget should go to the support of the research performed by its faculty, whatever the source of that support. The earliest NIH reimbursement rate for indirect costs was 8 percent. As federal subvention increased, however, the universities argued that they were in effect subsidizing government in ever larger degrees. In response, the regulations were changed to permit reimbursement of 20 percent of indirect costs and finally, in 1965, by act of Congress, the policy was changed to provide for a negotiated reimbursement of costs, but not full reimbursement.

The principle adopted was that of "cost sharing," a notion growing out of the original assumption that some of the charge for university research ought to be borne by the university. In practice, rates of indirect cost reimbursement now approximate 33 percent of direct costs. This is about half the average indirect cost rate of universities, which now runs about 60 percent of direct salaries and wages.[21] Actual rates of reimbursement depend upon negotiations and assumptions on both sides as to appropriate levels of cost and the research relatedness of various items. They are therefore subject to continual disagreement and compromise. Since there is no fixed standard, the universities are vulnerable to arbitrary moves, such as that recently made by HEW threatening to cut indirect cost reimbursement in half, a warning since withdrawn in favor of a compromise.

Among other items, HEW proposed new guidelines restricting the allowability of departmental administrative expense to heads and assistant heads of departments, limiting library reimbursement to the actual provision of library services in connection with contracts, and restricting department flexibility in permitting tuition remission and other compensation to students employed in subsidized research.[22]

The complex process of determining indirect costs has forced universities to expand both administrative staffs and data processing capacities. As Raymond Woodrow points out, the principles now in use "require a complicated computation of indirect cost rates supplemented by working papers, audit, and negotiation of indirect cost rates." Estimates of costs must include those incurred in complying with such regulations as the proper care of laboratory animals; avoidance of conflict of interest; and the provision of business and/or employment for small business, minority-owned business, veterans, the handicapped, and those affected by labor surplus conditions.[23] Woodrow also notes that these principles do not permit recovery of certain expenses allowed to industry and nonprofit organizations. These include the costs of independent research and development broadly related to government contracts, public relations and fund-raising costs, and the costs of patenting inventions (which are allowed to industry on condition that the government receives nonexclusive, royalty-free licenses).

In addition, universities cannot recover more than a fraction of the costs they have had to assume in recent years to implement a variety of federally mandated programs, including social security, equal opportunity, affirmative action, occupational health and safety, and environmental protection. It has been estimated that the combined cost of implementing these programs at six major institutions has been between 1 and 4 percent of their operating budgets, and that such costs have increased from 10 to 20 times during the past decade. The universities have been particularly hard hit by increases in employment taxes since they are comparatively labor intensive. These increases also vitiate the value of the universities' tax exemption since the exemption affects income, property, and sales taxation but not salary taxes.[24]

All these costs, moreover, have had to be borne by the universities during a period when both private and public sources of support have become more difficult to tap. State legislatures have tended to act on the theory that they are responsible solely or primarily for the instructional budgets of the state universities and colleges; and in order to alleviate unemployment while minimizing the costs of education, they have put greater emphasis than ever on low-cost postsecondary instruction, in which there is no need to support expensive research and graduate training. Enthusiasm for the promotion of economic growth by spinoffs from research-intensive universities has waned, as has the belief that employment opportunities in a post-industrial phase of the economy would require more sophisticated scientific and technological education for the majority of students.

The increase of costs and tasks associated with the accounting aspects of accountability has engendered a situation in which many universities are devoting what may well be regarded as an inordinate amount of their resources to administration. This cannot help but detract from other functions, unless increasing support is provided for these too. The quest for accountability has therefore come to impose heavy new economic burdens on the universities.

The Attack on Peer Review and Confidentiality

The system governing the distribution of research support to university scientists in the United States relies heavily on peer review—the process whereby qualified scientists sit in judgment (either individually or on panels) on project proposals submitted by other scientists. Even in the two agencies (NSF and NIH) in which it plays the most central role, however, peer review is only one aspect of the reviewing process. Applications are also subject to review by the agency staff, which considers their relevance to national objectives (including the balance of support among fields of research and geographical regions) and combines its own evaluations with those of the scientists in reaching its final decisions. The peer review system takes different forms, but all involve anonymous refereeing of the kind that has become a tradition in evaluating articles submitted to scientific journals or evaluating candidates for faculty appointments.

This system reflects the view of the scientific community that no one can judge a scientist's qualifications or the merits of his or her actual or proposed work as well as those who have achieved professional recognition. In a sense, therefore, the term "peer" is something of a misnomer, especially if compared with the democratic notion of a trial by one's peers, which implies a random selection of citizens. Peer review in the sciences subjects all alike to review by those whose accomplishments have shown them qualified to judge.

This emphasis on the qualifications of the judges as well as on the anonymity of their proceedings has led to a certain amount of criticism on the ground that in this instance, too, there is a problem of accountability. Critics say that the process smacks of an undemocratic elitism and permits research support to be controlled by unrepresentative cliques. The more prestigious, well-established researchers are thus in a position to discriminate against outsiders and potential rivals. Intellectual snobbery may preclude awards to those affiliated with lesser academic institutions or departments. Prejudices with respect to lines of investigation may also come into play to thwart efforts to challenge conventionally accepted paradigms and research strategies. The program officers who choose referees are also in a position to influence judgment by selecting those sympathetic to their own views. In addition, the Office of Management and Budget (OMB) has charged that NIH review panels deliberately approve more applications than can be funded in order to support appeals for higher appropriations.[25]

Congressman R.E. Baumann of Maryland has given political voice to certain of these criticisms, charging that research grants are being distributed "in an unregulated and secretive manner" through a system that "allows cronies to get together and finance their pet projects," as a result of which "many people are not devoting themselves to basic research needs but rather to feathering their own nests."[26] Other congressmen have occasionally criticized projects funded by NSF on the ground that they appear to be trivial or otherwise wasteful.

While this criticism does not necessarily indict peer review, it has induced program officers to nurture projects likely to be safe from such ridicule. This may only involve such cosmetic effects as the retitling of proposals but could conceivably inhibit approval of certain types of research (such as those concerning animal reproduction, which have sometimes appeared laughable to critics). Critics have lately proposed that in order to remedy what they regard as the deficiencies of the present system, reviewers' names and comments should be made public, and Congress should be apprised of individual research projects before they are given final approval.[27]

One NSF spokesman has responded that such criticisms oversimplify a complex and demonstrably fair process and threaten to replace it with one far more open to arbitrary—and political—judgment. He points out that when a proposal is received it goes to a program officer who may decide among a variety of review procedures, including staff review, consultation with other agencies, site visits, mailed ad hoc reviews, and panel reviews. On the average each proposal submitted to NSF receives 6.4 reviews in addition to a staff review. These are performed without compensation by scientists responding to the agency's request for assistance. In 1974, 120,000 reviews were performed in this way for NSF alone.[28] Although the outside reviewers are anonymous and the substance of their reviews is confidential, the names of the approximately 35,000 reviewers who advise NSF on project selection are now made available annually.[29]

In evaluating a proposal, NSF considers not only appraisals of its scientific merit but also the balance of support among various fields of research and geographical areas—the latter in pursuance of the mandate written into the NSF Act requiring that support be distributed in such a manner as to "avoid undue concentration of such research and education."[30] On a state-by-state analysis, research support is closely correlated with population, except in Massachusetts, New York, and California, states that also have a greater concentration of scientific talent (measured by such criteria as membership in the National Academy of Sciences and National Academy of Engineering). Studies of the reviewers used by NSF also show a distribution closely correlated with the distribution of population by state and by the measures of scientific excellence. The fact that applicants from the more prestigious universities tend to be comparatively successful in winning support is said to indicate only that the rankings are deserved.

Other studies of NIH and NSF procedures do not tend to substantiate charges against the motives or integrity of referees. A study of NIH review panels has revealed that average priority scores on new grant proposals have not changed significantly since 1967, thus tending to refute OMB charges that the sections have deliberately sought to generate pressure for more appropriations. As to NSF, one internal study shows that the pattern of its awards in chemistry correlates highly with the distribution of citation rates, thus indicating that funds tend to go to researchers whose work is seminal. Thane Gustafson has summarized the results of this study:

> Of NSF awards in chemistry, 80 to 85 percent go to departments whose faculty averaged more than 60 citations per author during the five-year period ending in 1972; the top four or five departments, which received the lion's share of NSF grants, averaged around 400 citations per author. If one accepts the premise that citation rates reflect the quality and impact of research results rather than simply the visibility of their authors, then the charges of bias leveled at peer review groups lose much of their force.[31]

The confidentiality requirement has been strongly defended by scientists. The Cornell University chemistry department, in a letter to the director of the National Science Board, asserted that the peer review process works as well as it does because the reviewer's identity is not disclosed to the applicant:

> Accordingly, reviewers feel free to provide honest and objective evaluations of proposals. For example, a junior scientist may criticize a famous scientist with no fear for his career. If this confidentiality were breached, the review system would break down because, as members of a common scientific community, reviewers would not want to alienate their colleagues by unfavorable reviews. Some expert scientists would simply refuse to review proposals if confidentiality was not guaranteed. Or, alternatively, reviews would tend to become platitudinous and meaningless and would provide no substantive input to the final deliberations of the award of grants. All objectivity would be lost and NSF would no longer be able to discriminate effectively between good and bad science. The nation's resources would inevitably be frittered away on much unproductive and poor science.[32]

The members of another chemistry department fully endorsed the view of the Cornell group, adding that "a procedure which allows an applicant to know the identity of critical reviewers is an invitation to nonscientific, emotional rejoinders from applicants against reviewers. Such exchanges must lead to the destruction of the review process."[33]

If peer review and confidentiality were undermined, in the name of improving accountability, the most likely outcome would be the weakened capacity of the federal agencies to allocate research support in accord with the most expert judgment. The alternative would be to distribute the support according to some formula that either would take only indirect account of merit (as in the case of institutional support tied to a formula weighted to reflect doctorates granted, academy memberships, and so on) or would ignore considerations of merit in favor of political criteria. The fact that such a patently dangerous alternative has been seriously proposed may reflect a heightened public concern with criteria other than excellence: a suspicion of all elites, including those claimed to be meritocratic; and last but not least, the discontent of those denied support in an increasingly competitive environment.

Peer review, however, is a critical element in the general structure of self-government that many scientists find essential to fairness and the continued advance of science. It functions as a way of preserving the applicability of professional norms and of avoiding external guidance and interference. It enables qualified scientists to identify research priorities, and it permits scientists themselves to map and advance the research frontier. A movement away from peer review would signal an effort to remove the capacity for self-determination from scientists and give it instead to those who influence political decisions. Inevitably there is a duality of decision-making power; scientists and the polity both affect the distribution of research support, but peer review protects scientists from undue interference at the same time that it protects the public against wasteful expenditure.

The Merit Principle and Discrimination

The shortage of academic employment opportunities has also aggravated a conflict between the academic ideal of appointment in accordance with merit and the social goal of remedying actual and presumed discrimination in employment. That such a conflict would develop was not apparent when efforts were first begun, in the decade of the 1960s, to press the cause of civil rights into the sector of education and employment. The Civil Rights Act of 1964 and later enactments sought rather to prevent discrimination on grounds of race, sex, and ethnicity—a goal eminently compatible with the academic principle. But as the legislation came to be implemented, the effort to assure equal opportunity and prevent discrimination turned into an effort to secure preferential employment in cases where designated groups had been previously underrepresented or underutilized. Ironically, the legislators who passed the 1964 Act had foreseen such a possibility and had deliberately taken pains to prevent it by inserting a provision in the Act clearly forbidding "preferential treatment" to correct any "imbalance":

> Nothing contained in this title [VIII] shall be interpreted to require any employer...to grant preferential treatment to any individual or to any group because of the race, color, religion, sex, or national origin of such individual or group on account of an imbalance which may exist with respect to the total number or percentage of persons of any race, color, religion, sex, or national origin employed by any employer....[34]

At the outset this law was interpreted to mean that all employers must take steps to eliminate any actual or potential discriminatory practices from their hiring procedures. Employers were to "act affirmatively," by advertising job openings widely and by making special efforts to recruit qualified women or members of racial and ethnic minorities, on the premise that such groups had previously been victims of discriminatory practices. As the various agencies created to implement the law became more organized, they began to interpret their role as a mandate to assure not simply that nondiscriminatory practices were being followed but that these practices resulted in the employment of more women and members of the designated minorities. In cases where discrimination was found to affect hiring practices, the implementing agencies decided that the law permitted preferential hiring for purposes of rectifying previous practices. As the rules and regulations promulgated by HEW stipulate in connection with Title IX of the Education Amendments of 1972:

> Where a recipient has been found to be presently discriminating on the basis of sex in the recruitment or hiring of employees, or has been found

to have in the past so discriminated, the recipient shall recruit members of the sex discriminated against so as to overcome the effects of such past or present discrimination.[35]

In order to ascertain whether such patterns of discrimination exist, the implementing agencies have required employers, including universities, to determine the race, ethnic identity, and sex of employees and to collect data on the identities of applicants considered for employment. Such data have been matched against other data indicating the pool of employable individuals in the affected categories in order to determine whether such groups are "utilized" or "underutilized." Critics have charged that by setting goals or targets for the employment of underutilized groups, the federal agencies are compelling discrimination in reverse and replacing the principle of equality of opportunity with an effort to secure sexual and ethnic balance instead. Thus, Nathan Glazer cites as a particularly blatant example of the result an announcement from San Francisco State College in 1971 of an affirmative action plan approved by HEW and calling for:

> an employee balance which in ethnic and male/female groups approximates that of the general population of the Bay Area from which we recruit. What this means is that we have shifted from the idea of equal opportunity in employment to a deliberate effort to seek out qualified and qualifiable people among ethnic minority groups and women to fill all jobs in our area.[36]

In the immediate future, such efforts can have little effect on employment in the natural sciences and engineering, at least where racial and ethnic minorities are concerned because as of 1972 only 4 percent of all scientists and engineers either employed or qualified for employment were members of officially designated racial and ethnic minorities.[37] Women have lately entered biology in increasing numbers, however, and the situation is quite different in the humanities and social sciences, with the result that controversy and litigation have been more intense in these areas than in the natural sciences. The very idea that the principle of appointment on the basis of sexual or ethnic identity could be forced upon the universities by the executive agencies, so far without judicial challenge,[38] is another indication that the autonomy of science is under assault. In the name of a broad concept of accountability, social goals are placed in conflict with scientific merit. The willingness of most universities to collaborate with the federal agencies may indicate sympathy with the intentions if not the methods of the effort; but it may also show that faced with the threat of a potentially crippling loss of federal support, the universities will not rush to defend the principles of appointment by merit or academic autonomy.

Accountability and the Special Role of the Research University

Broadening the concept of accountability to apply to nongovernmental as well as to government bodies and to take account of all the ways in which an institution makes an impact upon the public interest poses a danger to academic autonomy unless it can be shown that academic autonomy is itself in the public interest. In fact, a compelling argument can be made in favor of this proposition.

Any useful definition of accountability must consider the ways in which the techniques aimed at assuring accountability facilitate or hinder the efficiency of performance. The broad definition must also include an estimate of the effects of implementation. If these effects inhibit creativity, weaken educational effectiveness, and otherwise produce waste and inefficiency, they are open to criticism. They will have become an end in themselves rather than an instrument of public purpose. If for the sake of meeting publicly established noneducational and nonscientific standards, the governmental agencies make it difficult or impossible for the university system to serve its most critical function—the pursuit and transmission of knowledge in its most advanced forms—then these agencies will have succeeded only in transforming a great social instrument into a pliant tool of bureaucracy and the bureaucratic mentality.

The American university system is widely recognized to be a unique and impressive accomplishment, as foreign testimony will confirm. A study by the Organization for Economic Cooperation and Development (OECD) comparing research systems points out: "The United States is the only country in the world to have built up a university system which accommodates the maximum number of students and the greatest research teams, and which combines scientific excellence with universal access to postsecondary education."[39] The American system of higher education has won particular praise for the egalitarian access it makes available. As Ben-David notes, comparisons with other systems "all show that there is, and for some time in the past has been, less class discrimination in education in the United States than in other countries, including socialist countries."[40]

The peculiar virtue of the American system, as these observations suggest, is not that it excels in any single respect, but that it combines equality of access with scientific achievement and rich diversity. In the great universities, the unification of research and education arouses the admiration of knowledgeable educators and scholars everywhere.[41]

This consideration applies with special force to the institution that is in many respects at the vital center of the American system of higher education—the research university. In general usage this category is taken to comprise about 10 percent of the roughly 2,200 postsecondary institutions in the country, institutions that range from junior colleges to centers for research in which there is little or no instruction. These approximately 200 institutions, assigned to the category in the first instance because they confer the PhD degree, are the source of America's claim to world leadership in scientific research. It is of these universities that the OECD report speaks when it observes, "It can safely be said that United States research universities are the best in the world by virtue of the quality of their research and the scale of their contribution to knowledge."[42] Various standards of measurement bear out this claim, including international comparisons of scientific publications, citations of publications, and the award of prizes for scientific achievements.[43]

The reasons for the preeminence of the American research university are many, and some would suggest that its achievements are largely the result of political accident rather than design. The great increase in public support for research in the aftermath of World War II undoubtedly had a considerable effect. This increase, however, has been plausibly described as "largely a political accident incident to the arms race and massive public interest in health, not the result of a coherent policy for higher education or a firm national consensus concerning the value and importance of basic research to the economic and social health of the nation."[44]

Federal subsidization alone is not the explanation. American science has benefited from the voluntary and forced emigration of scientists from other countries. Most likely it has also benefited from the effects of the competitive ethic that motivates researchers and their institutions at least as much as other segments of the culture. The competition for support and prestige has undoubtedly had its harmful results as well. Universities have occasionally been induced to divert the focus of faculty attention from teaching to research; they have sometimes overextended, transforming already large universities into even larger organizations housing inharmonious activities or laboratories insulated from the rest of the university. Nevertheless, on the whole the availability of research support and the competition for it have greatly enhanced the university's traditional emphasis on research achievement, producing teaching that transmits an awareness of ongoing studies.

What is to happen to this system? In terms of student and faculty size, it has ceased to grow. Planning is based on steady-state projections and even these are subject to warnings of impending declines in enrollment and employment opportunities. It is conceivable that new "big science" projects similar to the space program will come to the rescue in the short run. The concern with the development of new energy technologies offers possibilities for expansion. It is also conceivable, though at present less likely, that Congress will respond to the urgings of educators by developing long-term public commitments to the support of higher education, however modest these may be, in order to allay fears of catastrophe and permit more efficient planning.

The most recent data are not overly encouraging on any score. In comparison with Europe and Japan, the position of the United States is deteriorating, both in scientific and technological accomplishments and in investments aimed at stimulating such accomplishments. Data comparing publications, citation indices, the certification of qualified scientists and engineers, patents, and attendance at international conferences tell essentially the same story, as do the statistics on public support. Whereas U.S. support of research and development reached a height of 2.99 percent of the Gross National Product in 1964, it is estimated to have dropped to 2.29 percent for 1974. Using the same standard, the Soviet Union now spends comparatively more of its income on research and development, 3.1 percent of its GNP, than does the U.S.[45]

It would be naive to posit a simple relationship between such expenditure patterns and either social welfare or economic growth, or to repeat an earlier folly and argue for increased support of American research on the grounds of the need to outrace the Russians. But it is equally naive to imagine that the defense of this country and its allies can be assured without an adequate research effort into military technology and the development of technical/political arrangements for halting the wasteful and futile pursuit of military supremacy.

In the face of the depletion of conventional energy sources, research will be needed to develop alternate sources and to support wise choices among alternatives. New technology is needed in almost every sector of the economy to increase productivity and meet domestic and international needs. If American foreign policy is to be more than hostile or reactive to the poorer nations' desire for independence and development, this country will have to mount a far more ramified program of technical assistance than has yet been attempted and must provide capital that can only be created by increased productivity.

If public health is measured by the success of researchers in understanding the causes of disease and epidemics and in learning how to prevent or deal with them, then surely the progress of medical science, in which the research universities have played a major role, ought not to be lightly discounted. Can there be any doubt that the great scientific achievements in chemistry and physics, and increasingly in biology, have already had enormous economic benefits for mankind and for the economic strength of this nation? As the United States comes to depend more heavily upon high technology exports and upon skilled scientists and technicians to develop and manage the technologies, it will depend more than ever on the research universities.

The public demand for accountability must, then, consider seriously the potential and actual role of the universities in meeting vital public needs. An unreflective undermining of this capability would scarcely be in the national interest.

Striking a Balance: Constructive Approaches to Academic Accountability

In considering academic accountability, then, it is well to remember that the ultimate test of its success must include a measure of the vitality and fecundity of the institutions of research and higher education. These characteristics, however, depend upon the maintenance of the pluralistic system that protects the autonomy of the university and allows it—without being diverted from its central task—to carry out its role with the support of beneficiaries that include the general public. In exchange the universities must be prepared to respond to legitimate efforts to regulate and audit public expenditures. They must also be prepared to cooperate with public agencies on mutually agreeable terms to assure that the knowledge and talents these agencies need are made available. In general the need is "to create understandings, and institutional arrangements, that will enable the government (in both its legislative and executive branches) to maintain a strong central policy direction over the apparatus of private institutions while giving the private institutions enough independence of operation to produce the maximum incentives for a distinctive and creative contribution to the government."[46]

How are the government agencies and the universities to develop an appropriate, balanced approach to academic accountability? To attempt to map out every detail would be futile, since the answers must come out of negotiation and cooperation. Some particular grievances and needs that are already well recognized have been mentioned or, as in the case of indirect costs, will be dealt with more explicitly in other papers in this volume. Less well recognized but worth consideration are several recommendations that could be addressed to each of the parties.

With respect to governmental policy:

(1) All agencies, state and federal, should be required wherever possible to adopt "self-denying ordinances" with respect to universities. To curb any bureaucratic penchant for the collection of useless or unnecessary data and reports, such requirements should be subject to review by a public commission or possibly the General Accounting Office. Before implementing a law that requires a proliferation of agency activities, and thus the time of researchers and administrators, the agencies should be required to perform an impact analysis.

An example from the practice of a federal agency may serve to illustrate the point. Title IX of the Education Amendments of 1972 prohibits discrimination on the basis of sex in educational institutions, but HEW has deliberately refrained from prohibiting the use of textbooks that perpetrate allegedly harmful sexual stereotypes on the ground that the ban would raise more problems than it solves. As the Department's analysis of the law points out, "The Department recognizes that sex stereotyping in textbooks and curricular materials is a serious matter. However, the imposition of restrictions in this area would inevitably limit communication and would thrust the Department into the role of federal censor."[47] The same principle should inhibit the government from interfering with academic determination of the curriculum, as Congress threatened to do in 1974 when it considered a bill to compel medical students to receive six weeks of training in a location where medical care was below adequate standards.[48] As a general rule, federal and state agencies should ask themselves, before embarking on some new regulatory tack, whether they are undertaking an effort for which they are ill equipped, whether it might better be accomplished in some other way, or whether it will raise more problems than it solves.

(2) Federal funding agencies should be required—and the state agencies encouraged—to develop uniform procedures and to share certain types of information so as to avoid wasteful duplication of effort. Wherever possible, reporting and auditing requirements should be waived altogether for those institutions whose procedures and staff qualifications meet agency standards. Certification requirements could be developed by the agencies, with the assistance of GAO, OMB, and the associations of university administrators, notably the National Association of College and University Business Officers. These procedures could include systems of external audit, as required for publicly held companies.

(3) As the Carnegie Commission on Higher Education has proposed, federal legislation should be considered to set aside a certain percentage (perhaps 10 percent) of research support for distribution in the form of institutional support, based upon the amount received by each university on a project basis.[49] The purpose of the provision would be to minimize the distorting effect of targeted support and provide the research universities with discretionary funds. To avoid the possibility that funds would be used to support relatively weak programs, which otherwise would not qualify for support, universities might be required to create faculty councils—perhaps to include some members from other universities—to establish policy. It would be advisable to restrict the use of such funds solely to the support of research or the infrastructure necessary for the conduct of research.

With respect to universities:

(1) It is clear that many universities need to improve their capacities for managing research facilities, equipment, and grant administration. Similarly, administrators must explain more articulately the need to take due account of the indirect costs of research. As the executive director of the National Association of State Universities and Land Grant

Colleges has put it, "University administrators must explain to faculty members what is done with federal money. The faculty member who complains publicly about his university 'ripping off' his research money is like a child playing with a loaded gun: a little ignorance is a dangerous thing."[50]

(2) Universities should consider developing a variety of innovative programs designed both to further diversify sources of support and to respond to vital public needs. Three alternatives are in fact already being pursued in relatively modest ways at certain universities. One involves cooperative arrangements with private industry, both in research and in student internship and apprenticeship programs. (The research accord recently worked out between the Harvard Medical School and the Monsanto Chemical Company is an example of a major development on the research front; the relationships already in existence between a number of engineering departments and industrial firms could serve as precedents for programs elsewhere.) Another involves the establishment of multidisciplinary policy study centers, some with a regional focus, others aimed at taking special account of the research strengths on a particular campus.[51] (The MIT Center for Policy Alternatives and the Graduate School of Public Policy at the University of California, Berkeley, are prominent examples.)

A bill introduced in the California legislature would establish a Public Policy Research Foundation under the auspices of the University of California. The Foundation would perform research needed by public agencies. The University has objected that the proposal would require the diversion of currently authorized research funds, but in principle it could serve a useful purpose and eventually alleviate pressures on research support. A third alternative is to create and administer centers for the provision of certain public services that are not well performed either under profit-making or governmental auspices. (Community health plans, such as the one administered by the University of Rochester Medical School, illustrate the principle. Another badly needed effort might involve the development of nursing homes, which could be undertaken by a consortium of universities and other public philanthropic agencies.) Universities could perform such services on a not-for-profit basis but charge a fee that would help spread general operating costs.

(3) To alleviate deteriorating economic conditions, the universities should consider making an appeal for federal relief, on the ground that the health of the nation's institutions of higher learning is essential to the quality of American life, quite apart from the direct and particular services they provide.[52] University administrators, faculty, and boards of trustees should take their responsibilities for preserving the integrity of the university very seriously, resisting improper pressures from external sources, including government agencies. In cases where this integrity is either thoughtlessly or deliberately invaded, they should be

prepared to undertake judicial appeals and to lobby for changes in legislation or executive revocation of administrative orders. As a last resort, university officials should establish contingency plans for cutting back operations in the event of a withdrawal of public support. This is, to be sure, a drastic action, and in all likelihood the declaration of the intention, coupled with the development of realistic plans, would inform the public in time to avoid such a strategy. The university associations can serve as useful brokers to ward off such ultimate dangers. Officials should also work for a degree of unity among universities—especially the major research institutions—which would permit cooperation of the kind that other nongovernmental bodies practice (trade unions, for example) when one of their members is faced with an assault.

Finally, both universities and government agencies should recognize that unless they cooperate to alleviate the increasing tensions, dire consequences could be in the offing. American higher education could well become much less rigorous than it is even now—and participants know better than critics how much room remains for improvement—and certification could become an increasingly empty benefit. If the present link between research and education, especially at the research universities, were seriously weakened, the quality of graduate education would suffer. The damage might not reveal itself immediately, but the pace of progress would certainly slacken not only in science but in the social applications that depend on science.

Increases of funding, from whatever source, could postpone such dire consequences perhaps indefinitely, but it would be more realistic, given the competing demands for scarce social resources, to achieve a new understanding of the sense in which the accountability of the universities must be measured. Above all it is necessary to judge the effectiveness with which their principal functions are performed. Tests of accountability must be made appropriate to their objectives and they must be administered with sensitivity and practical intelligence. The impersonal techniques made possible by advances in data-processing equipment and made necessary by the size and complexity of research activities should not be allowed to obscure the need for such sensitivity and intelligence. As one educational administrator has said, "None of us quarrels with pleas for increased accountability; however, none of us believes that the tools of cost accounting can quantify the life of the mind."[53] In the special case of the research universities, both the administrators and their overseers would do well to recognize that the life of the mind flourishes best when there is pride in accomplishment and confidence in the social system. Any attempt, however well intentioned, to require proof of exertion and evidence of conformity to social norms will only defeat the larger objective, which is surely to promote an environment for learning from which society will draw the greatest benefit.

188

1. National Science Board, *Science Indicators—1974: Report of the National Science Board, 1975* (Washington, D.C.: National Science Foundation, 1975), p. 61.
2. J. C. Furnas, "Coping With Sponsored Research: A Special Word to Presidents," in *Sponsored Research in American Universities and Colleges*, ed. Stephen Strickland (Washington, D.C.: American Council on Education, 1967), p. 34.
3. Derek Bok, "The President's Report, 1974-1975," *Harvard University Gazette*, February 20, 1976, p. 5.
4. Earl F. Cheit, "What Price Accountability?" *Change*, November 1975, p. 32.
5. Derek Bok, op. cit., p. 1.
6. Ibid.
7. Dael Wolfle, *The Home of Science: The Role of the University* (New York: McGraw-Hill, 1974), p. 124.
8. Committee on Science and Public Policy, *Federal Support of Basic Research in Institutions of Higher Learning* (Washington, D.C.: National Academy of Sciences, National Research Council, 1964), Preface.
9. John Locke, *Two Treatises of Government* (1690), ed. P. Laslett (Cambridge, England: Cambridge University Press, 1964), pp. 240, 444-445. The *locus classicus* of the theory in its ultimate form is probably Locke's *Second Treatise*: "The common Question will be made, Who shall be Judge whether the Prince of Legislative act contrary to their Trust?... To this I reply, The People shall be Judge: for who shall be Judge whether his Trustee or Deputy acts well, and according to the Trust reposed in him, but he who deputes him, and must, by having deputed him, have still a Power to discard him, when he fails in his Trust? If this be reasonable in particular Cases of private Men, why should it be otherwise in that of the greatest moment; where the Welfare of Millions is concerned, and also where the evil, if not prevented, is greater, and the Redress very difficult, dear, and dangerous."
10. Don K. Price, *Government and Science* (New York: New York University Press, 1954).
11. H. A. L. Nieburg, *In the Name of Science* (Chicago: Quadrangle, 1964).
12. Alice Rivlin, *The Role of the Federal Government in Financing Higher Education* (Washington, D.C.: The Brookings Institution, 1961), p. 43.
13. David Z. Robinson, "Government Contracting for Academic Research: Accountability in the American Experience," in *The Dilemma of Accountability in Modern Government*, ed. Bruce L. R. Smith and D. C. Hague (London: Macmillan, 1971), p. 114.
14. Raymond J. Woodrow, *Indirect Costs in Universities* (Washington, D.C.: American Council on Education, March 1976), p. 76.
15. Comptroller General of the United States, *Congressional Objectives of Federal Loans and Scholarships to Health Professions Students Not Being Met*, B-164031(2) (Washington, D.C., May 24, 1974), pp. 8-9.
16. Ibid., p. 35.
17. United States General Accounting Office, *Better Management Needed of Health Research Equipment by NIH Grantees*, B-164031(2) (Washington, D.C., July 17, 1973), pp. 8-9.
18. Ibid., p. 13.
19. Ralph K. Huitt, *The Indirect Cost Hassle* (Washington, D.C.: National Association of State Universities and Land Grant Colleges, April 29, 1976).
20. United States General Accounting Office, *Better Management Needed of Health Research Equipment*, op. cit., pp. 13-14.
21. Charles V. Kidd, "Levels and Trends in Federal Indirect Cost Payments to Colleges and Universities," draft cited with permission (Washington, D.C.: American Association of Universities, February 20, 1976).
22. Arthur B. Jebens and Norman H. Gross, *Indirect and Direct Cost Recovery Under Federal Contracts and Grants* (San Diego: University of California Statewide Administration and San Diego, 1976), pp. 35-36.
23. Raymond J. Woodrow, op. cit., p. 82.
24. Carol Van Alstyne and Sharon L. Coldren, *The Costs to Colleges and Universities of Implementing Federally Mandated Programs* (Washington, D.C.: American Council on Education, 1975), p. 4.
25. Thane Gustafson, "The Controversy Over Peer Review," *Science*, Vol. 190, December 12, 1975, p. 1063.
26. Ibid., p. 1060.
27. Ibid., p. 1064.

28. Richard C. Atkinson, Testimony before the House Subcommittee on Science, Research, and Technology, Committee on Science and Technology (Washington, D.C., July 23, 1975).

29. Thane Gustafson, op. cit., p. 1061.

30. Richard C. Atkinson, op. cit.

31. Thane Gustafson, op. cit., p. 1063.

32. Michael E. Fisher, Letter to Norman Hackerman, Chairman, National Science Board, December 4, 1975.

33. Murray Goodman, Letter to Congressman James W. Symington, Chairman, House Subcommittee on Science, Research, and Technology, Committee on Science and Technology, March 5, 1976.

34. Nathan Glazer, *Affirmative Discrimination: Ethnic Inequality and Public Policy* (New York: Basic Books, 1975), p. 44.

35. *Federal Register*, Vol. 40, No. 108, June 4, 1975.

36. Nathan Glazer, op. cit., p. 60.

37. National Science Board, *Science Indicators—1974*, op. cit., p. 241.

38. The Supreme Court declined to consider the challenge to preferential admissions practices in the *De Funis* case but is at this writing considering an appeal of the *Bakke* decision in which the California Supreme Court ruled that preferential admission on grounds of race is unconstitutional. The Supreme Court has not yet been asked to take a case concerning preferential employment, but lower courts have upheld the right of the federal government to compel other employers to adopt hiring quotas. As Glazer explains, the courts have reasoned by analogy with previous holdings in the areas of voting rights and school desegregation. In these areas, the test developed to determine whether discriminatory practices are in effect is whether a given percentage of the minority discriminated against is not registered to vote or enrolled in local schools. Similarly, the Court has reasoned, where women or ethnic minorities are not employed in reasonable proportion to their availability, a pattern of discrimination may be presumed to exist. (Nathan Glazer, op. cit., p. 50.) One problem with this reasoning is that in the cases of voter registration and school desegregation efforts to correct the presumed inequity need not involve preferential treatment, whereas in efforts to correct employment imbalances, preferential treatment is virtually inevitable, contrary to the explicit provision of the 1964 Civil Rights Act.

39. G. Caty, G. Drilhon, G. Ferné, N. Kaplan, and S. Wald, *The Research System*, Vol. 3, Canada, United States, General Conclusions (Paris: Organization for Economic Cooperation and Development, 1974), p. 37.

40. Joseph Ben-David, *American Higher Education: Directions Old and New* (New York: McGraw-Hill, 1972), p. 4.

41. Ibid., p. 113. Ben-David's acute commentary on the link between teaching and research is worth quoting at length: "As a matter of fact, there is a close relationship between the two, since researchers consider the communication of their results part of their institutionalized role. Probably the majority of competent researchers are good teachers of students who want to become researchers themselves. They may or may not also be good teachers to others, although in this respect, too, they have a natural advantage over other researchers; since they work in a field, knowing it intimately as artisans know their materials and techniques, they have something valid and valuable to communicate. Even if they are not very good communicators, they are unlikely to mislead their students through ignorance. The principle of the unity of teaching and research is, therefore, no mere ideology. It expresses something inherent in all real learning, and is well worth preserving."

42. G. Caty, et al., op. cit., p. 39.

43. National Science Board, *Science Indicators—1974*, op. cit., p. 2.

44. Harvey Brooks, "Have the Circumstances That Placed the United States in the Lead in Science and Technology Changed?" (New York: The Diebold Institute for Policy Studies, n.d.).

45. National Science Board, *Science Indicators—1974*, op. cit., p. 154.

46. Bruce L. R. Smith, "Accountability and Independence in the Contract State," in *The Dilemma of Accountability in Modern Government* (London: Macmillan, 1971), pp. 4-5.

47. *Federal Register*, op. cit., p. 24135.

48. Derek Bok, op. cit., p. 1.

49. Carnegie Commission on Higher Education, *Institutional Aid: Federal Support to Colleges and Universities* (New York: McGraw-Hill, 1972), p. 61.

50. Ralph K. Huitt, op. cit.

51. Dael Wolfle, op. cit., pp. 142-143.

52. Gerard Piel, "Public Support for Autonomous Universities," *Daedalus*, Vol. 104, Winter 1975, Vol. II, p. 150.

53. William H. Danforth, "Management and Accountability in Higher Education," *AAUP Bulletin*, March 1973, p. 135.

NOTES ON THE CONTRIBUTORS

Walter S. Baer is senior physical scientist and deputy director of the Energy Program of the Rand Corporation. He is the author of *Cable Television: A Handbook for Decisionmaking* and has coauthored and edited three other books in Rand's cable television series, as well as *The Electronic Box Office* (1974) and *Cable and Continuing Education* (1973). He served on the Office of Science and Technology staff in the Executive Office of the President, with responsibilities for federal communications, computer policies, and federal support of basic science. During 1966-67 he was a White House Fellow and from 1964 through 1966 a member of the technical staff of the Bell Telephone Laboratories. Dr. Baer holds a BS from the California Institute of Technology and a PhD in physics from the University of Wisconsin. He currently is a member of the faculty of the Rand Graduate Institute.

David W. Breneman is senior fellow in the Economic Studies Division of the Brookings Institution. From June 1972 through January 1975 he was staff director for the National Board on Graduate Education. He is the author of *Graduate School Adjustments to the "New Depression" in Higher Education* (1975) and coeditor of *Public Policy and Private Higher Education* (1978) and *Forecasting the PhD Labor Market: Pitfalls for Policy* (1974). His other publications include "The PhD Production Process," in *Education as an Industry* (1976) and "Predicting the Response of Graduate Education to No Growth," in *Assuring Academic Progress Without Growth* (1975). Dr. Breneman received his BA from the University of Colorado and his PhD in economics from the University of California, Berkeley. He is currently involved in research on federal education policy and on an economic perspective on community colleges.

Sanford A. Lakoff is chairman of the Department of Political Science at the University of California, San Diego. Before assuming that position in 1975, he taught at Harvard University, where he received his PhD in 1959, and at the University of Toronto. He is coauthor of *Science and the Nation: Policy and Politics* (1962) and editor of *Knowledge and Power: Essays on Science and Government* (1966). His essays and review essays on science policy have appeared in *Minerva, Political Science Quarterly, Science,* and *International Journal.* Most recently he contributed the chapter on "Scientists, Technologists and Political Power," to *Science, Technology and Society: A Cross-Disciplinary Perspective* (1977). Dr. Lakoff is a member of the Committee on Science and Public Policy of the American Association for the Advancement of Science, and the California Policy Seminar, a study group composed of members of the California legislature and University of California faculty. He has recently been elected to the Council of the American Political Science Association.

Dael Wolfle is professor emeritus of public affairs at the University of Washington in Seattle. From 1954 through 1970 he was executive officer of the American Association for the Advancement of Science; from 1950 to 1954, director of the Commission on Human Resources and Advanced Training; and from 1946 to 1950, executive secretary of the American Psychological Association. He has consulted for or served on the advisory committees of the Departments of Commerce; Defense; Health, Education, and Welfare; Labor; NASA; and the National Science Foundation. His books include *The Home of Science: The Role of the University* (1972), *The Uses of Talent* (1971), *Science and Public Policy* (1959). He is the author with others of *The Graduate Education of Physicians* (1966) and editor of *The Discovery of Talent* (1969) and *Symposium on Basic Research* (1959). Dr. Wolfle holds a BS and MS from the University of Washington and his PhD from the Ohio State University.

Carl M. York is a group leader in the Energy and Environment Division of the Lawrence Berkeley Laboratory of the University of California and serves as a consultant on energy policy and energy educational programs in Colorado and California. From 1972 to 1974 he was vice chancellor for academic affairs and dean of the faculty of the University of Denver. In 1969 he joined the White House Office of Science and Technology, where he served for three years as a technical advisor on basic research and academic science. He became a member of the faculty of the University of California, Los Angeles in 1960 and served there as professor of physics, associate dean of the graduate division, and assistant chancellor for research. He worked at Manchester University as a Fulbright Fellow and was a researcher in elementary particle physics. Dr. York received his PhD in physics from the University of California, Berkeley in 1951, while a predoctoral fellow of the Atomic Energy Commission.

Bruce L.R. Smith is professor of government at Columbia University where he has taught since 1966. He served as a senior staff member of the Rand Corporation from 1964 to 1966, received his PhD from Harvard University in 1964, and was a Fulbright scholar in Germany from 1958 to 1959. His books include *The New Political Economy* (1975), and *The Rand Corporation* (1966); he is coauthor of *The Politics of School Decentralization* (1973), *The Dilemma of Accountability in Modern Government* (1971), and Volume I of *The State of Academic Science* (1977). Dr. Smith has served in state government and the federal government and has consulted widely for government agencies and nonprofit institutions. Most recently he has been a consultant for the Office of Technology Assessment of the United States Congress, and he continues to serve as a member of the institutional review board of Rockefeller University.

Joseph J. Karlesky is assistant professor of government at Franklin and Marshall College. He is the coauthor of Volume I of *The State of Academic Science* (1977) and has just completed for the Sloan Commission on Government and Higher Education a Franklin and Marshall College self-study of the impact of federal regulations on the education effort. Dr. Karlesky received his PhD from Columbia University in 1972.